BATTLING FOR THE NATIONAL PARKS

BATTLING FOR THE NATIONAL PARKS

George B. Hartzog, Jr.

Introduction by Stewart L. Udall

MOYER BELL LIMITED
Mt. Kisco, New York

Published by Moyer Bell Limited

First Edition

Library of Congress Cataloging-in-Publication Data

Hartzog, George B.
Battling for the National Parks
George B. Hartzog, Jr.—
1st ed.
    p.   cm.
    Includes index.
    1. Hartzog, George B.   2. United States. National
Park Service—Officials and employees—Biogra-
phy. 3. United States. National Park Service—
History. 4. National parks and reserves—United
States—History. 5. Public Administration—U.S.
Government I. Title.
SB482.A4H37 1988   88-885
333.78'3'0978—dc19   CIP

ISBN 0-918825-70-9

Printed in the United States of America

TO HELEN—
Marrying her was the smartest thing I ever did

CONTENTS

ACKNOWLEDGMENTS

While serving as director of the National Park Service, I received a telephone call from a wealthy industrialist visiting in Washington saying that he and his family had just returned from a vacation in the national parks and that he wanted to meet me. The appointment was made and he came to my office. Racing day in and day out to achieve material success, he told me he had not taken a vacation in many years. Finally, his wife and children persuaded him to relax his harried pace and go with them to the national parks. Fishing and hiking with the children, attending the evening campfire programs as a family, he had rediscovered the joys of his youth and through the eyes of the rangers and naturalists he saw anew the lodestar of life—not material wealth of which he had an abundance but Who am I in the web of life. He concluded by saying, "I would gladly trade places with you; you have the best job in the world."

I demurred; "I won't trade because I know I have the best job in the world."

He ended the meeting saying, "This is why I wanted to meet you; I really had to know if you knew what you had."

For appointing me to the best job in the world, I am deeply grateful to Stewart L. Udall who has graciously written the

Acknowledgments

introduction to this book. My appreciation to Walter Hickel and Rogers C.B. Morton who confirmed me in that position. For success in that job I give thanks to Helen, our children, George, Nancy and Edward, and to the talented people of the National Park Service and their families who sacrificed and labored with me "for the good of the service."

To my mother and dad who encouraged me to "be somebody" and to Col. James F. Risher and Joe Moorer who helped me to become somebody, I am forever indebted.

Angus Cameron, Brian Kahn, our son George critiqued this manuscript, Britt Bell and Jennifer Moyer edited it; Dr. Charles S. Houston, Dr. Frank P. Sherwood, Bob Maynard and a host of my former park service colleagues, some retired (Joe Jensen, Dick Bowser, John Kauffmann, Manny Morris, Ira Whitlock, Howard Chapman, George Fry, Joe Brown, Helen Johnson, Bill Everhart, Bernie Meyer, Matt Ryan) and many nameless ones who are still in the deep and murky bureaucratic waters, supported me in this effort and contributed enormously to the content and organization of the material. To each of them I am most thankful. To acknowledge their assistance is not to saddle them with mistakes, if any, that may remain; those are all mine.

INTRODUCTION

by Stewart L. Udall

George Hartzog was one of the most inspiriting leaders I worked with during my years in the federal government, so it gives me immense pleasure to pen an introduction to this memoir. Indeed, part of that pleasure derives from the circumstance that I had the gumption, after one of our reminiscing visits two years ago, to "demand" that he owed it to history and to his friends to write an account of his adventures in public service.

George has neglected to relate how he grabbed the "brass ring" that opened the door to the office of the director of the National Park Service, so I will fill in that gap in his narrative. On becoming secretary of the interior, I made it a practice to inspect proposed new additions to the National Park System—and in the fall of 1961 I found myself floating on the Current River in the Ozarks with an exuberant group of Missouri conservationists who were mounting a campaign to preserve some of their state's finest free-flowing rivers.

As park superintendent of the Jefferson National Expansion Memorial at St. Louis, Hartzog had volunteered to work out the itinerary for this outing and, as I soon learned, had already formulated a political game-plan to turn the Show-Me State's rivers into a new kind of national park. George explained the elements of his plan while we were enroute to the Ozarks; he shrewdly analyzed the controversies that were swirling around this project, he provided vivid descriptions of the proponents and opponents, he offered insights about Ozark folkways—and he even ventured to tell me how I should "play my cards" to disarm the anti-biases of the "hillbillies" who lived along these rivers.

Our two-day tour to publicize the potential of the proposed park was, on several counts, a huge success: it paved the way for the creation of the nation's first national rivers parkland in 1964; it gave me invaluable insights into the art of marshaling local and national support for additions to the National Park System; and, not least, it established a rapport between me and George B. Hartzog that opened a door to the extraordinary public career described in this book.

Beyond his skill as a park planner, it was the winning, masterful touch George had in dealing with all kinds of people that made him an unforgettable person. From that first encounter there was a brotherly relationship between us; we were the same age, and we had both learned about life growing up during the Great Depression in small towns (he in rural South Carolina, myself in Arizona's high country).

As you read on, you will be delighted to discover that, although by present-day standards George had few formal educational opportunities, he learned enough by dint of what passed for self-improvement in those days to be ordained as a Methodist minister at 17, to acquire enough shorthand to be a court reporter at 18, and to "read" enough law to pass the South Carolina bar exam on his third try without attending a school of law.

In any event, indelible impressions of a man named George Hartzog were imbedded in my mind when Conrad Wirth decided in 1962 to retire as director, just as we were gearing up for what would become the largest expansion of the National Park System in our nation's history. There was a twinge of anguish among the old guard in the park service

Introduction

when it became known that I favored a generational leadership change and had selected George Hartzog as the new director. But I wanted a new dynamism—and I now believe that evidence adduced in this book vindicates the choice I made.

This book both documents the dynamism generated by Director Hartzog, and includes enough "combat stories" to inform us how George tackled some of the problems he encountered during his days in the park service. George is a wonderful storyteller, and we are fortunate that his editor lets his voice speak to us in the exact inflections he uses in everyday conversation. To read this book is to know a man.

In a decade when a president of the United States seeks out opportunities to denigrate the institution we call the federal government and belittle the work of its dedicated civil servants, we need antidotes like this book. George Hartzog's story reminds us of the glories of public service and the legacies our best bureaucrats leave to future generations.

George does not draw large conclusions about the outcome of his endeavors, but we who collaborated with him can perform that function. Everyone who saw him in action or who entered what he called his "command post" at the National Park Service remembers the sense of mission—and the zest and drive—he transmitted to his co-workers. Hartzog, as some of the episodes he cites attest, was a consummate negotiator: he enjoyed entering political thickets, and he had the self-confidence and savvy to be his own lobbyist and to win most of his arguments with members of Congress, governors, and presidents.

And George, as his words demonstrate on every page, was always the happy warrior who exuded reasonableness and good will. His signature was the greeting he invariably extended to ordinary citizens and senators alike: "Hello my friend, what can I do for you?" As an administrator, he set an exemplary standard for commitment, for candor—and for fair play.

Introduction

This is a timely, informative book, with a much needed message for public servants who hope for better days. I hope every person who esteems public service will peruse and ponder George Hartzog's heart-warming story of the best years of his life.

AN OPENING WORD

In our rootless, restless society, huddled together amidst the sterile plastic and concrete environment of congested urban centers, we need a sense of place in which to discover Who am I; a special place that is as constant as love, as never-changing as the cycle of the seasons, as joyous as the shriek of a child on Christmas morning, as exhilarating and re-creating as freedom itself. That special place is to be found in America's national parks—our unique creation that is admired and emulated around the world.

At Yellowstone, the Everglades, Great Smokies, and other parks, we have saved vignettes of our pristine landscapes. At Yosemite, Grand Canyon, Katmai and Mount Rainier, we stand in awe of the geological forces that have carved and shaped our land. At Mesa Verde, Gila Cliff Dwellings, Canyon de Chelly and other shrines of antiquity, we have preserved the remnants of aboriginal cultures.

From first blood at Bunker Hill, through the snows of Valley Forge, onto the battlefields of Cowpens and Kings Mountain and into the trenches of Yorktown, we commemorate the sacrifice, the courage and the valor of those who laid the foundations of our freedom.

At Independence National Historical Park, Hamilton

An Opening Word

Grange, Wakefield and in the historic district of Washington, D.C., we preserve the monuments and remember the legacy of those who wrote our Constitution and laid the foundations of our democracy.

At Gettysburg and scores of other battlefields we stand in silent reverence amidst the reminders of the purging fires of war that forged anew the bonds of union.

At Fort Raleigh where English settlement was first attempted, at Jamestown where it first succeeded, at Cabrillo, Castillo de San Marcos, Castle Clinton, Ellis Island, the Statue of Liberty, we remember those who came to this land. And at Cumberland Gap, St. Louis, Whitman Mission and at dozens of other landmarks along the trails of the American West we can walk where they walked in their painful, sacrificial trek westward to build our nation.

At George Washington Carver, Booker T. Washington, Saugus Iron Works, Edison's Home and Laboratory, Golden Spike, Wright Brothers, we honor the pioneers whose creative genius undergirded our industrial and economic might. At memorials to women's rights, Carl Sandburg, Frederick Douglass, Eleanor Roosevelt, Martin Luther King, Jr., Roger Williams, Mary McLeod Bethune, we lift up the hope that our love of justice, equality and liberty may be as matchless as our industrial and economic strength.

Perhaps second only to liberty itself, the national park idea is the finest contribution of the United States to world culture. These parklands are more than physical resources. They are the delicate strands of nature and culture that bond generation to generation. They are, moreover, the benchmarks of our heritage by which we may chart a new course of human and corporate behavior in our nation so essential to the restoration of quality in our daily lives and of a sense of community in our society.

The National Park Service—an elite cadre of career civil servants admired the world over for their professional discipline and dedication to public service—is charged with leadership in fulfilling the congressional mandate to manage these parklands "in such manner and by such means as will leave them unimpaired for the enjoyment of future generations." However, even as it struggles against the mounting threats to the integrity of our national parks, the National Park Service, itself, has come under political assault. At stake is whether our national parks shall be managed by a singular professional cadre of career public servants or have their management sink quietly into the squalor of political patronage.

I

WHOSE PARKS ARE THESE?

In the summer of 1970 a squad of horse-mounted park rangers rode into the midst of a group of young park visitors at Yosemite who had defied the superintendent's orders to disperse and vacate the meadow in the Valley. The ensuing melee was billed by the national media as a riot. Urban America had arrived in the wilderness park!

There were pot smokers in the group—perhaps even heavier stuff; wine and beer drinkers—perhaps even stronger stuff; and they had littered the park like millions of Americans before them, tossing their trash from cars, campers and trailers. I decided to go to the park and see for myself. I went incognito.

Dressed in old clothes I joined a remnant of the group one evening sitting in a circle on the floor of the valley. I was accepted as just another hippie—only older; a pretty lady—early 20's perhaps—sat down next to me and the common wine bottle was passed. After we both had taken our drink, she opened her purse and removed two joints offering one to me. I declined and suggested a cigarette. She put the joints back in her purse. I removed two cigarettes from my pack, put them between my lips, lit them both and passed her one.

She took a drag—coughed in revulsion and exclaimed, "I have never had one of these things before."

An hour or so after I joined the party, a young man hurried up to the group and said, "Hey, you know what? I just heard the big mutha-fucker himself is in the park." I cringed with embarrassment at such language in mixed company. A lively debate ensued as to whether the director was really in the park and, more importantly, whether he gave a damn about their complaints. They were not much for the establishment! After several hours, I told the two young people sitting on either side of me that I had to leave—it was getting late. I left with no notice from the rest of them and joined the plain clothes park policeman who was wandering around in the vicinity. No one had bothered to inquire as to who I was.

Earlier, I had dispatched a detail of park police from Washington to Yosemite to assist the rangers in keeping order. The next day I visited with them and the park staff about the melee and the ensuing events, including my experiences of the night before. We agreed that I should meet with the young people that night and hear them out.

The word spread that the director would be at the Campfire Circle that night to speak and answer questions. We had a good crowd, including quite a few surprised youngsters from the night before. When the tenseness subsided, the questions came fast and furious; one, in particular, etched itself in my mind:

> Why would you prohibit us from sitting in the meadow mashing down the grass when you are cutting down 150-year old Douglas fir trees to expand a campground for recreational motor vehicles?

Not too long afterwards, with the approval of the National Park Service, a conservation club gashed through another meadow in the park to install underground utilities to the club's privately-owned campground in the park.

Whose parks are these? What are their purposes?

I. Whose Parks Are These?

I caught unshirted hell for directing that the locked gates across some of the historic roads in the parks, especially at the Great Smokies, be unlocked so that the ordinary visitor could drive along these pioneer roads.

During the time that the controversy over letting the "public" into these old roads was underway, we had an outstanding special use permit for a local conservation club to use an old government-owned mountain cabin in the Smokies as a base for their convenience while hiking and camping in the park. The cabin was located on a similar historic road which had been gated and locked for many years. A parking lot had been built at the locked gate so visitors could park and hike along the old road into the park. The club members had keys to the locked gate which permitted them to drive their vehicles along the road to the cabin to unload their food and gear; thereafter returning their cars to the parking lot, locking the gate and walking back to the cabin to gather their grub and gear for a hiking and camping trip in the park. Some of these club members were in the vanguard of those criticising me for letting the "public" into these roads.

A mother in Detroit wrote to tell me of the joyous two-week vacation she, her husband and two children had in the national parks. They had tent-camped, she wrote, in ten parks from Yellowstone to Yosemite. She was complimentary of the rangers they had met, the clean campgrounds and the good roads. My road atlas indicated that the two-week trip must have involved at least 5,000 miles. They "windshielded" a lot of scenery.

In the sixties the poor people marched on Washington to seek redress from the blight of poverty and denial of basic human rights and dignity. On orders of President Johnson we

3

allowed them to establish Resurrection City on the great Mall in sight of the Lincoln Memorial, the Washington Monument, the Capitol and the White House. For two years thereafter when testifying before the committees of Congress, I carried a special briefing book outlining the sequence of events that led up to the granting of permission to camp there; the cost of overseeing the encampment; and the cost of cleaning up and restoring the site afterwards. A lot of congressional spleens were vented on me.

Whose parks are these and for what purposes?

The small, primitive tent camps that provided food and shelter for park visitors in the early decades of the parks have grown into expansive, modern resorts: their investments and leases now protected by an almost impregnable legislative shield.

In the Concessions Policy Act of 1965, the Congress decreed that concessioners should have a "possessory interest" in the capital improvements (hotels, restaurants, gas stations, souvenir/gift shops, etc.) they erected on parkland. "Possessory interest" was defined as all attributes of ownership, except naked legal title. In other words, the concessioner could not remove the facility without the approval of the secretary. Moreover, if the secretary wanted it removed he, first, had to pay the concessioner the fair market value of the improvement. As director, I testified in support of this legislation. But today mushrooming park visitation and economic growth have overtaken the policy. For example, the concession properties of the Yellowstone Park Company were sold in the mid-sixties for approximately $3,000,000; by 1971 they had increased in value (with insignificant improvements) to almost $10,000,000; and by the time the National Park Service bought them in the late seventies (still with no significant additions to capital improvements), the government paid $19,800,000 for them.

4

I. Whose Parks Are These?

Park concessions are coveted by mega-business conglomerates mindful of their unique exemption from competition, their favorable contract terms, and their preferential right to a renewal of the contract.

When many of the great western parks were established, notably Yosemite, Sequoia and Glacier, small enclaves of vacation cabins and modest year-round residences were included in the park boundaries. By law, the National Park Service fulfills the role of local government to these enclaves, with responsibility for health, fire, police, etc. Over many decades the park service has tried to acquire these properties to simplify administration and better preserve the park resources. Many were acquired—some by donation by their owners to the government.

I retained a consulting firm when I was director to compare the cost of acquiring these properties vis-à-vis the cost of letting them continue to exist and develop into town-sites. The study concluded that it would cost the government millions more to allow these environmental cancers to remain than it would to eliminate them.

Secretary Cecil Andrus, with the leadership and support of the late Congressman Phil Burton (California), attempted to complete the acquisition of these properties. When he did so a small group of owners organized to protest his decision. The shrillness of their protests amidst the raging "sage brush rebellion" brought this desirable policy initiative to a halt. Then, in a matchless gesture of contempt, Secretary of the Interior James Watt appointed the head of the property owners' association to the Secretary's Advisory Board on National Parks, and gutted the Land and Water Conservation Fund to finance the acquisition of these and other properties.

Whose parks are these and for what purposes?

In the beginning, the Congress decreed that the Yellowstone country is "reserved and withdrawn...dedicated and set apart as a public park or pleasuring ground for the bene-

fit and enjoyment of the people." It was to be managed for
"preservation from injury or spoilation" and be retained in its
"natural condition"—but not quite, for the act authorized the
construction of "roads and bridle paths" in the park. Lest it
be misunderstood that preservation of the "natural condition" took precedence over the "pleasuring ground," the Congress (Act of June 4, 1906) enlarged and extended the
secretary's authority from constructing "roads and bridle
paths" to entering into leases for the transaction of "business
in Yellowstone National Park...*as the comfort and convenience of visitors may require,* and to permit the construction
and maintenance of substantial hotel buildings and buildings
for the protection of stage, stock and equipment." (Emphasis
supplied).

Thus, was formulated a bifurcated park policy of use and
preservation that has fueled many a bull session, filled volumes of learned—and some not so learned—books and journals, and frayed many a friendship for nigh on to a century.

The dichotomy was restated in the Act of August 25, 1916,
establishing the National Park Service.

> The Service thus established shall promote and regulate the
> use of the federal areas known as national parks, monuments,
> and reservations hereinafter specified by such means and
> measures as conform to the fundamental purpose of the said
> parks, monuments, and reservations, which purpose is to con-
> serve the scenery and the natural and historic objects and the
> wildlife therein and to provide for the enjoyment of the same
> in such manner and by such means as will leave them unim-
> paired for the enjoyment of future generations.
>   [The secretary of the interior]...may also grant privileges,
> leases, and permits for the use of land for the accommodation
> of visitors in the various parks, monuments, or other reserva-
> tions....

To insure that park administrators were not ensnared by
the allure of the "preservation" emphasis of its park policy to
the exclusion of "use," the Congress by the Acts of April 9,

6

I. Whose Parks Are These?

1924 and January 31, 1931, authorized the secretary not only to construct and reconstruct roads inside the parks but also roads outside the parks "whose primary value is to carry national park travel."

As the Congress continued to add areas to the National Park System, the evidence indicates that the trend-line shifted: its mandated policies for management tended to emphasize preservation over use. For example, in the legislation establishing Cape Hatteras National Seashore, the Congress, for the first time, named wilderness as a value to be preserved. Since the beginning, each administration had accepted the necessity for a high order of preservation of the natural scene. The Congress acknowledged this fact in making the Wilderness Act applicable to the National Park System. It said:

> The purposes of this Act are hereby declared to be... supplemental to the purposes for which...units of the National Park System are established and administered.

The Congress was not content, however, to have the Wilderness Act as the last word in the ongoing debate of preservation vs. use. In 1965 it returned to the issue in the Concessions Policy Act. In glorious ambiguity it reaffirmed both preservation and use in its statement of policy. However, gone from the congressional policy was the concept of use "*as the comfort and convenience of visitors may require.*" In its stead Congress prescribed a new policy, namely: "*necessary and appropriate for public use and enjoyment.*" Clearly, a tilt to park preservation—wasn't it?

Many concessioners and their partisans in the Congress disputed this interpretation of a preservation tilt.

I persuaded Jim Evans, the chief executive officer of Union Pacific—and a dedicated park enthusiast—to donate its concession facilities at Zion to the park service rather than sell them to someone else. I sought the donation for the avowed purpose of removing the facilities from Zion. They had been

7

determined to be neither "necessary" nor "appropriate for public use and enjoyment" (the congressional criteria for concessions) of that fragile, tender valley. The facilities were to be allowed to continue in operation only on an interim basis while private enterprise developed adequate lodging and food facilities in the gateway area to the park.

When it came time to remove the facilities in 1975 (after my departure from the service), the trade association of concessioners, the Utah governor and some of the Utah congressional delegation mounted a campaign to retain them, and they succeeded. One of the more interesting arguments advanced to keep the facilities in the park, according to historian William C. Everhart, was made by Governor Calvin Rampton who "spoke of a 'devastating' economic impact, *predicting* [that if the facilities were removed] *the traveling public would bypass the region*, threatening the solvency of motel, restaurant, and service station owners." (Emphasis supplied). Remarkably illuminating: the throngs of visitors to America's national parks do not come to see the parks but to stay in the concession accommodations!

The Grand Canyon of the Colorado River in Grand Canyon National Park is a geological phenomenon so magnificent that when first viewed in awe by President Theodore Roosevelt he counseled simply to leave it alone.

Far from leaving it alone, more than twenty aircraft operators send their noisy machines daily soaring and chopping their way over the Canyon on sightseeing excursions that endanger the craft and the lives of their passengers, and destroy the tranquility of the park experience for hundreds of thousands of visitors to the Grand Canyon. For more than two years beginning in 1984, the professionals of the National Park Service monitored this environmental insult to the majesty of the park. During this study of both safety and noise intrusion, an airplane and a helicopter collided, killing all twenty-five of the passengers and crews aboard.

At six public hearings the National Park Service heard testimony and recommendations regarding flight safety and visitor reaction to the incessant noise intrusion in the Canyon. While the park service regional director was presenting his recommendations to the director to control these unrestrained abuses, representatives of the commercial operators were meeting with the secretary of the interior—who has jurisdiction over the National Park Service—to decry the modest controls proposed. Responding favorably to the operators' lament, the Interior Department Assistant Secretary for Fish, Wildlife and Parks, William P. Horn, stripped the noise abatement recommendations from the National Park Service report. He proposed implementation of safety controls only.

Mr. Horn also proposed that the Federal Aviation Administration and National Park Service jointly fund a two-year research program on the effect of aircraft noise on park visitors—this proposal on top of the costly two-year study just completed in 1986 by the National Park Service.

Replying to this two-year joint research proposal by Mr. Horn, the administrator of FAA said that "... the initiation of a joint study of noise impact would require a substantial commitment of resources by the agency and will, therefore, require evaluation on a cost/benefit basis before we can respond." How astonishing! In a society that seems to know the cost of everything and the value of nothing, even the tranquility of a national park is to be subjected to a cost/benefit analysis.

There are other less visible but equally serious threats to the survival of our national parks: the continued existence of privately-owned lands that impair the management of such national parks as Sequoia, Yosemite and Glacier; mineral leasing, mining and logging at park boundaries that disrupt the ecological integrity of such parks as Yellowstone and Grand Teton, thus endangering their big game populations, particularly the grizzly bears; the mounting pressures of commercial hunters, loggers and miners clamoring for access to the bounty of our newest national parks in Alaska; expansive commercial developments in and adjacent to fragile park environments; and much more.

Whose parks are these and what are their purposes?

Parks are an attribute of sovereignty and, of course, were known for hundreds of years prior to the establishment of America's first national park. Always those parks belonged to the sovereign—the king, the queen, the emperor, or whatever the title of the reigning monarch. The peasants were never allowed in them, except to serve the potentates and their friends.

In the United States, the people are the sovereign. America's national parks are the special creations of the people through their elected representatives in the Congress. These national parks belong to the people. This is the uniqueness of the national park idea as first expressed in the Yellowstone National Park legislation of 1872.

The purpose of national parks remains in hot dispute. Is it their purpose to be host to exhuberant youth on a frolic or privately-owned camping spaces for congenial club members? Protectors of gene pools to sustain life or parking sites for relaxing in recreational motor vehicles bringing all the modern conveniences from the home left behind? Preserves for scientists to search for knowledge and understanding of the web of life or a sanctuary for the poor and the underprivileged among us to protest against the ravages of poverty and the indignity of justice too long denied?

Are the parks' purpose to be destination resorts to assuage the feverish rich and networks of highways for sight-seeing Americans in a hurry or places to exult amidst superlative wildness and scenic grandeur?

Money machines, for purveyors of tasteless food and tawdry merchandise, subsidized enclaves for private second-home retreats or places to gain an understanding of the people and events that shaped our heritage?

And, one more question: though we have required our parks to serve all of these purposes, can they survive if we require them to continue to do so?

The national park idea set forth in the legislation estab-

I. Whose Parks Are These?

lishing Yellowstone National Park in 1872 decreed that some of our natural inheritance should be preserved in perpetuity for other than material gain and riches. This novel idea in public land policy is a unique contribution of the United States to world culture. It has inspired more than one hundred nations around the world to set aside national parks and similar preserves.

Slowly, over many years, the Congress implemented its new park policy by reserving additional parklands for the nation's patrimony. Then, in the tumultuous decade of the nineteen-sixties when great waves of environmental concerns swept America, hundreds of thousands of our citizens joined hands in a mighty effort to set aside vast new parklands. Responding to their insistent demands, the Congress established new kinds of parks; reserved dozens of traditional parks; laid the groundwork for an incomparable parkland heritage in America's last frontier of Alaska; created a dazzling array of monuments and memorials to commemorate our rich cultural heritage; and acquired expansive landscapes for outdoor recreation.

In an article on the national parks (July 28, 1986) *Newsweek* suggests that society needs

> ...to re-think the role national parks and wilderness play in the American psyche, to decide once and for all whether a given natural feature is worth any more than people are willing to spend for postcards of it. On the one hand, there is the romantic idealism of William Reilly, president of the Conservation Foundation, who considers parks the cathedrals of American civilization, "the quintessential American idea." On the other is the tough-minded utilitarianism of Assistant Secretary of the Interior William Horn, who reminded park directors in a memo last December that "natural features are conserved chiefly for the benefit, use and enjoyment of the general public." Put more succinctly: do the parks exist to conserve nature or to put it on display?

Ansel Adams, one of America's premier photographers and interpreters of the natural scene, focused on the crisis in his autobiography:

> The pressures of a growing population, self-interest, and shortness of vision are now the greatest enemies of the national park idea.

Your national parks, once described by former park service director Newton Drury as America's "Crown Jewels," have fallen on troubling times.

II

COMING TO THE PARKS

My father farmed the same land that his father had in the Edisto River section of Colleton County, South Carolina. The farm was located off State Highway 61, about 5 miles from the crossroads village of Smoaks. My two younger sisters and I lived with our parents in a small frame house, a short distance from the "big house" where our grandparents lived.

One of my first recollections of those happy childhood days was to tug at "Aunt" Lula—a black neighbor who helped my mother with the washing and ironing—until she came to see my infant footprint emblazoned on the stucco facing of the fireplace.

I was born on St. Patrick's Day in 1920 and soon thereafter, to the consternation of my mother, my father pressed my right foot into a mixture of ink and fireplace soot and imprinted it in the stucco. Many years later, my wife Helen and I would return there occasionally to see my footprint on the fireplace. The house had burned leaving the chimney—a forlorn sentinel—standing amidst the briars and the brush with my footprint.

I began school in a one-room schoolhouse on the "big road" (Highway 61) about one mile from where we lived. Our only teacher taught seven grades. Her son, my first cousin and I constituted the first grade. In my second year, we were consolidated with the Smoaks schools and bussed there by the county.

My mother cooked on a large black wood stove equipped with a reservoir on one side to heat water and a warming oven suspended from the back frame above the cooking surface. It was a huge contraption that devoured wood. It was my chore to keep the woodbox filled, taking precious time away from fishing with my grandfather. Along creek banks, at sink-holes and on the Edisto River he instilled in me his love of fishing. If in his hearing my dad would occasionally chastise me for fishing and not helping him in his fields, my grandfather would reply, "Remember George, the Lord does not count the time against you when fishing."

Nothing in those happy childhood years prepared me for the impending Great Depression. I was with my bewildered and distraught father and grandfather when the farm was sold to pay the mortgage. We moved into my grandfather's house so that the new owner could use dad's house for a tenant.

One day, walking home from where the school bus dropped me off, I broke out of the woods with a clear view of my grandfather's house engulfed in flames. Built with pine, it burned with the intensity of tar. All that was saved were the clothes we were wearing; the Hartzog family had lost everything but faith in God and my mother's determination.

We survived the poverty of the next years by the grace of God, the charity of neighbors and the welfare of the New Deal. I remember vividly my father walking the five miles to Smoaks for government hand-outs of "butt meat," sugar, flour and corn meal. Butt meat is hog-jowl, fatty but great when cooked with collards, turnip greens or black-eyed peas. But these supplementary foods were not enough to ward off the perils of malnutrition. My health was jeopardized by pellegra, my father's occasional asthmatic condition became chronic and my mother was stricken with what began as a severe cold, and from which she was bedridden for months.

II. Coming to the Parks

She was later diagnosed for rheumatoid arthritis that deformed her knee joints, causing her to walk with a limp for the rest of her life.

Despair descended upon our family. In 1933 my mother moved the family to Walterboro, the county seat, in search of employment. She was a talented seamstress, much praised for her beautiful work. With the financial assistance of friends, she rented two rooms in a private home with shared bath and kitchen privileges. Soon she found work as a seamstress in the WPA Sewing Room—a New Deal work/relief program—where clothes were made to distribute to the poor. Part-time jobs to supplement her meager wages were a way of life to me—mowing lawns, pumping gas, washing clothes for the local cleaner; bus boy, store clerk, dishwasher and cook.

Poverty clung to us like a sweat-soaked shirt.

As difficult as those times were, my mother and father never let us lose hope. They constantly held up to us the challenge of Lincoln's mother to him—"Be somebody." Not until years later when I was working for the park service as a young lawyer in Washington did I fully understand how much Lincoln meant to dad. On his sole trip out of South Carolina to visit my family, I had taken the day off to show him the monuments and memorials of the nation's Capital. To my great disappointment he was not interested in my sightseeing plans. Just before going to bed, however, he said, "There's one thing I want to see—Lincoln's Memorial." At daybreak I drove him to the memorial, parked along the curb in front of the reflecting pool and started to get out of the car with him. "No," he said, "I want to go by myself." I watched as he slowly climbed the great staircase to the seated Lincoln. After gazing upon the statue of the brooding Lincoln, dad walked around the inside of the memorial reading every word carved on its marble walls. He and Lincoln were all alone—for at that early hour we were ahead of the crowds. Returning to the street, eyes moist in the morning sun, he announced, "I'm ready to go home."

In the winter of 1936, at age 16, I left school and went to work full-time at two jobs—pumping gas in the daytime and working nights as a clerk at the Lady Lafayette Hotel. After midnight when all the guests had bedded down I could cat-nap on a couch in the lobby.

The following spring (1937), we were visited by Colonel James F. Risher, owner and headmaster of Carlisle Military School at Bamberg, South Carolina, and a childhood friend of my mother and father in the Edisto River community. He insisted that I graduate from high school. He offered to take me back with him, saying that if in the time remaining in the school year, I could pass the final examinations, he would graduate me from Carlisle. I went and graduated.

My mother and dad shared with me their love and pride in their church. Encouraged by them, it was my ambition to become a Methodist preacher. In the summer of 1937 I was licensed by the Methodist church as a local preacher—the youngest one in the state at that time. In our financial condition, however, going to college was out of the question. But in September our preacher informed me that an anonymous group of local businessmen had given him the money for my first semester at Wofford College. I was, also, he told me, to be hired as assistant to the pastor of Bethel Methodist Church in Spartanburg at a modest stipend.

Near the end of the first semester the donations of my Walterboro friends ran out. My father remained seriously ill and was unable to work. My mother's meager wages were not adequate to support the family. Overwhelmed by these circumstances, I left college at the end of the semester. I got a job on a bread truck in Gaffney, South Carolina. Later, I returned to Walterboro to work as a clerk for the National Youth Administration. My parents had insisted that I take shorthand and typing in high school and I had become proficient in both skills. This enabled me, a short while later, to get a better job in the county welfare department.

In the winter of 1938–39, I landed a job with a timber cruiser on a project at Brunswick, Georgia. In the spring of

II. Coming to the Parks

1939, I went to work as a secretary for Joe Moorer, a partner in the law firm of Padgett & Moorer in Walterboro. At that time, with a high school diploma, one was still allowed to "read law" in preparation for taking the South Carolina Bar Examination. The three-year curriculum was prescribed by the state supreme court which also required that the studies be directed by a full-time practicing attorney. I asked Mr. Moorer to supervise my studies. Before agreeing, however, he required me to read and pass his quiz on the four volumes of Sir William Blackstone's "Commentaries on the Laws of England." They were written in old English, meaning that the s's appeared to be f's. The purpose of this test was to satisfy him of my interest in and commitment to the study of law.

To augment my $10 per week salary I joined the local National Guard Company. In September, 1940, the guard was called into federal service and our company went to Fort Jackson. Because of family hardship, a number of us from Colleton County were discharged during the summer and fall of 1941. We were all offered appointments in the reserve. All of us were corporals, buck sergeants and above. I was a buck sergeant. All except me, accepted the reserve appointments. Immediately after Pearl Harbor those who had accepted appointments were recalled to active duty.

Upon my return from Fort Jackson in May, 1941, I resumed my study of the law and my work as secretary and law clerk to Mr. Moorer. To supplement my income, I sold casualty insurance and worked part-time during campaign time as a stenographer for some political candidates. I took down speeches for U.S. Senator James F. Byrnes, for Olin D. Johnston (governor, later U.S. senator), for Jesse Padgett (state representative) and for Col. Winston C. Pearcy in his campaign for the state senate. Colonel Pearcy was a leading businessman of the county who was running for the state senate seat vacated when the local senator, Richard Manning Jeffries, resigned to serve as governor.

Dick Jeffries had been senator from Colleton County for many years. He was the undisputed political "King" of the county, a better word than "Boss," for he ruled benevolently and with grace. He was a tall, distinguished appearing, charismatic man with a warm and engaging personality. Like a hawk, no movement escaped his attention. On January 17, 1963—20 years after I left South Carolina—he wrote me in St. Louis to congratulate me on my appointment as associate director of the National Park Service.

Through long service he had risen in seniority to become president pro tempore of the state senate. Burnett R. Maybank who had been governor was elected to the United States Senate; the lieutenant governor succeeded him as governor and died shortly thereafter. The president pro tempore of the state senate was next in line to succeed to the governorship. Jeffries resigned his senate seat and became governor. Early speculation was that he would seek to keep the office in the next election. Instead, he opted to run again for his old senate seat. In the meantime, Colonel Pearcy had announced his candidacy.

Colonel Pearcy frequently began his "stump speeches" as follows:

> I remember a little story about people in politics. It seems that not so long ago a stranger came into a community and drove up to this house and seeing no one around but a little boy he asked the little fellow where his father was. The boy replied that his father was down in the woods. He then asked the little boy if he had seen any candidates around. The boy replied, "I don't know but you can look around on the back of that shed, Pa's got a lot of hides back there." And I think we will have a great big hide stretched out this summer: one from a politician who has been around quite awhile. That is my platform for the present at least.

At every campaign stop, or "stump speakin" the first thing Dick Jeffries would do was head straight for Colonel Pearcy and the group of people around him. He would push his way in, shake hands with the colonel first and then work the crowd. One day after the speeches were over and the crowd was breaking up, an old farmer who had observed Jeffries' performance on several occasions said to Colonel Pearcy: "Winston, if you are so much opposed to Dick Jeffries, why are you always shakin' hands with him?"

It was an uneven contest. Dick Jeffries won the election handily.

On the campaign trail with Colonel Pearcy, Dick Jeffries taught me that if pressin' the flesh of your adversaries doesn't convert them, it sure disarms them and confuses the bystanders.

Years later when I was director of the National Park Service I put this lesson to good use. Stan Hathaway, a Republican, (later to be named secretary of the interior) had been elected governor of Wyoming. He and a group of sport hunters in Wyoming were leading a campaign against our elk management program in Yellowstone. We had an overpopulation of elk and notwithstanding our efforts to trap and remove them to other ranges and zoos, we had, finally, been forced to shoot the remaining surplus. Our rangers shot and field dressed them, giving the meat to the Indians.

Direct reduction through shooting by the rangers had always been a bone of contention with the hunters who contended that the park should be opened for them to hunt and kill elk.

The controversy had generated so much heat for Senator Gale McGee, a Democrat of Wyoming, that he felt compelled to air the matter through a senate subcommittee hearing in the state. I was summoned to attend.

The hearing was held in the courtroom of the Casper Courthouse. Senator McGee, the presiding officer, was sitting in the judge's chair behind the raised bench. A witness table and chairs had been arranged at floor level in front of the bench, and behind the witness table were two rows of long pew-like benches for spectators on either side of the center aisle.

I was scheduled as the last witness of the day. However, I arrived early and took the first seat, first row, left side of the center aisle—immediately behind the witness chairs. All the witnesses when departing had to pass me.

The governor led off the parade of witnesses critical of our program. As each witness finished and was excused I rose from my seat, blocked the aisle, stuck out my hand and greeted them with, "Thank you very much, I'm George Hartzog."

The governor and the first few witnesses I greeted in this manner were startled and bewildered. By the end of the day when I had finished my testimony I was surprised by a round of applause from what had begun as a very disgruntled crowd.

After two failures, I passed the bar examination and was admitted to the bar of the supreme court of South Carolina on December 17, 1942.

My mentor, Joe Moorer, was a wise and good man who greatly influenced my life not only by supervising my reading of law but also by the counsel he shared with me. Shortly after I was admitted to the bar, in order to give me some courtroom experience, he permitted me to assist him in the trial of a criminal case. We represented the defendant. With suggestions from him I was allowed to examine the witnesses and make the defense argument to the jury.

Throughout the proceedings, Mr. Moorer sat at the counsel table. It had been agreed that if he had any suggestions for me he would write them on a note and put it at the end of the table. As I paced back and forth, I was to keep an eye on the table. If I saw a note, I was to pick it up as unobtrusively as possible, read and heed the instruction. About midway into my closing argument to the jury a note appeared. I palmed it and read its contents with consternation. It read, "You Won, Shut Up, Sit Down!" In the thousands of hours of testimony that I gave before committees of the Congress I never forgot that advice.

On March 17, 1943 (my 23rd birthday) I was drafted into the army and assigned as a clerk in the Judge Advocate's Office of the 75th Infantry Division at Fort Leonard Wood, Missouri. There I met Cpl. Paul H. Gantt.

Paul and I became lifelong friends. Because of a severe asthmatic condition he received a disability discharge early in 1944 and returned to the solicitor's office of the Department of the Interior in Washington where he had reemployment rights as an attorney. In the meantime, I was selected for officer's training. Commissioned in the Transportation Corps, I was assigned to the Military Police. After my release from service in March, 1946, I looked up Paul Gantt in search of a job. He arranged for interviews by the Solicitor's Office and by the chief counsel of the General Land Office (now the Bureau of Land Management). I was offered attorney jobs in both offices and accepted the one offered in the Oil and Gas Leasing Division of the General Land Office in the belief that it offered greater opportunity for moving into private practice.

In six months I had an opportunity to join a private Washington law firm and I left the government.

Within a matter of weeks I received a telephone call from the chief counsel of the National Park Service, Jackson E. Price, asking if I was interested in being interviewed for an attorney job with him in Chicago. The salary was more than I was then earning and double what I had earned with the General Land Office. I was interested. I got the job and in October, 1946, moved to Chicago where the headquarters of the National Park Service was then located.

Jack Price was an able and talented lawyer devoted to the park service. He insisted that his lawyers be helpful in solving management's problems. The first matter referred to me involved a proposal by the superintendent of Petrified Forest to combat theft of petrified wood from the park. His proposal was unacceptable legally. I prepared a reply for Jack's signature saying so. When he got my draft reply he called me in to his office and began, "I have read your memorandum and agree with your conclusion, but you have done only half the job; the other half is to tell him how he can cope legally with the problem he has. Take this draft back and do that."

A couple of weeks after my arrival Jack assigned me the job of writing a law enforcement handbook for the park rangers. Its purpose was to provide guidance on how to handle the most frequently encountered problems in the park— disorderly conduct, theft, trespassing, poaching, etc. The director had called a conference of chief rangers and chief clerks to convene in Chicago to discuss park operations. Jack and I met with the chief rangers to listen, ask questions and gather issues to be dealt with in the handbook. There were twenty-five to thirty of them from the major national parks —Yellowstone, Glacier, Grand Teton, Grand Canyon, Sequoia-Kings Canyon, Yosemite, Great Smokies, Everglades and many more—places known to me only on a map. Seasoned, savvy professionals, they each loved their parks, knew every inch of their terrain and all of their problems. At twenty-six, I was by far the youngest man at the meeting; a real tenderfoot in their world. They were tolerant and understanding. These were "people" people who each year served tens of thousands of tenderfeet like me who visited the parks. As the discussion ebbed and flowed their personalities came through—individualistic, tough, self-reliant men bound to a common code of service above self. Their comradarie was spontaneous and catching. By the end of the meeting I had found my career. I didn't know the parks but I knew these park service people and it was among them that I wanted to be.

III

FIRST EXPERIENCES

One snowy night in Chicago in December, 1946, while working late on a ranger law enforcement handbook, my office door opened and in came Minor (Tillie) Tillotson, director of the National Park Service southwest region with headquarters in Santa Fe, New Mexico. Small, wiry, leathery of face, in cowboy boots topped off with a ten-gallon roll-sided Stetson, he epitomized the self-reliant, can-do rangers and superintendents whose selfless service created the legends of the early National Park Service. "You're never going to be a success in this outfit," he said, "you are spending too much time on paperwork. Come on, let's go have dinner."

Over steak and beer he explained his paperwork management program. He had three boxes on his desk. Every day for a month, his secretary put all the park service mail in the box on the far right side of the desk. He never read it. If at the end of the month, no one had inquired about it, she moved the whole stack to the middle box where it remained for a month. If headquarters inquired about any item, it was removed, read and answered; otherwise, at the end of the second month the whole stack was transferred to the third box where it continued to rest for another month. If inquiry was made about a matter, it was handled; at the end of the

23

month, the contents of the third box were dumped in the trash.

"It's amazing," he concluded, "how much time I have available to run my region."

In June of 1947 Helen Carlson of Arlington, Massachusetts, and I were married. Because of the lack of new housing during the years of World War II and immediately thereafter, we were unable to lease an apartment in Chicago. But a National Park Service colleague was going to the field with his wife and daughter for a month's assignment. In exchange for sitting for their cat, they let us occupy their apartment in Evanston. Upon their return we moved to a hotel. Those were the days of rent control. If a residential hotel let you occupy a room for more than five days they were required to give you a weekly rate. The number of transient rooms in these hotels was very limited. Accordingly, we had to move to a new hotel every fifth day. The frustration of constantly moving had about convinced my bride to return to Massachusetts until I could find an apartment. In the meantime, I hit upon the idea of just "checking out" my shaving kit each fifth day and then reregistering that evening without requiring her to move. I broached the subject to the manager and we struck a deal. That was our last move until we returned to Washington in October, 1947, when the headquarters was moved back from Chicago.

Almost immediately upon our return to Washington, I learned that I was soon to be bumped from my position by an attorney in another bureau of the Interior Department who was being "riffed" (reduction in force). He had more seniority. This was a serious blow because I had fallen in love with my work in the National Park Service.

Apparently my work had been satisfactory to my superior because Jack Price solved the problem, in cooperation with Regional Director Tillotson, by transferring me to Lake Texoma National Recreation Area in Denison, Texas, and abolishing my job in Washington.

Lake Texoma was a Corps of Engineers project on the Red

River (Texas-Oklahoma border) on which the National Park Service managed the land and recreation resources. It was my job to lease the land for purposes of agriculture and business use (marinas, stores, etc.) to serve the visitors.

In August, 1948, the leasing program had been largely accomplished. The displaced attorney who desired my job in Washington had found another and I was transferred back to the chief counsel's office in Washington.

Upon my return, I applied for admission to the bar of the U.S. Supreme Court. The requirements for admission were modest: good character and in good standing at the bar of one of the states for a minimum of five years.

It was customary to invite the departmental solicitor (general counsel) to move admissions to the Court for Interior attorneys. The solicitor was Mastin G. White. He was a graduate of the University of Texas Law School with a master's degree in law from Columbia and a doctorate in law from Harvard. Before World War II he had distinguished himself as a special assistant to the attorney general and as general counsel of the Department of Agriculture. Upon his return from the War, he had joined the Interior Department. Jack Price asked Mastin to move my admission. He agreed and invited me to ride to the Supreme Court building with him in his chauffeured government car. Helen and a few of our friends who were giving us a luncheon afterwards went separately to the Court.

During our brief ride from the Interior building to the Supreme Court building, Mr. White asked me where I was from, (his ancestors had migrated from my home state of South Carolina to East Texas after the Civil War); how long I had been in the department and where I had attended college and law school. I told him I was only a high school graduate and that I had read law in a law office in South Carolina. He lapsed into silence. Fortunately we were almost at the Court.

At the appointed time he moved my admission and with the ceremony completed, greeted Helen, said good-bye to me and departed. A short time later, a memorandum was issued from the Solicitor's office to the several bureau chief counsels advising that, henceforth, only lawyers who were law school graduates would be hired in the department.

In 1948 I enrolled in the night program of the School of Business Administration at American University in Washington. During the next seven years I completed the B.S. degree program and all but three hours of the M.B.A. degree program before I was transferred again to the field.

In the meantime, in 1951, I was promoted and assigned to the concessions division in the Washington office of the service as the assistant division chief. This was the division responsible for negotiating contracts for the operation of commercial visitor services (concessions) in the parks. High on the priority of my assignment was to write a concessions manual (handbook) for use by the field personnel involved in the administration of the concession contract operations.

In August, 1955, I was transferred to the assistant superintendent position at Rocky Mountain National Park. My boss at Rocky Mountain was James V. Lloyd, who had been superintendent at Lake Texoma when I was assigned there as the regional attorney for the Southwest region.

Jimmie grew up in Washington, D.C. He started work as a "chain-man" on a government survey crew where he met Arthur Demaray, later to be a director of the National Park Service. When the National Park Service was authorized in 1916, Mr. Demaray, then in the Geological Survey, was transferred to the new bureau. He was instrumental in getting Mr. Lloyd a ranger job in Yosemite working for the legendary chief ranger there, Forest Townsley. He was a resourceful, tough—sometimes tyrannical—boss who worked interminably long hours to perfect the new ranger organization, and demanded that his rangers do likewise. Mr. Lloyd was trained in the "School of Hard Knocks." On his way to being superintendent he had progressed slowly through all of the Civil Service grades.

Jimmie loved to tell the story about the day while on patrol as a young beginning ranger in Yosemite he came across a bear who had caught his toes in a steel trap. Poaching was rampant in the early days of the national parks.

The bear was hurting and furious. Jimmie raced his horse back to the chief ranger's office and reported the incident to Chief Townsley.

The chief said to this city boy, "Here's a pair of shears. Go back and cut off his toes; you can take another one of the rangers with you." Back to the trapped bear these two rangers went. Fortunately, the trap with the bear in it was on a hill. As Jimmie told the story, his companion got on the downhill side of the bear and started challenging him. The bear became more angry, lunging the full length of the chain at his tormentor. In the meantime, Jimmie was easing down the hill to the trap. When the bear was fully extended, he reached behind him with the shears and cut off his toes. Off-balance, the bear rolled down the hill. Meanwhile the rangers grabbed their guns awaiting his charge. Instead the bear went limping, growling off into the brush.

Jimmie married the superintendent's secretary and they went on to have a great 50-year career together in the National Park Service. Ethel was charming and sensitive, and always salving the egos that Jimmie had busted!

Trail Ridge Road traverses Rocky Mountain National Park, across the Continental Divide, from Estes Park, Colorado on the East to Grand Lake on the West. About 3 miles of the road, above the 12,000-foot elevation, slices through the tundra at the top of the mountain range. On the east side of the Divide is a visitor service complex: store, food counter, restrooms, interpretive exhibits, parking lots and short walks.

Shortly after my arrival, we received an emergency call about a couple in trouble at the top of the mountain. The parking lots were full, so they parked along the sloping shoulder of the road and got out to have a better look at the awe-inspiring view of the park. The husband forgot to leave the car in gear or set the hand brake. Soon they observed their car rolling across the tundra toward the Thompson

River Canyon thousands of feet below. The husband ran to catch his new car; fortunately for him just as he caught the door handle he tripped over a boulder and fell. The car continued downhill, gathering speed as it went. One witness described it as fairly leaping like a rabbit and with each leap the boulders smashed the bottom of the car scattering parts and metal fragments for several yards on either side of its self-made trail to the bottom where it settled in plain view from the top of the road.

Such a visual intrusion could not be left there. The chief ranger position was vacant at the time and the rangers decided the newly arrived assistant superintendent should accompany them into the Canyon to decide what disposition to make of the wreckage. Mr. Lloyd agreed.

Two rangers and I set out to inspect the wreckage. There was no trail across the tundra, so we followed the route of the car to the bottom.

I had spent seven years in Washington. My exercise consisted mainly of repairing an old house and walking to night school about six blocks away. I was not excited about the test of stamina on which I was about to embark. But I had wanted a field assignment and now I had one. At 12,000 feet the air was thin, oxygen was scarce and the terrain was rough, strewn with boulders against which the car had crashed on its descent. My work uniform and boots had not arrived so I was attired in ranger gray dress shirt, green trousers and a new pair of cordovan leather sole dress shoes. While the ranger's work boots gripped the tundra, my shoes slid over it. In places the descent was quite steep necessitating my walking side-step and in some instances inching painfully downward on my rump. Gasping for breath and struggling with and against the boulders, I arrived at the edge of the Canyon. It was a harrowing and distressful experience.

It is not without purpose that the rangers say "one mile down and three miles up." The return trip was even harsher —my shoes sliding out from under me, requiring, at times, that I crawl on my hands and knees, muscles quivering from exhaustion.

Our decision was to require the visitor's insurance company to have the car cut into pieces and placed under a ledge in the canyon wall so that it would not be visible from the road.

As devastating as the trip had been physically, the ego-busting was even worse; for, during the ordeal it had become obvious to me that I was needed on the trip about as much as a "Buick needs a fifth hole."

The following Sunday one of the rangers invited me to go fishing with him in Bierstadt Lake—named for the great western artist. He suggested that we take our families and have a picnic lunch. We were thrilled to accept.

Bierstadt Lake is an easy, short walk from one of the main roads in the park. It is small, nestled at the foot of the mountains that are mirrored in its quiet, placid waters. Away from the bustling crowd, it is an idyllic spot for a family outing.

We decided to fish awhile before having lunch. The ranger and I hooked up poles for the children and lines for ourselves. The area was pleasantly bug free—only an occasional mosquito. After more than an hour without so much as a nibble, the children lost interest. We recessed fishing for lunch. The children did not care to resume fishing after lunch, so the ranger took the ladies and the children for a walk around the lake. I would not be deterred—for another three hours after lunch, I continued to beat that lake, but never a bite.

The next morning I was telling Mr. Lloyd of my fishing trip with the ranger to Bierstadt Lake. He laughed uproariously. There had never been a fish in Bierstadt; its a sterile lake.

My hazing by the rangers over, we settled down to work.

I learned a great deal about park operations from Jimmie Lloyd—both things to do and not to do. He was an absolute stickler about ranger entrance station operations, clean restrooms and roadsides. If his rangers didn't smile when greeting the visitors on arrival, they didn't work long in Jimmie's organization. Woe to the maintenance supervisor on whose beat he found a dirty restroom or roadside litter.

As that first summer season was winding down, Mr. Lloyd took me with him for a trip across the mountain to inspect the west side operations. On our return we stopped on top of the mountain to view the glorious sight of the setting sun and to watch the pikas in their frenzied labor to harvest grass for the approaching winter. As we stood there chatting, a lady walked up to me and asked, "Ranger, what are those little creatures?"

"They are pikas," I replied.

"No they are not," she retorted, "I know what a pika is."

I was stumped. Stuttering around and flustered I parried, "Well, that's what they look like to me."

She persisted, "I know they are not."

Mr. Lloyd leaned over and whispered in my ear, "Tell her they are golden-crested pikas."

I peered into the rocks again and said, "You know, I do believe they may be golden-crested pikas."

She had observed Lloyd's whisper to me. "Well, that's better," she replied victoriously, adding, "I knew you didn't know what they were."

We got in the car and started down the mountain for home. Embarrassed at having made an idiot of myself in my first opportunity to interpret the fauna of the park, I said to Mr. Lloyd, "Ed Alberts (the park naturalist) didn't tell me anything about golden-crested pikas when he brought me up here the other day on an orientation trip."

"I am not surprised," Lloyd replied, "for there isn't any such thing. But why would you want to argue with a visitor?"

About all of these things Jimmie Lloyd was right; I learned later as director that every visitor has one representative in Congress and two senators. If the visitor believes he/she got a bad shake, off go the letters and the director has a problem.

Jimmie was not much for negotiating, however. The park concessioner, Ike James had a bad septic field at one of his lodging accommodations. Ike was a fiesty, self-made man who like Jimmie, also did not negotiate well. Jimmie ordered the field to be repaired and the concessioner agreed to fix it by spring. For some reason, he did not get the job done.

When Jimmie found out about it, he came into my office and said, "I want you to write a letter for me to Ike telling him to have that field fixed in a week or else." I drafted the letter, but left off "or else" and took it into him for signature. He read it, looked up and said, "I thought I told you to tell him to fix it 'in a week or else.'" I explained that I left out "or else" because I didn't think Ike would respond very well to an ultimatum. Never mind, he replied, do as I say! I took the letter back and added the ultimatum.

A week went by and there was no reply from Ike. Jimmie had the rangers check and the field still had not been fixed. Upon learning this, he came in the office in a towering rage. He walked right by my door, saying to his secretary, "Get me Ike James." Our offices were back to back with a paper thin wall between. Each of us could hear all that was going on in the other office, if you listened closely, and on this occasion I did.

In a moment, I heard his secretary call out, "Mr. James is on the line," then I heard Lloyd's side of the conversation.

"Hello." Pause. "Ike, did you get my letter?" Pause. "Well why isn't that field fixed?" Pause.

Bang—down went the receiver.

I got up and went into his office. "What did Ike say?" I asked.

"He said he is waiting on 'or else.'" Whereupon, without stopping, he continued, "You get a hold of Ike's brother and get that field fixed."

We had several saddle horse operators at Rocky Mountain. Each spring we had to issue them a concession permit to carry on their pack operations in the park. That was one of my assignments. The park had a much better permit form than the one I had incorporated in the concessions manual I had written when I was in the Washington office, so I used it.

In those days, a copy of each local permit was sent to the regional office. Shortly after I issued the saddle horse permits, the superintendent received a memorandum from the region wanting to know why we had not used the form in the manual. I explained to Mr. Lloyd that I had used the local form because it was better than the one in the manual and since I had written the manual I didn't think there was a problem. We gave the region's memo the "Tillotson treatment." The episode did raise a question in my mind, however, about the efficacy of the handbook series.

In the meantime, two good things happened to me. I was selected for one of eight government-wide scholarships offered, annually, by the American Management Association for its management course, then given at the Astor Hotel in New York, and I was offered the assistant superintendent's job at the Great Smoky Mountains National Park (Tennessee/North Carolina), a larger park operation.

In the fall of 1957, my family moved to park headquarters at Gatlinburg, Tennessee, and I was detailed to Washington to write my last manual—the one on land acquisition.

After several weeks in Washington—I joined my family at the Smokies. My bride had done a remarkably fine job of moving in and getting the children settled down and in school. The government house assigned us was one of three at the end of a cul-de-sac behind park headquarters at the Gatlinburg entrance (Sugarlands) to the park. The chief ranger and the park engineer and their families lived in the other two houses. From the front porch of our house we could look several miles down the main park road to the Chimneys —a prominent geological feature of the park. On that first night home, as my bride and I were inspecting the basement and the newly installed washer and dryer, I happened to look up to the ceiling over the washer. Wrapped around the hot water pipe was a Copperhead snake; their bite is highly poisonous. Casually, I thought, so as not to alarm Helen, I asked, "How long have you had him with you?"

"Who?" she asked.

III. First Experiences

"That Copperhead up there on that pipe," I replied. She blanched and bolted for the door. At Rocky Mountain we had lived above 7500 feet and had no poisonous snakes; in fact, we seldom saw one of any kind.

As she raced up the stairs, I yelled after her to call Corky Johnson the chief ranger.

Momentarily, I heard her on the telephone in the kitchen above.

"Corky, come over here right away. I got a Copperhead in my basement." Pause.

"No, I'm not drunk."

Bang! Up went the phone.

In two or three minutes Corky arrived. We greeted each other and surveyed the situation.

We decided our line of attack: Corky got an eight-foot piece of one-by-two so he could pin the snake to the basement wall while I bashed him with a two-by-two. Murphy's law overrode our plan of operation. Corky succeeded only in knocking the snake off the pipe and onto the floor behind the washing machine. The senior leadership of the park responsible for the safety of millions of visitors each year were now in a full state of alarm for their own safety. Since we had awakened the snake from his comfortable hibernation, we certainly could not leave him where he fell. There was real danger in trying to get in close enough to move the washer and dryer because we didn't know just where he might have crawled. While we were standing there silently pondering our plight, I'll be doggone if that critter didn't crawl out on his own. Wood still in hand we quickly ended the encounter.

Hunting black bear in the Smokies was a part of the heritage of the natives. The establishment of the park, with its prohibition of sport hunting, was an unwelcome intrusion on their recreation. For many years after the park was established, poaching of bears in the park was a serious problem; occasionally it was a dramatic one. One day a terrified elderly couple came into park headquarters. After we got them calmed down, we learned that they had stopped along the road at the top of the mountain; she was feeding a black bear and he was taking pictures. Suddenly a young man walked up to the bear and shot it. Two companions quickly appeared and the three of them stuffed the bear in the trunk of their car and took off in the direction of Cherokee on the North Carolina side of the park. When the couple feeding the bear could gather their wits they headed in the opposite direction toward Gatlinburg. They had the license number of the culprits, but by the time we could alert the patrol rangers our bear-harvesting friends had departed.

Ed Hummel was regarded as one of the outstanding superintendents in the system. He was a creative, supportive manager who gave his staff the opportunity to achieve. I was especially fortunate to serve as his assistant. He was also blessed with a talented, attractive bride. They were both highly respected participants and leaders in community affairs. Ed encouraged his staff to join service clubs, be active in Boy and Girl Scouts, Little League, etc., and accept speaking engagements in the small towns surrounding the park.

In May, 1958 Ed Hummel was promoted and transferred to the superintendency of Glacier National Park. He was succeeded by Fred Overly, the superintendent of Olympic National Park.

Fred Overly was an extroverted, gregarious, back-slapping fellow who never met a stranger in his life. As assistant superintendent it was my assignment to introduce him to the people in the local communities around the park.

Hazel Creek on the North Carolina side of the park was rated as one of the ten best trout fishing streams in America. Before the land was condemned by the Tennessee Valley Authority for the Fontana Dam more than 1,000 people lived in the valley. Most of the land was taken not because it was needed for the reservoir, but because when the reservoir was filled access to the valley was cut off, except for boats. There had never been a hatchery trout put in Hazel Creek and we allowed fishing only with artificial lures. The trout were wild, beautiful and plentiful—even our seven-year-old son could catch them on a fly.

Ed Hummel had fixed up one of the old farmhouses on Hazel Creek as a summer seasonal ranger station and living quarters. When not used by the rangers, Ed and I would use it occasionally to take a community leader or two over for some fishing.

Soon after Fred arrived I suggested we go to Hazel Creek and take along four prominent leaders in Gatlinburg who were avid trout fishermen. The trip was set.

Fred had served in the Washington office of the service before he was assigned as superintendent at Olympic. He had never had any experience with the chiggers (sometimes called red-bugs—actually a form of mite), ticks, no-see-ums (gnats) and other pesky insects of the Southern forests. We were going to be at Hazel Creek at the height of chigger-time. I suggested that Fred take along some sulphur to put over his shoes, socks, pants and shirt. It smells bad but it beats having chiggers. I also suggested that he not sit down on any logs, old stumps or other forest materials—the native habitat of the chigger. Fred rejected the sulphur and was heedless of where he sat down to rest. I looked up once while fishing and saw him sitting on a huge, rotting log. When we got back to the station that night I suggested he at least take a hot, soaking bath as quickly as possible. He preferred to have a drink and dinner. Before going to bed, he did take a hot bath, but too late. The next morning what seemed like a million chiggers were feasting on his rear end, backside up to his belt and the backs of his legs. Every spot is an itch and if you break the skin it's a pain. He itched and hurt so bad that by noon we called the boat to take him to the doctor. That was the first—and last time—he ever offered "fresh western meat" to Smoky Mountain chiggers.

Upon my arrival at the Smokies in the fall of 1957 I had joined the Gatlinburg Rotary Club. The club sponsored a number of projects, including a recreation program for the local children. Because of the age of our twins, then eight, I took on the job of organizing a baseball program for youngsters ages seven to ten. I almost ruined the program.

There were only enough boys in that age group to make up one team. Our twin daughter, Nancy, was a real tomboy and so was Corky's daughter, Loretta. They were the same age and they loved baseball. It seemed perfectly logical to me, therefore, to organize a boy's team and a girl's team. Moreover, I told the boys that they should allow the girls to bat first. I quickly discovered how stupid I was. Every time Nancy or Loretta got to bat they cleared the bases with home runs! Only after batting around a couple of times did the boys manage to get the girls out. With Nancy pitcher, and Loretta catcher, it was three boys up and three boys down. We never did get to the end of the game; the boys quit in disgust. Like those boys, I was mystified by the "weaker sex" bit. To salvage the program for the balance of the summer, the girls agreed, albeit reluctantly, to split up and some go over on the boys' team with some of the boys going over to the girls' team. Fortunately, before another summer rolled around I was transferred to St. Louis.

IV

THE GATEWAY ARCH

"What the hell did you do now?" one of my National Park Service friends wrote to me when it was announced in December, 1958 that I was to be the new superintendent of the Jefferson National Expansion Memorial National Historic Site (JNEM) in St. Louis—the location of The Gateway Arch. After my arrival on duty, I learned that I was not the preferred choice for the job. But as indicated by my friend's question, among National Park Service careerists, at that time JNEM was not the preferred duty station in the National Park System.

JNEM was the first national historic site established pursuant to the Historic Sites Act of 1935 authorizing the preservation of places of national significance in the interpretation of our national history. The purpose of the area is to commemorate Jefferson's Louisiana Purchase and the Westward Expansion of the United States.

But there is another less scholarly explanation for the Memorial at this location on the waterfront in St. Louis. Apocryphal, in part, perhaps, but told many times in the presence of Barney Dickmann, a former St. Louis mayor, without disapproval or correction. The story is important because it illuminates more than most, the vital role of politics—sometimes rawhide—in the establishment and preservation of America's parklands.

The father of the idea for a Memorial on the Mississippi River in downtown St. Louis was Luther Ely Smith, Sr., a distinguished local lawyer and civic leader. The grand political strategist who made the dream a reality was his ally and friend, the mayor of St. Louis, the Honorable Bernard F. (Barney) Dickmann. When I arrived in St. Louis in January, 1959, Barney was retired but still active in behalf of St. Louis as an elder statesman. Luther Ely Smith, Sr. was dead.

In 1933, Luther Ely Smith, Sr., Barney Dickmann and a large contingent of St. Louisans had been invited to Vincennes, Indiana, for the dedication of the George Rogers Clark Memorial. The group made the roundtrip by train.

They were impressed by the Clark Memorial and its favorable impact on the city. On the way home there was discussion among the group about how they might have such a project to rejuvenate their downtrodden St. Louis Waterfront. Brilliantly, Smith conceived the idea of a memorial to the Louisiana Purchase—Dickmann agreed enthusiastically but, alas, there was not adequate city money for such an undertaking.

In 1935 Dickmann came to Washington to seek federal help from his friend, President Roosevelt. Roosevelt was sympathetic but uncertain how he could assist. He sent Barney to see the attorney general. Barney was frustrated by his meeting at the Justice Department.

Roosevelt was looking forward to another run for the presidency. Dickmann was the unchallenged leader of the political apparatus of St. Louis. Carrying St. Louis in the next election was crucial to carrying the state of Missouri. Armed with knowledge of this reality, Barney returned to the White House where he told his friend, the president, "You can forget Missouri next time around." This was a threat the president could not ignore. He summoned the attorney general and instructed him to be helpful. As occasionally happens with lawyers, the attorney general had not heard all the facts clearly the first time—mainly, the one about carrying Missouri in the next election. When this fact was understood fully by him, he discovered the newly enacted Historic Sites Act which was the perfect vehicle for accomplishing what the mayor sought.

The agreement between the city and the federal government provided for financing the project on a matching basis of one dollar of city money to three dollars of federal money. A 91-acre site was acquired and cleared for the project. World War II intervened and the project was closed down and remained in limbo for more than a decade. In retrospect, this was not bad because no clearly defined development plan had been agreed upon for the memorial.

While the nation was mobilized for war, the business leadership of St. Louis, through the Jefferson National Expansion Memorial Association, kept alive the interest in the Smith/Dickmann dream for a memorial. Between 1945 and 1947 they raised $225,000 to sponsor a nationwide architectural competition for a design of the memorial.

A young architect, Eero Saarinen, the son of the renowned architect, Eliel Saarinen, had just left his father's firm and launched his own practice. Eero was an unknown. Both he and his father submitted proposals in the competition. Eero's design was one of five selected by the panel to be fleshed out for final evaluation.

Inadvertently, however, the panel of judges sent the telegram notifying the semi-finalists to Eliel Saarinen—not to his son, Eero. It was some time later before the mistake was discovered and with many red faces, Eero was advised that it was he—not his father—who had been selected as the semi-finalist. Eero's design of a heavily landscaped park from which rose a soaring, stainless steel arch—symbolic of St. Louis as the Gateway to the West—won the competition.

When I was assigned to JNEM, Howard Baker, the regional director of the Midwest region (headquarters in Omaha) met me in St. Louis to introduce me to the mayor and the JNEM Association.

I had arrived in St. Louis amid a rainstorm on January 31, 1959. The temperature dropped during the night and the next morning the city was an icy wonderland. The hazards and inconvenience of trying to move around were minor disturbances compared to what I learned that day from Howard.

In 1956 Congress appropriated $2,640,000 to start the relocation of the railroad tracks of the Terminal Railroad (an association of all the rail carriers in St. Louis) which separated the site from the river. The tracks were to be put underground in a tunnel. Even though the Congress had appropriated the money on May 19, 1956, the plans had not even been drawn. The mayor was rightly frustrated and upset. Howard told me that in a rather testy meeting in Washington the mayor had extracted a commitment from the park service director that work would be underway by July 1, 1959. Most of the first day of February was already gone!

Howard and I paid our courtesy call on the mayor. The mayor was proper and formal as we all were: Howard because he was still smarting from the recent Washington meeting, me because I was plumb scared, and the mayor, in typical Missouri "show me" fashion. Like my friend said, what in hell had I done to land in this situation?

Raymond Tucker had been an engineering professor at Washington University before being elected mayor. He was charismatic, smart as a whip and very organized. I liked him immediately. When Howard departed the next day, I called the mayor for another appointment to get better acquainted with him and his staff. I was very anxious to get off on the right foot with the mayor.

I went over my background with him: country lawyer from a small town in South Carolina, four years in the army in World War II and thirteen years as a career employee of the National Park Service. I explained to him that I knew the "paper chase" of the bureaucracy but I knew nothing of big city politics; my only exposure to the game never having involved a town of more than 3,500 people. With all the confidence of a real champion, which he proved to be, he said,

IV. The Gateway Arch

"That's great, we got a winner; you move the paper and I'll handle the politics." With that partnership established, I turned my attention to Eero Saarinen & Associates who had been retained to design and supervise the construction of the project.

Joseph Jensen, an engineer by training, and a partner of Saarinen's was the manager of the project. He arrived in St. Louis during my first week on duty. A strapping, personable man, 6 foot 4 or thereabouts, he proved to be resourceful, bright, talented and hardworking. He was so good, as a matter of fact, that after I became director, I persuaded him to join the National Park Service as my associate director in charge of professional services.

He had come to St. Louis to bring me bad news. It would be several weeks before even preliminary plans for the relocation of the railroad tracks—the first phase of the project—would be available for review. He promised me they would expedite the plans as much as possible. Based on my experience with plan review inside the park service, I realized that there was no way we were going through preliminary review with the railroads, their unions, the city, the Missouri Public Service Commission and the National Park Service, make revisions, prepare final plans, advertise and sign a construction contract by July 1. I reported this depressing development to the mayor and to Regional Director Baker. Their response was, *you must make that deadline.*

Howard was a landscape architect by training. He had been in management for many years and was respected by all of us as one of the most able of the regional directors. He wanted his field operations run by the book, but he was flexible. We had known each other for a dozen years or so and were friends. Later when I became director, I invited him to Washington as my associate director for operations—from which he retired from government service.

Toward the end of February, Joe Jensen called to say the preliminary plans would be ready for review in March. I called Howard with this information and told him that if we

41

were going to be under contract by July 1 we were going to have to dispense with the routine.

Cautiously, he asked, "What do you have in mind?" I told him that we were going to have to assemble all interested parties in St. Louis for one all-day review session, advertise the work on a unit price basis—so much per yard for excavation, concrete, foot of track, etc. This then would permit us to use the preliminary plans as a basis for contracting. He was agreeable to the one review session, but he was not too sure about the unit price bidding.

We scheduled a date for the review and issued the invitations to those involved in the project. More than one hundred engineers, architects, estimators, construction superintendents, union representatives, state, city and railroad officials showed up. I had expected a bunch, but this was ridiculous! The out-of-town park service people were overwhelmed. Realizing the impossibility of meeting the deadlines through the bureaucratic processes, Howard quickly approved advertising on the basis of the preliminary plans and unit prices.

The construction contract was signed on June 18, 1959, and a groundbreaking ceremony was held on June 23. The original contract was for an estimated $2,400,000.

My park service colleagues involved in government contracting were duly upset by Howard permitting me to proceed in such an unorthodox—though completely legal—arrangement. *They hadn't seen nothin yet!*

In late summer, Saarinen's office finished the preliminary plans for the north and south overlook structures and retaining walls—essential elements for completing the railroad relocation. Joe Jensen had taken off the estimated quantities and based upon the unit prices of the low bid on the first work, these structures were estimated to cost $2,506,000— an amount in excess of the original contract. In the meantime, the prices of concrete and steel had increased modestly. MacDonald Construction Company, the general contractor agreed to undertake this new work at the unit prices bid in the spring. If we brought in another contractor he would have to work on top of MacDonald; that's a mare's nest of coordination.

All of the work had to be completed before we could switch over train operations to the relocated tracks and get on with building the Gateway Arch. I recommended to Howard that we proceed with the additional work as a change order to the original contract. A change order is an amendment to the contract, negotiated without advertising, between the government contracting officer and the contractor. The General Accounting Office has carefully prescribed criteria which must be met before the change order can be negotiated. The principal criteria are that the additional work must be directly related to the contract work underway and that the change is essential to a useable project.

My recommendation set off a fire storm. Howard's staff was aghast. After analyzing all of their objections, I concluded that the real basis for their disapproval was simply the size of the change order vis-à-vis the original contract. I persuaded Howard to send the question to the Washington office. The Washington office staff was in lock-step with the region and turned thumbs down. And, to spike the issue they even got a lawyer in the solicitor's office to agree with them.

My favorite definition of a lawyer is: a person professionally trained to help you become confused in an orderly manner.

During my time in the chief counsel's office, one of my tasks was to review government contracts and change orders for legal sufficiency. I was confident in this instance the staff and the lawyer were wrong.

The final arbiter on such contract issues is the comptroller general, the head of the General Accounting Office. I could get the issue there, however, only with the approval of the director. I called and asked his permission to come to Washington to argue the issue before the lawyers at the General Accounting Office. I did not want his "doubting Thomases" to do it for me. He agreed but insisted I take them along too.

The meeting was scheduled and I came to Washington to

present my position to the General Accounting Office. GAO agreed with me and approved issuing the change order, which I did in January, 1960. The mayor was elated; this meant we could keep the work on schedule.

The second phase of construction involved excavation for the footings for the Gateway Arch and the Underground Visitor Center to house the Museum of Westward Expansion, theaters, offices and other administrative space. It was estimated this work would cost approximately $3,500,000. The work was expensive because of the limestone bluffs that had once existed along this stretch of the river. Thousands of yards of limestone had to be excavated.

Alas, however, the administration had included only $1,650,000 in the 1961 fiscal year budget for the project. Immediately the community leadership began a campaign to get the Congress to increase the appropriation. The local newspapers—the St. Louis Globe-Democrat and the St. Louis Post Dispatch—joined in the chorus. The focus of the attention was Clarence Cannon, chairman of the House Appropriations Committee and one of the most senior and influential members of the House of Representatives.

Mr. Cannon was from the little country town of Elsberry to the north of St. Louis on the way to Hannibal. He was small in stature—almost elf like—but woe betide the person that misread that canny countenance. He was unmoved by the pleas to increase the budget. His position was simple. "If President Eisenhower wants the money, ask for it." The newspapers were highly critical of his obstinate, downright obstructionist disregard of their crusade.

I remarked to Mayor Tucker about this continuing drumbeat and expressed dismay that Mr. Cannon could stand his ground under such an onslaught. "It's simple, George," he said. "Not a soul in Elsberry reads either the Globe-Democrat or the Post Dispatch."

Finally, Tom Curtis, the Republican congressman from Webster Groves to the south of St. Louis, prevailed on President Eisenhower to ask for the additional money in a supplemental appropriation. Clarence Cannon promptly complied and we were back on schedule.

Eero Saarinen was a genius. Reserved but not introverted, brilliant but not bookish, demanding perfection of himself and of others but not bullying, he was by every measure a gentleman. He was blessed with a vivacious, talented, extroverted bride, Aline, who, by profession, was a journalist and art critic for the New York Times. Writing about Eero's Gateway Arch before they were married, she called it, "Timeless, but of our time." Mayor Tucker said of Eero, after their first meeting, "He's the greatest damn salesman I ever met." He possessed the easy grace that enabled him to dominate a meeting without being boorish.

Eero did not frequent the project—he left that pretty much to Joe Jensen—but occasionally he did look in on it. One such visit occurred just as the contractor was bringing the north retaining wall out of the ground. The exterior of the wall, facing the river to the East, was flat—perpendicular to the ground. After standing at the corner of Wharf Street (now Leonore Sullivan Boulevard) and Washington Street for what seemed like an interminable time, he turned to me and said, "That will not look right. It must be curved, wider at the base tapering inward to the top." I ordered the contractor to stop work until Eero could redesign the wall.

At the corner of Washington and Wharf Streets, the wall of the north overlook structure impacted the flood plain. Accordingly, we had been required to obtain a permit from the St. Louis District of the Army Corps of Engineers for the construction. Now that we were going to change the configuration of the wall, we needed an amendment to the permit. The Corps refused on the basis that the expanded base of the wall for perhaps six feet above ground level was too serious an obstruction in case of flood. Joe Jensen did not agree. Nevertheless we were at an impasse and the contractor was threatening increased costs as a result of the delay. I called Mayor Tucker for help. He had his city engineer check out the situation. He agreed with Joe—no big deal. The mayor assembled the Corps (district engineer and staff), National Park Service, Joe Jensen and the city engineer. He carefully explained to the district engineer his concern over the delay, his interest in seeing that Mr. Saarinen's views were accommodated, if feasible, and then inquired as to the amount of the adverse flood impaction of the redesigned wall. The Corps knew there was one—everybody did—but the colonel could not tell the mayor how much.

Apparently, his staff had failed to recompute the flow based on the redesigned wall—they just knew it reduced it. Unfortunately for the colonel, however, the mayor had computed it—and it was *de-minimus*.

This meeting taught me that you want to make sure who you are dealing with *before* the meeting! The colonel discovered that in meeting with the mayor, he was meeting with a politician and with his peer—an engineer. Before close of business that day I had my amended permit.

The Gateway Arch is in the shape of a classical weighted catenary curve. A catenary curve is the form assumed by a free falling chain when it is suspended freely between two points. The depth of the curve is the result of the distance between the points to which the chain is attached.

In 1959, it was contemplated that the Arch would be 590 feet high. However, Eero continued to study the "right shape of the curve." He had a series of chains suspended in his office. Joe Jensen says of this period:

> A visitor or client being ushered into Saarinen's office might find several of us lying flat on the floor, discussing the proposed height of the Arch span by assuming the floor as the sky and the ceiling as the earth. No doubt several clients may have speculated on their wisdom of choice of architect. On returning home at night to Helene and the kids, I explained my dusty front suit appearance by paraphrasing Aline's comment, 'Dusty and dirty, but of our time.'

On my visits to Eero's office, usually once every month or two, I noticed that the chains were getting longer. This meant the Arch was getting higher; and each change in height meant a redesign of the foundations and of the tunnel for the relocated railroad tracks.

Several months into 1960, Eero announced the new height of the Arch at 600 feet.

The Arch design contemplated that there would be an elevator inside the legs to take visitors to a viewing platform at the top. In addition, there were to be stairs for egress in the event of an emergency. As design work proceeded, the major elevator companies lost interest. Elevators are supposed to run in a straight line—not track a catenary curve. Some even said it couldn't be done.

But, then, events took a fortuitous turn in Eero's favor. A young man on his way to Washington to look at a parking garage elevator stopped by Montgomery Elevator Company in Moline, Illinois to visit with a friend.

Dick Bowser's father had designed an elevator system for parking cars in a rampless garage. The elevator not only traveled up and down but also horizontally and diagonally. Dick at this time was temporarily unemployed.

His friend at Montgomery told him of the elevator problem in the Arch and suggested he might be helpful.

With Saarinen and his partners, he reviewed the Arch design, explained his theory for solving the problem and was told by Eero to proceed.

Bowser's design was not an elevator—it was a transportation system. As such, he had provided a solution to another problem we didn't then know existed.

On August 3, 1961, the Congress appropriated $9,497,000, all but approximately $500,000 of the remaining amount of federal money for completion of the project. Available matching city funds amounted to approximately $3,000,000. Based on the estimates then available, we had adequate balances to finance the Gateway Arch, Visitor Center, Museum of Westward Expansion and landscaping. Eero was continuing to eye-ball his longer and longer chains!

Joe Jensen told me that during the long months of study

one model of the Arch reached 640 feet. Eero finally settled on a height of 630 feet. Severud, Elstad & Krueger of New York, the consulting engineers retained by Saarinen, began the structural drawings in preparation for advertising for bids.

At a height of 630 feet, the Arch is approximately 63 stories high. It rests on foundations 630 feet apart at ground level. The cross section of each leg is an equilateral triangle with sides 54 feet wide at the base, diminishing to 17 feet wide at the top. The wall thickness is 3 feet at ground level, tapering to 7 ¾ inches above the 400 foot level.

The Gateway Arch was the first structure built in the United States using the orthotropic design as contrasted with box-girder type construction.

The frame of the structure resembles a sandwich—a sheet of structural steel on the inside and a sheet of stainless steel on the outside—bound together with structural members welded to the inside face of each sheet. Up to the 300-foot level the sandwich is filled with reenforced concrete. The center of the triangle contains the staircase, the transportation system and the electrical power supply.

With these design decisions now made, Joe Jensen reworked the budget. It was tight but we were optimistic that it was adequate.

The big imponderable was what the stainless steel was going to cost; the Arch would require the largest order of stainless steel ever placed. From time to time, we had discussed seeking bids for both aluminum and stainless steel for the outer skin of the Arch. Structurally, aluminum would have worked and we believed that the head to head competition between aluminum and stainless steel may hold down the cost. In the end, however, Eero ruled out aluminum. We were now in the market for stainless steel alone.

Before we received the bids, Eero died tragically on September 1, 1961, of an inoperable brain tumor. The low bid of MacDonald Construction Company far exceeded the engi-

neer's estimate. All kinds of proposals were advanced to reduce the cost. In the end common sense prevailed. Neither
the design of the Arch nor the material chosen by Eero were
changed. We did eliminate some of the work, such as the
transportation system, in order to get the bid within the
available funds. Even so, it was obvious that we could not
complete the project with the available funding—importantly, we did not have enough money left for the Museum of
Westward Expansion and the landscaping.

Mayor Tucker was confident that the citizens of St. Louis
would approve an increase in the bond issue to provide
matching funds to complete the project. He was in favor of
proceeding with the reduced package even though it meant
going back to the voters for a new bond issue and to the Congress for additional authorization and appropriations to complete the project.

The federal funding for the project had been very controversial all during the post-war years. In light of this history,
the director was not sure that we should proceed to accept the
pared down bid package.

Leonore Sullivan was the congresswoman in whose district
the project was located. She represented the central business
district and South St. Louis. She had succeeded her late husband in the Congress and continued to actively support the
project as he had.

With grace, poise, intelligence and hard work, she had
earned the respect of her colleagues in the Congress and the
love of her constituents. She was an especially close friend of
Mayor Tucker who lived in her South St. Louis district.

I had done all that I could do to squeeze down the package
—both with the architect/engineers and the low bidder. The
final decision of whether to proceed was a political one. In
accordance with our partnership agreement, the burden was
now on the mayor. He grasped the thistle and called Lee Sullivan.

Mrs. Sullivan arranged a meeting with Clarence Cannon,

the St. Louis delegation and Missouri's two senators. Cannon chaired the meeting. The status of the project was explained and the question was posed: shall we accept the pared down low bid and come back for additional authorization? All of the participants contributed to the discussion. Finally, Clarence Cannon, eyes twinkling and the barest sign of a smile creasing his face, turned to Mrs. Sullivan and said: "Lee, what do *you* want *me* to do?"

"Mr. Chairman," she began, addressing her old friend, "I want you to tell us to proceed and that you will help us get the additional money."

He broke into a smile to reply, "I think that is a perfectly reasonable request and why don't we do it." Meeting adjourned!

The deletion of the transportation system from the contract was going to reduce greatly the potential for visitors to experience and enjoy the unique Memorial. After we had made this painful decision and announced it to the public, I received a telephone call from Colonel Smyser, the executive director of the Bi-State Development Agency. He invited me to lunch at the exclusive, downtown Noon Day Club.

The Bi-State Development Agency was created by compact between Missouri and Illinois. Its mission is to provide transportation facilities and services in the metropolitan St. Louis/East St. Louis areas. It is authorized to finance its program through self-liquidating revenue bonds.

"If you can convince our lawyers that the lift in the Arch is a transportation system, I might be able to help you build it," he said as we sat down to lunch. That was music to my ears.

"I sure will try," I replied, "if you don't call it a lift anymore." He didn't.

He made the appointment with his attorneys. They were friendly but dubious. After all, Bi-State is authorized to build transportation facilities, such as airports, and operate transportation systems, such as bus and rail lines. There's nothing in the charter about building and operating contraptions in-

side of a "wicket," as the skeptics had derisively referred to
the Arch for many years.

"First, it seems to me," I parried, "we must agree on a
definition of transportation." We didn't have much trouble in
agreeing that it involved moving people and property between two points.

Having agreed on that, is there anything in the compact
agreement that says Bi-State must transport them horizontally?

No.

Is there anything that prescribes the type of vehicle that
may be used?

No.

Is there any limiting factor on the distance over which people may be transported?

Yes, it must be within the metropolitan area defined in the
compact.

We all agreed that the Arch—being in downtown St.
Louis—was located in the prescribed area in which Bi-State
could operate.

Is the "contraption" in the Arch an elevator?

No.

Is it an escalator?

No.

Well, if it's not an elevator and it's not an escalator, yet it
transports people from point A to point B what could it be
other than a transportation system?

Since none of us could think of anything else that Bowser's
system might be, we agreed it was a transportation system.
Once we cleared that hurdle, the lawyers quickly concluded
that Bi-State was authorized to build and operate the transportation system even though this one traversed a catenary
curve and not a city street.

With approving legal opinion in hand, Colonel Smyser and
I then approached bond counsel. Will anybody use this transportation; if so, how many. Will that be enough to pay off the

bonds and interest—the real bottom line because these are self-liquidating revenue bonds.

After several meetings and much data on tourism and visitor use—Disney, Statue of Liberty, Washington Monument and much, much more—counsel was convinced.

Colonel Smyser and I negotiated the cooperative agreement for Bi-State to build and operate the transportation system in the Arch. On March 14, 1962, when the director and MacDonald signed the contract for the Arch and Visitor Center, the director and the chairman of Bi-State also signed the cooperative agreement for the transportation system. It has proven to be a fabulous success.

I resigned from the National Park Service in July, 1962, to become executive director of Downtown St. Louis, Inc., an association of businessmen devoted to the revitalization of downtown St. Louis. My government career was over, I thought. I would be a "sidewalk superintendent" looking on as others completed the projects I had started. But through the good fortune of having met Stewart Udall on the Current River in 1961, such was not to be the case. I returned to the National Park Service in February, 1963, as associate director.

In the meantime, MacDonald Construction Company subcontracted the Arch to Pittsburgh-Des Moines Steel Company (PDM). There was intense competition for the subcontract. MacDonald had a chief estimater, Joe Minner, who Joe Jensen and I quickly learned had the "sharpest pencil in town." He was a bright, personable man of unimpeachable integrity and a resourceful, tough, skilled negotiator. The word around town was that PDM in its quest for the subcontract left some of the Arch money on the table. At any rate, PDM had the Arch contract when I returned to the service.

Because the construction involved a construction theory never before used in the United States, Fred Severud, retained Dr. Hans Karl Bandel of Germany to assist him. Dr.

Bandel was a leading authority in orthotropic design and construction. He supervised preparation of the plans and specifications and maintained close and detailed supervision of the project.

Not too long into construction, PDM requested a change order, contending the structure was unsafe. The request was denied. PDM appealed to me because by then, I had been appointed director of the National Park Service.

When notified of the appeal I met with Joe Jensen, Fred Severud and Dr. Bandel. They convinced me that the structure was designed properly. At the heart of the difference between PDM's engineers and Severud was an argument as to the efficacy of orthotropic construction vis-à-vis box-girder construction. Technicalities aside, the two theories are mutually exclusive. Not understanding the nuances—perhaps, even more not understanding much of either theory—but having unquestioned confidence in Jensen, Severud, and Bandel, I agreed to meet with PDM's engineers and let them have their say. At my conference table, PDM's engineers were arrayed to my right and Severud, et al, to my left; the discussion began. Quickly, the meeting became a dialogue between Mr. Severud and an academician employed as a consultant by PDM. Back and forth went the discussion, becoming more esoteric all the while.

Finally, Fred Severud said, "Doctor, we are imposing on Mr. Hartzog—he does not understand what we are talking about. The only way we will resolve this issue is to fabricate a scale model and wind tunnel test it. I'm agreeable to doing that on this basis—we agree on a laboratory to build and test it—if it fails the test I will, personally, pay for the test and recommend a change order; if it passes the test, you pay the costs."

With that little statement by Fred, PDM's engineers quickly began stacking their papers and the meeting adjourned.

After the meeting, I inquired of Joe as to how much Fred

had just put on the line for the model and tests he proposed. Joe replied, "Perhaps, as much as a million dollars." That sure did fortify my confidence in Severud.

But PDM was not through with the argument. They hired Gen. Donald Dawson, a distinguished Washington lawyer, who had been military aide to President Truman, to take their appeal to Secretary Udall. Udall listened to General Dawson and to Bill Jackson, president of PDM, and to me. I recounted to them my meeting with Severud and PDM's engineers and consultant. The secretary promised to look into the matter.

When they had departed, he told me that he thought he should have the engineers of the Bureau of Reclamation assess the dispute. I protested that they did not have a single engineer that I knew of who was qualified in orthotropic design and the argument was really about which of two theories was valid and appropriate in this instance.

He was insistent, however, and I retained the Bureau at a cost of $100,000 to do the analysis.

They agreed with PDM.

When Stewart got the report he called me to his office. In the meantime, Joe Jensen and Severud had been advised of the Bureau's report and their opinion was that it was $100,000 worth of bunk! Moreover, Severud told me that if we accepted the Bureau's conclusion and issued PDM the change order he would withdraw from the project.

The secretary was clearly worried, as was I, that a major bureau of his department had told him that I was leading him into a debacle: the Arch was going to fall down if he didn't approve the change order. I had just told him that if he issued the change order, we would have to complete the Arch without Severud and, importantly, Bandel who was the only engineer then readily available who had worked with orthotropic structures.

I said to Stewart as we both paced the floor of his huge ornate office, "You can always get another director but, in my

IV. The Gateway Arch

judgment, Severud is irreplaceable. Why don't you let me stay on course? If it comes out OK, you are home free. If the damn thing falls down, fire me, have a news conference and announce the appointment of another director to clean up the mess!"

Before he could respond, the buzzer went off on his desk. He answered, listened and said, "Just the man I need to see, send him in."

In walked Nat Owings, senior partner of Skidmore, Owings & Merrill, one of America's most distinguished architects. Without even inquiring about the purpose of his visit, Stewart immediately began to outline the problem he and I had been discussing. When he finished, I then told Nat my proposition to let me stay the course and if it fell down, to fire me and have another director clean up the mess.

Stewart asked, "Nat, what do you think I should do?"

Nat began, "I have known Fred Severud for many years—he is one of the best. He challenged them to a test and they didn't take it. I'd do what George suggests. If he's wrong fire him."

Nat Owings through an incredible coincidence had saved Eero Saarinen's Arch.

I went back downstairs, called General Dawson and told him that the secretary had just given me full responsibility for the decision. "We are not going to issue any change order; PDM should proceed in accordance with the plans."

About this time, the secretary had asked me to participate in a team study of historic preservation in Europe. Helen and I arrived in New York to join the group prior to departure. We were staying at the Pierre Hotel. About 9:30 that night I received a telephone call from Bill Jackson once again pressing for a change order. He insisted that the Arch was going to fall down when they lifted the keystone.

My response, "Lift it, Mr. Jackson; if she falls I'm fired."

On October 28, 1965—the day scheduled for lifting the keystone—Joe Jensen, wrote of the occasion:

55

To lift the final section into place there had to be about a million pounds of pressure exerted on the two legs of the arch to allow the keystone to be placed and then the legs depressured back to (close on the key section still with good pressure) maintain the total arch in continuous pressure. The sun shining intensely on the south leg was going to cause the leg to lengthen and twist which could produce havoc with the closing. The decision to spray water from fire hoses at elevations up to the top of the arch saved the day by keeping both legs approximately the same temperature. Thank heavens for a brilliant fire department and good new hoses.

"What a beautiful sight to behold," Jensen concluded, "when the keystone fit perfectly."

Despite the daring project, PDM did not experience a single major mishap and there was not a single disabling injury or death.

When I returned from Europe, my friend, Ted Rennison—Saarinen's project inspector—sent me a photograph of him and our son George standing atop the Arch, having climbed out through the trap door used to replace the navigational hazard light.

Within a matter of a few weeks, a single engine airplane jock flew through the Arch. The staff got his plane number and were all for prosecuting him. "No way," I said. "We will leave him in the same fix as the preacher who, playing golf on Sunday morning, made a hole-in-one—he may be proud of it, but he can't talk about it!" Fortunately, no one else has done such a recklessly stupid thing.

If the Gateway Arch were looked on simply as an architectural-engineering marvel, one would miss the transcendent significance of Eero's creation and the genius of his concept.

Historians have said one could stand at Cumberland Gap, St. Louis and South Pass in Wyoming and watch civilization moving west through the virgin land to fill the continent. This epic of Westward Expansion wrought major changes in the economic, political and social history of the new nation. Towering above the banks of the Mississippi, the Arch sym-

IV. The Gateway Arch

bolizes St. Louis as the gateway of the gigantic migration to the West.

But in choosing the revolutionary orthotropic design for his Arch, Eero caught a broader vision than that of a memorial to a place and a time in our history.

The theory of the orthotropic design is that the strength of the structure is greater than the sum of the strengths of the individual parts. The Arch consists of hundreds of sheets of stainless and structural steel. Slowly and painfully each piece, different in size and shape, was fitted and welded into place. From the *diversity* of shapes, sizes and materials the builders fabricated an arch that is, "Timeless, but of our time."

In like manner, from the *diversity* of colors, cultures and national origins—crafted by compromise, consensus and compassion—the peoples who came to these shores have fashioned a nation of hope, of opportunity and of personal freedom unmatched in the annals of human history. Our diversity is a source of pride—our oneness is the bulwark of our freedom. And, the Gateway Arch is symbolic of this greater strength derived from our oneness.

V

THE OZARKS: A NEW KIND OF PARK

Wendell uncapped a fifth of Cutty Sark scotch and threw the top out the window.

"Wait a minute," I exclaimed, "you just threw the top out."

Without changing expression, he replied, "That's the way we always drink in the Ozarks." It was the beginning of a great park experience.

The unique people of the Ozarks as I came to know and cherish them were creative, insular and suspicious. I remember once asking a businessman in Van Buren his assessment of the local support/opposition of the park proposal. I really can't tell you, he responded, I ain't a native; I've only lived here fifty years. Remarkably self-reliant, some capable of hunting small game (rabbits, squirrels, etc.) with stones— not rifles and guns; fishing by noodling fish from under bluffs, rocks and fallen trees—not with fish hooks and lines. Most were poor as church mice. Engaging and cagey, they were cautious and not likely to be snookered.

Lennis Broadfoot, a native artist, painted and wrote of them. He lets Jess Thompson tell us of their resourcefulness:

I'll bet I can kill more squirrels with rocks than most fellers can with a gun! Now, boys, I can really knock 'em. . . . Hit's plum easy for me to get all the squirrels I want, an' don't have to pay nary a cent for ammunition.

When I go fishin' I never use hooks an' gigs an' things. All I do is jist wade around very slow an' feel around under rocks, an' logs, an' ol' tree roots, an' catch all the fish I want with my hands....

While I was serving as superintendent of the Jefferson National Expansion Memorial in St. Louis, in 1960, Regional Director Howard Baker asked me to take on the additional assignment of Ozark Rivers National Monument proposal in Southeast Missouri, and see what, if anything I could do to move it along. Wendell Howard, a local businessman in the Ozarks owned a summer house on the Current River. Wendell agreed to meet with me in Ellington and show me several locations on the Current River. Leaving St. Louis in the dark of night I met Wendell about 7 a.m. in Ellington. In the meantime, he had invited Coleman (Cokie) McSpadden from Van Buren (on the Current River) and Bill Bailey from Emminence (on the Jacks Fork) to join us. Soon the four of us were on our way to Wendell's cabin. It was located on a bluff with a sweeping view of the Current River. A sloping dirt road ran down from the parking lot to the river for launching the johnboats. The johnboat is indigenous to the Ozarks, and unlike a canoe, it has a wide flat bottom and a wide stern — very stable in the water and ideal for floating and fishing the Ozark mountain streams.

We poked around several other spots on the river. About noon we headed for Van Buren for lunch. Shortly, Wendell reached under the seat and pulled out a fifth of Cutty Sark. "Want a drink?" he asked.

"Well, I'll join you, if you fellas want one." From the backseat Bill spoke up. "We always have a drink before lunch." Without cups, water or other chaser, the four of us finished the bottle before lunch.

I didn't see any more of the project that day, but I survived their initiation and our friendship blossomed.

V. The Ozarks: A New Kind of Park

Cokie, Bill and Wendell became three of my greatest supporters and advocates for preserving the Ozark Rivers as a part of the National Park System. They were instrumental in soliciting local supporters, prominent among whom was G. L. Davis, a highly respected teacher and farmer at Birch Tree, Missouri. They arranged several opportunities for me to meet with local groups in the area. On one such occasion I attended an evening meeting in Ellington.

It was a long and testy affair lasting until about midnight. After shaking hands all 'round, I got in my government station wagon and started back to St. Louis about one in the morning. Forty miles or so from St. Louis the car started sputtering. I managed to get it started several times but finally it died on a long, lonesome, desolate section of the highway. It was now well after two in the morning. I could see no lights any place, and I was unfamiliar with the territory. Occasionally, I could hear a dog in the distance barking at the moonless dark. A couple of vehicles passed, and as I heard and saw each one approaching, I would get out on the road and try to thumb a ride, but none would stop. Finally, about five-thirty in the morning, a logging truck came by and stopped. The driver gave me a lift into the suburbs of St. Louis, where I called Helen who came and picked me up. I called the government dispatcher and told him where the vehicle was and he sent a wrecker down to pull it in. When we got the car to St. Louis, we discovered that someone had filled the gas tank with fine white sand, a great deal of which I had pulled through the fuel system into the carburetor before the carburetor became solidly packed and would let no more gas through.

During the meetings that I had along the river, I noticed that there was one particular couple—Mr. and Mrs. Clark—who came regularly to every meeting. Mr. Clark was the banker in Ellington and very much opposed to the National Park Service program for preservation of the Ozarks. It was my practice immediately following my presentation and answering questions, to hurry to the back of the hall or meeting room to shake hands with every person that had come. After about the third meeting at which I greeted Mr. and Mrs. Clark on their way out, I finally said to him, "Mr. Clark, I really do appreciate your interest in the proposal and I'm looking forward with great enthusiasm to your support."

"Oh," he said. "I don't support you at all."

"Well," I said, "if you don't support me, I'm puzzled as to why you keep coming to every meeting."

To which he replied, "I just keep coming to find out when you're going to lie."

Mr. Clark had made a telling point. A lot of good people do like to gossip and a lie goes around the world before the truth can get its britches on!

One of the greatest problems I had to cope with were the misrepresentations of those opposed to the preservation of the rivers. According to them if the rivers were put in the National Park System, their whole economy would be wrecked. Generally, the very opposite was true because of the benefits of tourism to the new park area. With the help of Joe Jaeger, the Missouri State Park director, and Dunie Bollinger, a member of the state house of representatives from Van Buren, we persuaded Governor Dalton to come to the Ozarks and make a speech on the value of tourism. In his speech he explained it quite succinctly: "A tourist is worth twice as much as a bale of cotton and is twice as easy to pick."

After spending every weekend for several months on the Ozark rivers and driving down there (300 miles round trip) for meetings one or two nights a week, I realized I was making precious little headway. I was in a fight and it was going to get worse before it got better. The fight was going to be won or lost in the Congress. Naively, being a career park man, I had thought "people are for parks" and that getting this park would be a cakewalk. What a sheltered view I had.

From the beginning of my assignment to the Ozarks

project I had been keeping a card file with the name and address of every person I had talked with and the date(s). The cards were kept in three categories: those for, against (with reason if known), and indifferent. The "aginers" and the apathetic far outnumbered the supporters. I decided to back up and look at the situation again.

I sought the advice of Tony Buford—a skilled and savvy political operator, and Leonard Hall who lived at Ironton, Missouri, who also owned property near the proposed project along the Current River. Len Hall was a dedicated conservationist who wrote an outdoors column for the St. Louis Globe-Democrat. I also sought the advice of G. L. Davis of Birch Tree and Bill Sponsler, field assistant to Richard (Dick) Ichord, the Democratic congressman in that district.

A consensus quickly developed that we needed an organized, on-site group that could "evangelize" our cause, disseminate information, monitor opposition meetings, challenge their misinformation and arrange speaking opportunities for me. Tony, Len and Bill, likewise, agreed that Mr. Davis was the ideal person to lead such an organization. He was born and raised in the Ozarks, had lived and worked in the area all of his life, was then in his seventies and semiretired. He was much loved and highly respected and his integrity was unimpeachable. At the time, there were not enough Republicans to answer a mating call, and he was a Republican, making the group nonpartisan. I approached Mr. Davis—G.L. as he was affectionately known throughout the region.

G.L. was enthusiastic about saving the beautiful rivers, but he was not too sure that he wanted to get out front in leading the charge. We had several long and thoughtful visits together. At the very onset, he wanted to be reassured that he would not be leading a front for a bunch of Democrats. I assured him that the organization would be nonpartisan, nonprofit, educational in nature and managed by a local board composed of his neighbors, all of whom would be acceptable to him. We agreed, too, there would be no freeloaders or interlopers. Every member would be required to pay dues, although dues should be modest. The organization, of course, would need money, but of equal importance we needed a rallying point for the relatively small number of our supporters, most of whom were of modest means.

G.L. had the mutual respect of many of our strongest opponents: large land owners (who stood to lose the opportunity to exploit their holdings for timber, pulpwood, mining, etc. and summer home site subdivisions); the State Conservation Commission whose recreational hunting programs would be eliminated; the U.S. Forest Service which would lose jurisdiction over the federal lands it administered along the Eleven Point River; most of the local bankers and businessmen who believed their future was tied to timber harvesting, farming and mining—not tourism. They were all—with a rare exception here and there—honorable, upstanding people who honestly disagreed with the proposal either out of misunderstanding, misinformation or because their "ox was being gored." G.L. agreed to try to convert the opponents. He was prepared to debate the merits of their arguments but not their motives, questionable as I thought they were. He insisted on my agreeing with his idealistic, tough rule of conduct, summarized as:

> There is so much bad in the best of us,
> and so much good in the worst of us,
> that it behooves none of us to condemn any of us.

There were times when I was hard pressed to live up to this commitment but it taught me another lesson which served me well when I became director: fight for your program on its merits; don't trivialize the debate by attacking the motives of your adversaries.

The organization was formed with G.L. as president. As I recall, we named it the Ozarks Natural History Association. With a handful of members aboard—and the active but not publicized help of Bill Sponsler, Tony Buford and Len Hall— we went to work again. Slowly but surely we picked up momentum. Our efforts were given a big boost when Congressman Ichord brought Secretary Stewart L. Udall to visit the area.

In the fifties, the National Park Service had proposed to preserve portions of three rivers and springs in a national monument: Jack's Fork, Eleven Point River, Current River and their series of springs. The term monument had been commonly used in Europe to designate any natural object regarded as a monument of nature's handiwork. Alexander von Humboldt, a scientist and explorer, had described tropical trees as "monuments de la nature" early in the nineteenth century. In the United States, a monument generally referred to statuary, but at the beginning of this century the term national monument gained widespread recognition as an area of unique scientific distinction or antiquity. In 1906, for example, the Congress authorized the president to set aside by proclamation areas of scientific significance or antiquity from lands owned by the United States. Several of the existing national parks, such as Grand Canyon and Grand Teton, were first reserved as national monuments by presidential proclamation.

National parks and national monuments, generally, differ in these significant respects:

Parks are relatively spacious—monuments may be any size.

Parks, generally, possess two or more unique scenic or scientific values of superlative quality—monuments need only one attribute of scientific or prehistoric significance.

Parks must be established by act of Congress—monuments, if composed of federally-owned lands may be established by presidential proclamation; otherwise, they must also be established by the Congress.

The policies governing national parks and national monuments are, for the most part, the same. In both types of areas (with rare exception) recreational hunting and consumptive resource utilization, such as timber harvesting, mining, etc. are prohibited. These policies which would have brought about radical changes in the historic uses of the rivers and adjoining land were at the heart of the controversy involving the proposed Ozark Rivers National Monument. After a year, or so, it became clear that the original proposal was never going to fly. For example, there was almost solid opposition, locally, to the prohibition of all hunting within the boundaries of the proposal. On the other hand, the national conservation groups, such as the Sierra Club, were never going to support inclusion of a national monument in the National Park System that permitted sport hunting. With the support of the local congressman and my regional director, I set about to explore alternatives with the newly organized association, the affected state agencies (state parks and the Conservation Commission) and the local elected officials—commissioners, judges, representatives and state senators.

A great deal of the land along the Eleven Point River was already in federal ownership under the administration of the U.S. Forest Service.

The forest service was established in 1905 under the leadership of the legendary Gifford Pinchot. A personal friend of President Theodore Roosevelt and one of America's first professionally trained foresters, he was a politician of extraordinary talent. After leaving the federal service as chief forester in 1910 he was elected governor of Pennsylvania.

For most of its existence, harvesting the virgin forests, mineral extraction and cheap grazing have been the engines that drove the forest service. Ingeniously, Pinchot had cloaked his new agency in the more attractive garment of multiple use—a euphemism of dubious intellectual merit but of overwhelming political appeal.

The theory of multiple use holds that forest lands may be used for a variety of benefits including water, forage, wildlife habitat, wood, recreation, wilderness and minerals. The extent of the area within which these mostly incompatible multiple uses may occur is never mentioned. On the contrary, the concept is packaged, locally, to leave the impression that one may have all of these goodies at the same time from the same acreage. Moreover, revenues received by the forest service from uses on the national forests are shared with the local governments in whose jurisdictions the forest lands are located.

Skillfully wedding the special interests seeking to exploit America's natural bounty with local politicians receiving a bonanza of public funds without the pain of local taxation, the forest service is, indeed, a powerful political force.

The forest service was adamantly opposed to surrendering jurisdiction of its lands along the Eleven Point to the National Park Service. Moreover, in that whole area along the Eleven Point, I could not find a half dozen people with enough "fire in the belly" to join the charge for taking the river from the national forest and putting it in the National Park System. The remainder of the proposal—the Jack's Fork and the Current—was still viable as a unit of the National Park System.

A wise man once said that everyone should have three sets of objectives: one set that he announced to the world; one set that he discussed only with his spouse and kept in his desk drawer; and one set that he talked over only with God. I didn't immediately abandon the Eleven Point but it was in the third set of my objectives.

The biggest problem in building local support for the Jack's Fork and the Current was the hunting issue.

We were fortunate in having a charismatic, young articulate congressman who had served previously as the Speaker of the Missouri House of Representatives—the youngest in the history of the state at that time. He was in his first term in the Congress. Philosophically he supported saving the rivers but he was not about to run over the full-throated opposition of the hunters. Without at least his tacit support we were never going to get the needed legislation.

The *de facto* leader of the hunting opposition was William Towell, director of the Missouri Conservation Commission.

He was a forester by training and a dedicated conservationist. Not only did he bring distinguished leadership to his commission but he was a high official in the councils of the International Association of Fish and Game Commissioners. That association as a matter of policy, principle and practice fought every national park proposal that would close off public hunting.

I spent a great deal of time with Bill Towell and we developed a warm personal friendship which has endured over the years. For a long time we could make no headway in resolving the issue. To him it was a matter of principle—and you can't negotiate principles. We never stopped talking, probing and exploring all the what ifs. What if hunting was to be allowed, should it be permitted in campgrounds and picnic areas? Obviously, not. Gradually, we began to change the focus from principle to problem and therein lay the opportunity to resolve the matter. We started exchanging drafts of language. Slowly we narrowed the gap until we arrived at language the substance of which was included in the Ozark legislation:

> The secretary shall permit hunting and fishing on lands and waters under his jurisdiction within the Ozark National Scenic Riverways area in accordance with applicable federal and state laws. The secretary may designate zones where, and establish periods when, no hunting shall be permitted, for reasons of public safety, administration, or public use and enjoyment and shall issue regulations after consultation with the Conservation Commission of the state of Missouri.

With the hunting issue resolved we had broken the back of the local opposition and we began to pick up speed. The association grew and prospered as new supporters came aboard.

Congressman Ichord was successful in moving the bill for congressional hearings both in the field and in Washington.

For the Washington hearing G.L. and Bill Sponsler were able to recruit a sizeable contingent of local supporters to come to Washington, including our friends Len Hall and Tony

V. The Ozarks: A New Kind of Park

Buford. Some of the "good ole boys" led by Wendell Howard rented a white Cadillac and set about to enjoy the night life of Washington. After partying, they returned to the hotel one morning about 2 o'clock. I remember the time exactly for one of them started beating and kicking on my door to get me up to go out with them. I got up because I had to unless I wanted to wake up the whole hotel. They had also rousted Len Hall from bed. In the meantime, a half dozen of them—a couple without shoes—got in the Cadillac and brought it around to the front of the hotel with Wendell riding western saddle style—barefooted—on top of the hood, feet resting on the bumper. Before they could get out of the driveway and into the street a police officer drove by. Observing this scene he swung around in front of the car and inquired where they were going. They gave the right answer—to bed!

The Ozark National Scenic Riverways legislation was the first park bill enacted by the Congress in 1964 after I became director.

It was the first of the national rivers and the harbinger of the Wild and Scenic Rivers System.

VI

APPOINTMENT AS DIRECTOR

There are no secrets in Washington; it's a question of who has the information first.

Stewart Lee Udall's family is deeply rooted in Arizona. A site closely associated with his forebearers is Lee's Ferry on the Colorado River, now a part of Lake Powell National Recreation Area administered by the National Park Service.

Shortly after he appointed me director I received a note from him in a blue envelope. Blue envelopes were the medium for sending priority mail internally to the personal attention of the addressee. The note asked me to insure that the two remaining buildings at historic Lee's Ferry were preserved. By similar blue envelope, I transmitted a copy of his note with a covering memorandum to the regional director of the Southwest region at Santa Fe, asking that he implement whatever measures were needed to insure that we complied with Secretary Udall's request.

Not long afterwards, I received a telephone call from a friend in Utah advising that he had been by Lee's Ferry and that all remnants of the ferry operation had been bulldozed. I was incredulous.

I telephoned the superintendent immediately, bypassing the region because I was in a hurry to reassure myself that my friend was mistaken. Unfortunately, he was not mistaken. The remaining buildings had been bulldozed. Not only had we carelessly lost heirlooms of our nation's history but I had failed the man who appointed me in carrying out his first request.

I telephoned Orren Beaty, the secretary's executive assistant, and told him I had to see the secretary immediately. Orren explained that his schedule was full and that he didn't see how he could work me in. I told Orren it was an emergency and it could not wait. I needed only five minutes, to which he replied, OK.

I hotfooted it up to Orren's office, adjacent to the secretary's office, and he took me in through a side door that connected the two offices. Stewart was reading and signing mail. I told him straight out that we had bulldozed the buildings at Lee's Ferry. Without looking up or changing expression, he said, "I know. When did you find out?"

In astonishment I replied, "I just found out."

"Well," he said, "I knew it sometime ago—I was just waiting to see if you had the guts to tell me."

I had first met Udall in 1961 when he came to the Current River in the Ozarks of Southeast Missouri with Congressman Richard (Dick) Ichord. The purpose of the visit was to review the proposal of the National Park Service to preserve the Current, Jack's Fork and Eleven Point Rivers as a national monument. The group consisted mostly of Dick Ichord's constituents but also included representatives from the agencies of the state government, whose jurisdictions were affected by the proposal. We stayed at Wendell Howard's cabin, a very large house on the Current River, a magnificent scenic spot within the boundaries of the proposed national monument. From the very beginning a tremendous comraderie was established in the official party.

After dinner, while I was getting ready to put on a slide show of the area, one of the local good ole boys suggested we go for a swim. No one had bathing suits. The secretary in his exuberant, spontaneous way said, "Let's do it!" and fifteen or twenty of the group took off for the river to swim in the nude. In the meantime, I carried on with the slide show for the remaining twenty-five or thirty who stayed behind.

At Wendell Howard's cabin life never stopped; someone was always up all night and the coffee pot was always boiling. If you wanted something stronger than that, that was also available. This night was no different. Congressman Ichord's field assistant, Bill Sponsler, and I were responsible for ram-roddin' the trip. In addition to doing any and all tasks for the comfort of the party, this also meant staying sober and staying awake all night.

About 4 o'clock in the morning, I decided to check the boats to make sure that we had adequate fish for the fish fry at noon along the river. When I got to the river I found that the fishermen—after too many beers the night before—had pulled the boats up on the bank just far enough so that the fish boxes were out of the water. Every single fish—bass, pike, perch—was dead. I aroused Cokie McSpadden, our lead fisherman and told him of the disaster. Cokie is one of the finest Current River fisherman in all of Missouri. He immediately gathered together four of his friends and at daylight, they hit the water.

We cooked a real country breakfast for the party with piles of bacon, ham, eggs and plenty of toast and grits. As the sun began to sparkle on the riffles of the sand bars, we put in the johnboats and started down the river. Soon we were joined by large groups of opponents of the NPS proposal. Most of them were standing along the banks carrying posters telling the secretary to "Get out and go home" and telling NPS to "Stay away and leave us alone." Some joined our flotilla in their johnboats. I soon recognized among the group some who not only didn't live along the river but who did not even live in Congressman Ichord's district.

As our flotilla passed Cokie and his fervent fishing partners, Cokie had just hooked a bass. The only problem was that the bass was on the opposite side of a fallen tree from his johnboat. Cokie was standing up in the boat playing the fish. The contrary bass was running back and forth just under the water but he wouldn't jump like bass normally do; unless he jumped so that Cokie could jerk him across the log, he was going to be hung up. We stopped the boats to watch. Cokie played that bass until he finally made him jump and when he did so, Cokie snatched him across the top of the log. This event gave the secretary a real insight into the resourcefulness, skill, intelligence and ability of the great people that lived along those magnificent rivers.

When we arrived at the designated spot at noon for lunch, Cokie and his crew of fishermen and cooks had ample fish frying for everyone in the party. In keeping with our efforts to convert our adversaries, we even invited some of the opposition to have lunch with us and meet the congressman and the secretary.

I did not see Secretary Udall again until August of 1962. By this time I had left the NPS to become the executive director of Downtown St. Louis, Inc. The secretary was coming to St. Louis to make a speech and he was to be hosted and introduced by the mayor, the Honorable Raymond R. Tucker. Mayor Tucker had been my guide and counsel in getting the Memorial project underway. During this time we had developed a warm personal friendship. Mayor Tucker called me on the morning of the secretary's arrival and asked me if I would like to ride out to the airport with him to meet the secretary. I quickly accepted and went to City Hall to accompany the mayor. We met the secretary, had a pleasant visit on the way in to town during which time Mayor Tucker told the secretary that I had left the NPS and was now working with Downtown St. Louis, Inc. The secretary expressed surprise. When we arrived at the Jefferson Hotel, the mayor preceded the secretary and me through the door. Instead of following, Stewart hung back and asked me why I left. I said, "Well, I had no future."

He replied, "Would being director be enough future?"

I said, "Mr. Secretary, it sure would." He followed the

mayor through the door with me behind him. The subject was not mentioned again during his visit.

Three months later, Helen and I were invited to Washington to a Department of the Interior Honors Convocation to receive the department's Distinguished Service Award. Each recipient marched across the large stage in the department auditorium, was greeted by the secretary and presented with the award. When I was greeted by the secretary, instead of the usual pleasantries about the award, he said simply, "Come to my office after the ceremony."

The National Park Service had arranged a reception in the departmental cafeteria after the ceremony for its honorees, their friends and families. When the program was over, I said to Helen, "You'd better go to the reception because I have to go see the secretary." She was surprised by this announcement but didn't tarry or question me. I took the elevator to the sixth floor and told the receptionist who I was and why I had come. I was immediately taken into the secretary's office, where he and Assistant Secretary John Carver were waiting. Udall had a fire burning brightly in the fireplace in the huge magnificent paneled office built by and for Harold Ickes during his term. The secretary greeted me, introduced me to John Carver, and pulled up his rocking chair in front of the fireplace. John and I pulled up chairs to join him. He launched the conversation by saying that he had asked me to come up to see him because of our conversation in St. Louis in August; he wanted me to be the director of the National Park Service. I was stunned and elated. After recovering from the initial shock I asked, "Is Connie Wirth retiring?"

"Well," he said, "he is going to." He said it in a way that left me with the impression that the plans to do so may not yet have jelled.

I said, "Mr. Secretary, I want that job more than anything in the world, but I do not want to be a party to pushing Connie Wirth out."

We exchanged a few more comments and he turned to John

Carver and said, "John, why don't you and George go down to your office and talk about this for awhile and then come back and see me." John and I departed.

John's secretary fixed us some coffee and we sat down on the couch at the far end of his office, almost as large as the secretary's office but not nearly so handsomely appointed. He said, "George, I think you are exactly right not to want to be a party to pushing out Connie Wirth. If you did that, you would bring with you your own enemies and all of Connie Wirth's friends who would become your enemies."

I related to John my three discussions with Connie prior to leaving the National Park Service. I had told Connie that with the Gateway Arch now under contract and all of the authorized money appropriated and obligated, the major work at the Memorial had been accomplished and that I wished a new assignment. Also, Downtown St. Louis, Inc. had offered me the job of executive director at a substantial increase in salary but I really preferred to stay in the service if I could get a new assignment.

Connie had pointed out that there were no major superintendent vacancies, that I had no regional office experience and that I would have to get in line. However, the associate director's job was vacant and had been for months. I suggested that if he filled it, there would be a vacancy— never dreaming that he would appoint me as associate director. He would make no commitment to fill the job.

Accordingly, I told John that after these discouraging and inconclusive conversations with Connie, I had decided to go ahead and accept the offer from Downtown St. Louis, Inc. I told John that I would be perfectly happy to return to the National Park Service in the associate director's position provided Connie invited me back; that I had the assurance of the secretary that when Connie did retire, hopefully within less than a year, I would be appointed the director of the service; and that in the meantime, I would have some say in what transpired in the service. John agreed completely and he and I returned to the secretary's office. John outlined our discussion and our conclusion. The secretary quickly responded that he thought this was an ideal solution.

My absence from the NPS reception soon became obvious. Helen told me many people inquired where I was. She has an incomparable ability to smile, be gracious, say something and tell nothing. Still, it was not long before word swept the first corridor that I was meeting with John Carver and the secretary. I never did get to the reception.

Immediately after meeting with the secretary I returned to the director's office. My purpose was to brief Connie on my visit with Udall. He was tied up, so we made arrangements to have lunch the next day.

In substance, I told Connie that the secretary, John Carver and I had discussed the associate director's job. I did not tell him that the secretary had offered me the director's job. I also told Connie that I had advised Udall that I would be pleased to return to the service as associate director provided Connie wanted me back in that capacity. It was then that Connie told me of his appointment of the Eivind Scoyen Committee to recommend replacements for Eivind at the time he had announced his retirement as associate director. Connie told me that my name was on the list of five candidates recommended by the committee but he had not sent the names to the secretary. I learned later that the other candidates were much senior to me in rank and years of service. The Scoyen Committee had completed its work well in advance of my discussions with Connie about the St. Louis job offer and my desire for a new assignment.

Connie also told me that he proposed to retire after the Yosemite National Park Service Superintendents' conference, scheduled for October, 1963.

Helen and I returned to St. Louis, excited about the possibility of returning to the National Park Service, but cautious in our optimism.

Almost two months went by before I heard anything else about the matter. Then one day the telephone rang in my office with Connie Wirth on the line offering me the job of associate director. I quickly accepted. We tentatively agreed on a reporting date in February of 1963 because I had to communicate this information to my board and seek some mutually satisfactory termination schedule with them.

I reported for duty in Washington as associate director of the National Park Service in February, 1963.

The groundwork had been laid for Connie's retirement at the superintendent's conference in Yosemite in October, 1963, the secretary would announce my appointment as director, and I would announce my selection of Clark Stratton to be associate director. Clark was a talented, personable man who was a longtime park service career employee, having entered the service during the Civilian Conservation Corps days.

John Carver was a featured speaker on the first day of the conference. John unloaded on the NPS bureaucrats and, inferentially, on Connie. The speech was widely reported by the national media. Many in and out of the National Park Service agreed with the major thrust of the speech—the service was insular, rigidly bureaucratic and politically unresponsive. But that was hardly the time or the place to say it. He really roiled up the conference.

John must have forgotten the story about the old mule skinner who was an expert with the whip. He delighted in showing off his prowess. One afternoon he had given a demonstration by striking the blossom from a dandelion and, later, hitting a fly in midair. Finally, a bystander pointed to a hornet's nest, but the old man shook his head.

"A blossom is a blossom," he said, "and a fly is a fly, but a hornet's nest, man, that's an organization."

The secretary appeared on the last day of the conference. His words of praise for Connie dissipated much of the rancor that John had stirred up. The announcement of Connie's retirement and of my appointment was made as planned.

On November 22, President Kennedy was assassinated in Dallas. This threw my appointment into doubt because no one knew whether President Johnson would retain Udall. The appointment of the director is a secretarial appointment, and until Udall's status was clarified by President Johnson things were in limbo. Prior to the end of the year, the president affirmed his confidence in the secretary, asked him to remain, and things were back on track.

Connie retired and I succeeded him in January, 1964.

In the first half-century of the existence of the National Park Service, I was only the second director to have pulled duty in the parks—Albright was the other. When I was sworn in as director, John Carver remarked, "If you hadn't got out you never would have got up."

In the hierarchy of the department, the director reports to the secretary through an assistant secretary who has oversight of two bureaus: the National Park Service and the Fish and Wildlife Service.

The National Park Service is operated with three levels of management: the director's office in Washington which is responsible for translating the secretary's objectives into action; regional offices (six during my tenure—now ten) are responsible for coordination of field management; and the parks, each in the charge of a superintendent, responsible for on-site accomplishment of the service mission, namely: preserve the park resources and serve the visitor.

The operation is not nearly as smooth as the outlines of the organization chart. Park people are intensely committed to their mission, hard working, strong-willed and fiercely independent. Dr. Stanley Cain, a former assistant secretary and a former chairman of the secretary's Advisory Board on National Parks, once likened the director's job to that of a university president. "They each," he said, "have a job that requires the skill to herd wild hogs on ice." He should know —he was a distinguished scientist, teacher and administrator who spent most of his working career in academia, first at the University of Tennessee and later at the University of Michigan.

That skill, rather than any particular professional discipline may be the key qualification for being director.

The founding director of the National Park Service in 1916 was Stephen Tyng Mather, an influential industrialist who had made millions from *Twenty Mule Team Borax*. Mather was a dedicated conservationist and an avid mountain climber. On a trip through Sequoia and Yosemite National Parks in 1914 he was shocked by the conditions he found. Upon returning to his home in Chicago, Mather wrote Secretary Franklin Lane a highly critical report on the mismanagement of the national parks. Quite succinctly Lane responded, "Dear Steve: If you don't like the way the national parks are run, why don't you come down to Washington and run them yourself." That challenge prompted Mather to come to Washington to see Lane who offered him a job as assistant to the secretary to oversee the parks.

But Mather, then 47, had never worked in the government and had no intention of doing so. Lane pressed the case, "I can't offer you rank or fame or salary—only a chance to do some great public service." When Lane agreed to give Mather a young assistant, Horace Albright, to handle the myriad bureaucratic details, Mather agreed to accept the job for one year.

Albright had come to Washington in 1913 as a 23-year-old to clerk for a year for one of his former professors at the University of California who had been appointed an assistant secretary of the Interior. His year nearly complete, Albright had made plans to return to California to marry and to enter a prestigious San Francisco law firm. In the meantime, Lane introduced him to Mather. Falling under the spell of the dynamic, charismatic Mather, Albright accepted the invitation to remain as his assistant for the year Mather had agreed to serve. To the good fortune of all generations, they both stayed

VI. *Appointment as Director*

much longer. Mather remained as director until 1929 when
ill health forced his retirement. He was succeeded by his
young assistant Albright.

He was succeeded by his associate director, Arno Cammerer, a longtime career government employee. Ill health
forced his retirement seven years later.

Mather and Albright saw *use* as the engine to drive public
support for preservation and expansion of the system. Their
challenge was to build the park system, establish a professional ranger/manager corps free of the taint of patronage,
partisan politics, and ward off the thrusts of the miners, loggers and grazers who would compromise and destroy their
beloved parks. To a remarkable degree they succeeded.

In 1940 Newton Drury, the executive director of the Save-
the-Redwoods League, was appointed director. Drury was an
English major graduate of the University of California in the
same class (1912) as was Horace Albright. Mather was also a
California graduate in the class of 1887.

If the seventeen years of Mather and Albright (1916–
1933) may be said to be the years in which the promotion of
use was the emphasis, the eleven years of Drury (1940–1951)
may be characterized as the *preservation* emphasis years.
Some suggest that the war-time limitations of money and
manpower and the onslaught of the loggers, miners and
grazers seeking access to park riches—in the name of the
war effort—may have pushed Drury to the *preservation* emphasis. I think not. Long before his appointment as director,
he had earned his spurs as a preservationist. He was one of
the organizing cadre of the Save-the-Redwoods League in
California. He coined the phrase "the Crown Jewels" to describe his beloved parks. Moreover, he had an antipathy for
the seashores and the reservoir-based recreation areas with
their emphasis on outdoor recreation. In his judgment, they
did not belong in the system. He gladly surrendered Santa
Rosa Island (Florida) to the war-time navy, banished Shasta
Recreation Area in California from the National Park Sys-

tem, and, to the downright annoyance of Secretary Julius Krug returned Lake Texoma Recreation Area to the Army Corps of Engineers.

Following the superintendent's conference in Yosemite National Park in 1950, Newton asked me to accompany him to Sequoia National Park to review a concession problem. Because of the sudden death of the chief of concessions in Washington, Newton had designated me to serve in that capacity on an interim basis.

The park superintendent at Sequoia was Eivind Scoyen— a patriarch among the superintendents. Eivind was born in Yellowstone and had spent his entire career in the National Park Service. In 1956, Connie Wirth named him associate director, from which he retired in January of 1962. He was, indeed, "Mr. Park Service."

The concessioner was Howard Hayes, owner of the Riverside Press and a prominent California business leader. Hayes was a friend of Mather and Albright, having met them in 1915 at Yellowstone National Park where he operated the Wylie Camps. After Hayes moved to Riverside, California, Mather persuaded him to develop tourist camps at Sequoia. Howard was a brilliant businessman; warm, empathetic, always courteous, never forgetting a name. You could tell when he was in the Washington office; the staff was always excited. Though a wealthy and busy man, he never passed a desk without stopping to shake hands, say a pleasant word and call the employee by name.

The problem Newton and I had gone to look at involved a giant Sequoia that had begun to tilt in the direction of some of the concessioner's cabins in Giant Forest as a result of a recent storm in the area. There were several cabins that would be demolished should it fall. Moreover, should it fall while the cabins were occupied, conceivably, there could be loss of life. Hayes wanted to cut the tree. The park service foresters had investigated the situation and classified the tree as hazardous but, of course, no one had any idea how long the giant could remain standing.

VI. Appointment as Director

Hayes and Drury walked round and round the tree—Hayes pressing his case for removal, Newton saying nothing. After what seemed like an interminable time, Drury said to Hayes, "Howard, I am not so sure: my first obligation is to the tree. Perhaps you should remove the cabins." Hayes exploded with anger—the first and only time I ever saw him in that state of temper. He thundered dire predictions of adverse publicity in his own newspapers and with the California press for putting trees ahead of property and possibly, people. Drury remained glacially calm and unmoved.

Eivind, who had been standing to one side with me listening and observing, stepped in. He suggested to Newton that in a heavy windstorm the tree, if it fell, could be blown somewhat from the expected line of fall destroying cabins other than those anticipated; thus, he suggested it be removed.

His countenance reflecting grief, Drury, reluctantly, agreed. His devotion to *preservation* over *use* was indisputable.

Drury's tenure as director came to an end in the bitter battle sparked by the proposal of the Bureau of Reclamation to build a dam in Dinosaur National Monument. Oscar Chapman, then secretary, approved of the proposal. It was a bitter pill for Drury to swallow but loyally he accepted the secretary's decision. The conservationists did not!

Led by the Sierra Club and the Wilderness Society, the citizen conservation organizations joined the battle with the secretary and the Bureau of Reclamation. It was a protracted and fierce political fight. Eventually, the Congress said "no" to the dam and it was Chapman's turn to swallow the bitter pill. His legendary political touch had just gone cold.

Over lunch in 1973, Oscar and I were reminiscing about our time in government. I brought up the Drury episode. He expressed his strong view that Drury had been disloyal to him during the fight over the dam in that Drury was not vigorous in his support of the secretary's decision. He went on to say that he really felt like firing him. Up to that time however, no park service director had been fired. Chapman did not choose to break that tradition, even though Drury was not a career park service employee.

What Chapman did do when the fight was over, was offer Drury a job of equal rank and pay as an assistant to the secretary. Drury was reluctant to accept. The issue was resolved when Governor Earl Warren (also California Class of 1912) offered Drury the job of director of California State Parks. Drury accepted and resigned as director of the National Park Service on March 31, 1951.

Chapman immediately appointed Arthur E. Demaray director. Demaray had come to work for the Geological Survey, also in the Department of the Interior, as a young clerk before the National Park Service was established. When the new service was being organized by Mather and Albright, the survey loaned them Demaray to help put their fledgling organization together. When funds were appropriated for the National Park Service, Demaray transferred to the new agency. He proved to be an extremely able, sensitive administrator thoroughly at home in the bureaucratic politics of Washington. Mather promoted him to assistant director; Cammerer named him as his associate director. He served Drury in the same capacity. Nearing the end of a long and illustrious career, his appointment as director was a fitting tribute to one of the most loved and respected of the small group that brought the new agency to life. Arthur served less than a year, retiring on December 8, 1951.

Chapman named Conrad L. Wirth, a landscape architect by training, to succeed to the directorship. Wirth had entered the federal service with the National Capital Planning Commission. Albright brought him into the National Park Service as an assistant director in 1931. He remained in the Washington office as assistant director under both Cammerer and Drury, becoming associate director under Demaray on April 1, 1951.

Wirth was confronted with a physical plant in the parks that had deteriorated during the war years when the parks were, largely, mothballed. Millions of Americans, denied the opportunity to travel in the gas-rationing war era, were pouring into the parks like robins returning in the spring. The annual incremental increases of the normal budgetary process would not soon correct the obvious needs of the parks. Brilliantly, Wirth conceived Mission 66—a ten-year program "designed to overcome the inroads of neglect and to restore to the American people a national park system adequate for their needs."

Connie involved the field personnel of the park service in formulating the program, and Secretary McKay and President Eisenhower in validating it politically. In one swoop, he had leapfrogged the routine annual budget process with a ten-year budget package. It was a stroke of genius. The Congress endorsed the program enthusiastically. Until political action committees came along, ribbon-cutting was a Congressman's love second only to a constituent—and Mission 66 promised a lot of ribbon-cutting for its development projects.

The tilt in the dichotomy of park policy had returned to *use*. In ten years with a development package of roads, trails, visitor centers/offices, employee housing, modernized and new campgrounds, lodging and eating facilities, the parks were to be made ready for the visitation of 1966 and beyond.

Fueled by ever-increasing appropriations, the construction program picked up speed. It perked up the concern of the increasingly involved citizen conservation organizations.

All applauded the removal of the concession facilities from the rim of the Grand Canyon of the Yellowstone but should they have been relocated in the vicinity in what later was identified as grizzly habitat or should they have been eliminated from the park entirely?

Connie awarded a thirty-year concession contract to the Yosemite Park & Curry Company for all of the lodging, food, gasoline, transportation and a host of other commercial merchandising operations in Yosemite for a nominal franchise fee of ¾ of 1 percent of gross receipts. The concessioner promptly subleased the gasoline concession for far more than the company would pay the government for all of the operations. This brought the ire of Congressmen John Moss (California) and Jack Brooks (Texas) down upon the park service. The contract could not be cancelled. Moreover, the franchise fee could not be increased without the consent of the concessioner, which it refused to give. As a result, a new policy was adopted that required concessioners to pay to the Government ½ of their receipts from sub-concession agreements in addition to the franchise fee set forth in the contract. This controversy was but a symptom of a larger question that has persisted since, namely: what is the role of privately-owned concessioners in the parks and the terms and conditions under which they should operate if, indeed, many of them should even remain?

Others were sparked into flame by the size of campgrounds, straightening and improving existing roads, building of new roads, etc. Perhaps the most publicized and heated dispute involved the Sierra Club under the leadership of Ansel Adams over the widening and improvement of the Tioga Road in Yosemite.

These mounting disagreements over what many considered the development excesses of Mission 66 were but the tip of the iceberg. The needs of an increasingly urban America for outdoor recreation; the establishment of a wilderness preservation system to embrace major portions of the parks; and the validity of NPS policy of "let nature take its course" in park resource management were other controversies that engulfed the National Park Service.

From the establishment of Yellowstone in 1872 the objective of management was to preserve the park forests against commercial timber harvesting and the ravages of fire, bugs and disease. The "good" animals—elk, deer, buffalo, moose, etc., were, likewise protected but not so the "bad" animals— predators. By the time management understood the role of the predators most of them were gone from the park scene. Moreover, with man's developments moving ever closer to the park boundaries, the natural habitat of park wildlife was appropriated or otherwise adversely impacted. With little or no predation, no sport hunting and diminished habitat, park wildlife populations, elk and deer particularly, exploded beyond the carrying capacity of their available range. If they were not to starve, the options for control were trapping and removal to other ranges, zoos, etc., and direct reduction (shooting by park rangers). Trapping, usually, was not successful in removing all of the surplus. Shooting by the rangers raised the hackles and howls of sports hunters who contended the parks should be opened to them for hunting. Hunting clubs, state fish and game commissioners, members of Congress and others were calling into question the historic wildlife management policy of the park service.

In the meantime, a few scientists were beginning to question NPS forest management policy. A landmark study of the giant sequoias in Sequoia National Park established the fact that wild fire played a significant role in the survival and perpetuation of the species. The study contended that as a result of NPS policy protecting the understory (brush) from fire, a dense cover had grown up and should there be a wild fire out of control it could threaten the survival of giant sequoias.

By the time the Kennedy Administration arrived in 1961, the conservationists, by and large, were cooled toward if not turned-off by Mission 66. Moreover, with the environmentally sensitive Stewart Udall, Mission 66 had a less hospitable climate than it had known in the Eisenhower years.

Confronted with these volatile issues and having no independent body of knowledge to establish policy, Secretary Udall sought the counsel of the National Academy of Sciences. He appointed a panel of distinguished scientists and wildlife managers to examine the wildlife management policy of the park service. The reports of these learned bodies arrived just before I became director. They were destined to change park management policy for all time.

The academy report highlighted the need for an organized, well-financed research effort. The natural sciences research budget was only $28,000 annually.

The Leopold Report (named for the Committee Chairman A. Starker Leopold of the University of California at Berkley) went far beyond consideration of wildlife management. In the words of the committee the emphasis of the report was "...placed on the philosophy of park management and the ecologic principles involved. Our suggestions are intended to enhance the esthetic, historical and scientific values of the parks to the American public, vis-à-vis the mass recreational values."

The committee articulated a new goal of park management: "As a primary goal, we would recommend that the biotic associations within each park be maintained, or where necessary recreated, as nearly as possible in the condition that prevailed when the area was first visited by the white man. A national park should represent a vignette of primitive America."

It was my good fortune to become director at a most propitious time in the history of the National Park System. Great tidal waves of environmental concerns were beginning to move.

First, the Outdoor Recreation Resources Review Commission authorized by the Congress in the Eisenhower administration completed its work in 1961—the first year of the Kennedy administration. Under the creative leadership of its chairman, Laurance S. Rockefeller, the commission had made a searching examination of the demand and the needs for outdoor recreation in an increasingly urban America. Two of its imaginative recommendations were to have an enormous impact on the National Park System, namely:

1. The federal government should take the initiative in providing additional recreational areas in close proximity to our urban population; and

VI. Appointment as Director

2. The federal government should vastly increase the appropriations for the purchase of parkland.

This latter recommendation resulted in the Land and Water Conservation Fund of 1964, earmarking receipts from park entrance and user fees, motorboat fuel taxes, receipts from sale of surplus government real estate and a portion of the revenues from off-shore oil leases. The money accruing to the fund was set aside and remained available until appropriated for federal land acquisition and matching grants to the states for land acquisition and development of recreation facilities. Prior to authorization of the Land and Water Conservation Fund, parks had been added to the system from the federally-owned lands of the public domain (Yellowstone, Yosemite, Glacier and most of the other western parks); private philanthropy (Acadia, Virgin Islands); and donation to the federal government by the states (Mammoth Cave, Great Smokies, etc.).

Secondly, the remnants of wild America—its lakeshores, seashores, virgin forests, wild rivers and alpine environments—were rapidly disappearing.

This nation was blessed with one of the richest natural inheritances (land, water, forests, wildlife, minerals) of any country on earth. The creative genius of the people who came to these shores transformed these natural blessings into the mightiest cornucopia of economic riches of any society in history. Yet, for the most part, we had preserved of our cultural heritage only presidential birthplaces and battlefields.

The fields were white for harvest. Now was the time, if we were to preserve the remaining vignettes of our natural inheritance and reach out to commemorate and memoralize the cultural heritage of the industrial revolution, discoveries in the sciences, medicine, the arts, music and literature, and the remarkable growth in understanding of individual worth and human rights.

Third, stirred by such giants as Ira Gabrielson and C.R.

(Pink) Gutermuth of the Wildlife Management Institute, Clarence Cottam of the National Parks & Conservation Association, Howard Zahnizer and Sigurd Olson of the Wilderness Society, Ansel Adams and David Brower of the Sierra Club, Gordon Gray of the National Trust for Historic Preservation, Tom Kimball of the National Wildlife Federation, and a host of others, the citizen conservation organizations were mobilizing for combat to protect a livable environment.

Fourth, the political climate was conducive to growth.

Mrs. Kennedy, in 1961, inaugurated the program to restore the historical integrity of the White House and expand its fine arts collection.

In 1964, Mrs. Johnson began reaching out to restore beauty to a natural scene too long neglected. Her enthusiasm stirred President Johnson to leadership and support.

I was privileged to work for an enthusiastic, supportive Secretary, Stewart Udall. He was the first secretary to articulate the interdependence between people and their natural world. He was in the forefront of those visionaries whose leadership ushered in the environmental era, and was perhaps the greatest leader the Department of the Interior has seen. Both of us shared similar backgrounds as rural small town lawyers and were of the same age—only 60 days difference in our birth dates. We quickly developed a trusting, warm, personal friendship which has endured more than two decades. He gave me wide latitude to pursue our mutual objectives with the Congress.

Local, regional and national media, notably the Washington *Post*, Miami *Herald*, the New York *Times*, the Los Angeles *Times* and the *Christian Science Monitor*, were focusing public attention on the needs, the opportunities and the urgency of rescuing and preserving our natural and cultural heritage.

Morris Udall (Arizona), John Saylor (Pennsylvania), John Dingell (Michigan), Alan Bible (Nevada), Tom Kuchel (California), Henry (Scoop) Jackson (Washington), Gaylord Nelson (Wisconsin), Clinton Anderson and Tom Morris, both of (New

Mexico) were in the vanguard of members of Congress responding to the political involvement of growing numbers of citizens across the land concerned with the preservation of their patrimony.

Lastly, Udall embraced the Leopold Report and directed the National Park Service to implement its recommendations for ecologically based park management, replacing the historic policy of "let nature take its course."

To help me keep my bearings for the exciting journey ahead, I set three signposts:

Expand the National Park System;

Make its programs and its parks relevant to an urban America; and

Update park management policies and reinvigorate the agency's personnel management system.

VII

KEYS
TO GOVERNMENT
MANAGEMENT

The United States government is the biggest business in the world. It is a service institution engaged, as Lincoln said, in doing for the people those things they cannot do for themselves. The president of the United States is its chief executive officer.

Like any business, the performance of the executive branch is commensurate with the talent, the vision, the leadership, the motivation, and the creativity of its employees and its managers.

In private enterprise, managers are in two categories: corporate officers (president, vice presidents, general counsels, etc.), and operating division heads (directors, chiefs, or other such senior management title).

In government it is similar: the corporate officers are the departmental secretaries, deputies and assistants, the political bureaucrats appointed in every new administration. The operating division heads are the bureau chiefs, directors or other such senior management title: the career bureaucrats with on-line supervision of the work force. They (the political bureaucrat and the career bureaucrat) are interdependent; each is indispensable to the success of the other. The political bureaucrat provides credibility to the process of government by articulating philosophy and establishing policy/objectives to achieve the president's platform. The career bureaucrat provides the expertise in the innumerable disciplines needed to put muscle and sinew into the philosophical body of each administration.

The political bureaucrat and the career bureaucrat interface very much like two sprocket wheels. When these gears mesh properly our government is responsive, responsible and efficient; when they don't the people suffer. Sadly, in far too many instances they do not mesh. The problem arises from a basic misunderstanding of their roles—and that problem begins at the very top of the political leadership. I have been angered, frequently, by the criticism leveled at the career Civil Service by almost every presidential candidate ranting against "the damn bureaucracy," oblivious to the fact that he is running like hell to become the chief bureaucrat among all of the bureaucrats. Imagine the CEO of General Motors damning its employees in public and then expecting them to build competitive Chevrolets. It is a bad scene.

This is often exacerbated by the reciprocating attitude of the career bureaucrat toward the political bureaucrat: "What the hell, this politician will soon be gone!" And, most times they are right. The average tenure of departmental secretaries is about three years; for deputy and assistant secretaries it is even less. Such an attitude begs the question, however: the names may change but the position of the political bureaucrat remains. Indeed, it must remain if government is to be responsive to the changing priorities of the people as expressed through the electoral process.

A great many highly successful business men and women enter each new administration as political bureaucrats. None would dream of trying to run their large corporations without a carefully thought-out management system—policy/objectives; annual goals; product and personal performance standards; evaluation of operating results—yet, inexplicably, many do not approach the management of the government business with the same management philosophy.

One of the most serious deficiencies in the management of the federal government occurs because the *political* bureaucrat does not take the time to sit down with the *career* bureaucrat and establish at the outset a clear frame of reference to govern their work together in getting the public's business accomplished. As a result there builds misunderstanding which feeds mistrust which compounds into horrible inefficiency and waste. Like the male alligator, they eat their own. For example, not since Secretary Hubert Work's memorandum of March 11, 1925, to the first director Stephen Mather had any secretary clearly enunciated his policy/objectives for the management of the National Park System.

There are five keys to successful management of a government bureau: appointments; appropriations; legislation; clearly defined secretarial policy/objectives; and operations evaluation.

I decided to start my tenure as director in 1964 by establishing a clear understanding with Secretary Udall about what his policy/objectives were for the management of the National Park System. After reviewing together the draft I had prepared, he signed the memorandum on July 10, 1964, establishing six policy/objectives: to provide the highest quality of use and enjoyment; to responsibly conserve and manage the parks; to expand the National Park System; to cooperate with other conservation organizations; to communicate the significance of the American heritage through the National Park System; and to increase the effectiveness of the National Park Service.

When Wally Hickel replaced Stewart Udall, I drafted another memorandum of policy/objectives for Hickel. He was truly excited about the draft I showed him. He made a few changes, passed it to Carl McMurray, his executive assistant, who also suggested a few changes. Then the secretary said to Carl, "As soon as this is signed, I want you to have every bureau head in the department write such a statement for my signature."

Hickel issued his memorandum setting forth policy/objectives for the National Park Service on June 19, 1969. In that memorandum he validated most of the policy/objectives then in place and accepted several new initiatives I had recommended to him: Parks to People, Volunteers-in-Parks, limitations on automobile access, etc. The only Udall policy he scrapped was to contract with concessioners for the operation of park campgrounds.

Every new administration has its own distinctive style, tone and objectives. This is a great opportunity for the career bureaucrat and a critical time for him to support the new political bureaucrat with whom he will interface.

I had become convinced during the Johnson presidency that the National Park Service needed a legislatively-approved Corps of Volunteers to assist with our accelerating programs, especially interpretation. Secretary Udall agreed. We completed the staff work on the Volunteers-in-Parks (VIPS) legislation. But before we could send the package to the Congress, President Johnson announced that he would not seek another term. Within a few months we were going to have a new administration.

Stewart agreed with me that if we sent up the legislation then, it would be shopworn for the new administration. I put the whole package in my desk to await the new administration.

Soon after Hickel settled in, I produced the VIPS package. He embraced it enthusiastically. The Congress quickly passed the legislation.

The new First Lady, Mrs. Nixon, inaugurated the program at Arlington House. We were off and running with what has become one of the most popular—and useful—of park programs.

VII. Keys to Government Management

When Rogers Morton succeeded Hickel, he and I reviewed Hickel's memorandum and he confirmed those policy/objectives.

With these memoranda clearly setting forth secretarial policy/objectives for the National Park Service, I never had a single serious dispute in the nine years I served three different secretaries of the interior. That is not to say that all was sweetness and light. I did have arguments—some heated—with their staff. I never let that disturb me, however, for the appointment hanging on my wall was signed by the secretary—not by his staff. My view was that like all good staff "they should be on tap but never on top." I ran the National Park Service. They knew it and I knew it. More importantly, the people in the National Park Service knew it.

In 1964, we had to change attitudes and motivate people to respond to the emerging needs of an urban America. That was a secretarial objective; it, therefore, became my imperative. Subject to compliance with applicable laws and regulations, the secretary delegated to me the personnel appointment authority to get the job done. I personally, appointed or approved the appointments of all superintendents, regional directors, deputy, associate and assistant directors, as well as all appointments and promotions to grade GS-13 and above. This allowed me, early on, to get complete control over the bureau and to tighten up our personnel management program. It needed tightening.

One of my assistant directors came in one day to demand that I allow him to fire an engineer that he believed was incompetent. Surely, if his assessment was supported by the record, I agreed; the government should be shed of such an incompetent. I called the personnel officer and asked him to come to my office with the man's personnel folder. I flipped it open and the top document was an efficiency rating of excellent given less than three months previously. Obviously, he could not prove a case of incompetency with a rating like that.

Another favorite trick was to kick 'em upstairs.

When I was superintendent in St. Louis at JNEM I got a promotion list from the regional office for a vacancy on my staff. I got on the telephone and started calling, not the top candidate's supervisor but his peers. He's a goof-off, I was told with citations to chapter and verse. Then I called the superintendent who had recommended him for promotion. After first trying to snow me, he reluctantly admitted he was trying to unload a problem.

I told my regional directors that if I ever found that happening while I was director, I was going to move the employee back to their personal staff, make them fund the moving costs both ways, and they were going to have a traveling companion for the rest of their career, or until they took action to get rid of him. I only had to do it once; thanks to the watts telephone line the word got around!

The competent career employees applauded this new look. Based on my experience at JNEM I had been sure they would. When I arrived as superintendent there we had a ten-point preference veteran in our administrative division. He would, invariably, show up thirty minutes to an hour late, take an hour or more for lunch, rather than the standard thirty minutes and, generally, leave for the day fifteen minutes to one-half hour before quitting time. His supervisor had talked with him, I had talked with him numerous times and over several months had documented his misconduct in letters of reprimand to him. Nothing helped. Finally, I concluded the only thing left to do was fire him—but firing a career civil service employee with ten-point veterans' preference is no cakewalk. Before starting down a road that I may have had to back-travel, I decided to talk it over with the senior division chief—not the man's supervisor—who had spent his whole career at JNEM. He was an outstanding employee of great integrity. I called John Smith to my office late one evening and laid out my problem.

His response: "Mr. Hartzog, we've been wondering how long it was going to take you to fire him."

VII. Keys to Government Management

I fired the man. He hired a lawyer and they took me through the Civil Service hoops, as was their right to do. My case was solid and the dismissal stuck.

I noticed almost immediately that the floors were a little more polished, the tardiness dropped off, the telephone didn't ring so many times before being answered, and the whole organization seemed to have a little more snap in it.

As Lawrence Appley, the distinguished former president of the American Management Association once said, the employees probably know before the boss does when someone should be fired, and firing an incompetent employee is as important to the integrity of management as rewarding a deserving one.

The National Park Service was established in 1916. We interpreted more sites of Indian culture than did the Indians but we did not have a single superintendent who was an Indian.

We administered the George Washington Carver and the Booker T. Washington National Monuments and the Frederick Douglass Home, sites associated with three of the greatest leaders in American history, but we did not have a single black superintendent.

And except for the talented, gracious lady we inherited with the Adams Mansion National Historic Site in 1946, when the property was donated to the government, we did not have another woman superintendent.

Moreover, we seldom searched for the most talented person available for a position: we looked only inside the organization.

As one old-time superintendent said, "To get to the top you have to polish the seats of the right chairs in the right order." One superintendent even contended that an entrance grade ranger was not qualified for promotion until he had served five years!

History records that the two most creative periods in the growth of the National Park Service occurred during its founding years beginning in 1916 and again in the 1930's when President Roosevelt transferred to it the Military and Historical Parks and assigned it responsibility for the Civilian Conservation Corps programs in the national and state parks. In both of these glory periods, the leadership of the park service reached out to bring in the most creative, innovative, talented people available.

I opened up the system establishing seven goals for personnel management including equal opportunity, and rewards for productivity and initiative.

The goals were printed on plastic, wallet-size cards and distributed to every employee. I unnerved a lot of people when I promoted the GS-12 superintendent of Richmond National Battlefield Park over many more senior, but less productive and creative people, to the GS-15 superintendency of Independence National Historical Park at Philadelphia.

On the reverse side of the cards we printed the National Park Service *Pledge of Public Service*: a statement of our organization goals, our shared ideals and our commitment of service to the American people, the owners of our national parks. This pledge was the unifying theme of our management. It was a positive force in building confidence, cohesion and organizational character.

I retained the management consulting firm of James M. Kittleman and Associates of Chicago for an organizational study of the park service. Thereafter, I retained Jim Kittleman, personally, on a part-time, as needed, consulting basis to monitor and advise on the implementation of the study recommendations.

We contracted with the Federal Executive Institute at Charlottesville, Virginia, to devise and implement an organizational development (team-building) program to bring cohesion to our changing organization.

The Institute was established by the Civil Service Commission (now the Federal Office of Personnel Management) to train senior management personnel of the Federal Career Service. The University of Southern California loaned Dr. Frank Sherwood, Director of its School of Public Administration, to the government to head the Institute. The sixty-day residential program designed by Sherwood and his distinguished faculty for senior bureau managers was the most creative, innovative effort made by the government during my career to improve the quality of government management. I attended the first session and sent one or more of my principal assistants to each session thereafter until each deputy, associate and assistant director and each regional director completed the program.

The explosive growth of the National Park System during the next nine years—beginning with ten new parks in 1964—enabled me to implement this action program with a minimum of grumbling. The few who were disgruntled with the new emphasis chose to retire.

Upon the recommendations of the Outdoor Recreation Resources Review Commission, President Kennedy created the Recreation Advisory Council to coordinate federal policy for outdoor recreation. The council was composed of the secretaries of interior, agriculture, health, education and welfare, commerce, defense and the administrator of the Housing and Home Finance Agency later to become the Department of Housing and Urban Development. On March 26, 1963, the Council issued its policy circular no. 1. setting forth the administration's outdoor recreation policy and decreeing that National Recreation Areas (National Seashores, National Lakeshores, National Waterways, National Riverways, National Recreation Demonstration Areas, and areas with similar names) "should be readily accessible at all times for all-purpose recreational use" and that federal investment in such areas should be "more clearly responsive to recreation demand than other investments that are based primarily upon considerations of preserving unique natural or historical resources."

The areas included in the National Park System were to be governed by management policies different from those applicable to the national parks. For example, sport hunting was to be permitted in the recreation areas but not in the national parks.

Ever since the park service began managing recreation on Bureau of Reclamation reservoirs in the 1930s, it had made a distinction in management practices between recreation areas and the parks. For one thing, the service did not even identify recreation areas as a part of the National Park System. Rather than a separate set of policy guidelines for management, however, the distinctions were exceptions to normal park policy. One classic distinction that always amused me was the one that *prohibited* grazing in the parks but *permitted* pasturage in the recreation areas. It was enough to confuse even the cows!

Bob Coates, a thoughtful and scholarly park service policy analyst, after long study had concluded that we should develop distinctive management principles and administrative policies to reflect the values and the purposes of each category of areas in the system: natural areas (parks, monuments); historical areas; and recreation areas as defined by the president's council. I thought it was a brilliant solution to a real dilemma; so did Secretary Udall who, in his memorandum of July 10, 1964, establishing policy/objectives for the National Park System said:

> In looking back at the legislative enactments that have shaped the National Park System, it is clear that the Congress has included within the growing System three different categories of areas—natural, historical, and recreational.
>
> Natural areas are the oldest category, reaching back to the establishment of Yellowstone National Park almost a century ago. A little later historical areas began to be authorized, culminating in the broad charter for historical preservation set forth in the Historic Sites Act of 1935. In recent decades, with exploding population and diminishing open space, the urgent

VII. Keys to Government Management

need for national recreation areas is receiving new emphasis and attention.

...a single, broad management concept encompassing these three categories of areas within the system is inadequate either for their proper preservation or for realization of their full potential for public use as embodied in the expressions of congressional policy. Each of these categories requires a separate management concept and a separate set of management principles coordinated to form one organic management plan for the entire system.

Udall then set forth the principles that were to govern the administrative policies for management of each of the three categories of areas in the system. Based on these directives we developed a separate set of administrative policies to guide management of each category.

Implementing the Leopold Committee report was a more vexing problem.

Following the statement of its goal for park management, "A national park should represent a vignette of primitive America," the committee added prophetically, "the implications of this seemingly simple aspiration are stupendous."

I cannot begin to explain how stupendous and difficult it was to translate the recommendations from policy (which the secretary approved) to practice (which I had to do). Several illustrations come to mind.

First, I went to see Congressman Michael J. Kirwan, the chairman of the Interior Department Appropriations Sub-Committee, to discuss funds to beef up our natural science research effort. Flat-out, he bombed the idea. "Research is a function of NIH [National Institutes of Health] not the park service," he advised me. As chairman, his power over park service appropriations was like that of a Roman emperor: thumbs up and you got your money; thumbs down and you were dead. Research was dead—so be it. So I changed the name from research to resource studies and began financing it from a reserve which I withheld as a percentage of park management funds to handle emergencies.

In the winter of 1966–67, we had a surplus of elk at Yellowstone. Our trapping efforts had not controlled the herd successfully so we initiated direct reduction. This was consistent with the Leopold recommendations. The rangers who shot the elk would field dress the carcasses and give the meat to the Indians. The sport hunters were furious.

Wyoming, shortly before, had elected a new Republican governor. He saw the hunters' complaints as an opening to embarrass Democratic Senator Gale McGee, the senior senator from Wyoming. He jumped to the head of the line of critics, forcing Senator McGee to air our elk management policy in a congressional subcommittee hearing at Casper, Wyoming.

The governor demanded that we stop the shooting and begin trapping again. Senator McGee, a member of the Senate Appropriations Committee, agreed to provide additional funding to do the trapping, and I agreed to stop the shooting.

At the hearing Senator McGee asked the governor how many trapped elk he wanted delivered to the ranges in Wyoming. "One thousand," he replied.

In the back of the room you could hear the ranchers audibly catch their breath as they began to murmur among themselves: the elk hunting season in Wyoming was over. Elk are notorious competitors with cattle for the ranchers' hay stacks in the winter. It was then March of 1967; snow was blanketing the landscape.

I agreed to provide the governor with his 1,000 elk and directed the superintendent to start trapping. When we had trapped and shipped about half of the elk, the decibel level of the ranchers' complaints had begun to drive the hunters' complaints from the governor's ears. He called the superintendent to stop the shipping. The superintendent called me. "What shall I do?" he asked.

"Tell the governor," I replied, "if, in the future, he will stay the hell out of my wildlife management program, I'll stop shipping; otherwise, keep shipping, even if you have to unload them on the Capitol grounds." The governor agreed. The trapping and the shipping stopped and the Leopold wildlife management recommendations were in place at Yellowstone.

I had less success with the park service employees in Hawaii where, in accordance with Leopold's recommendation, I approved deputizing local hunters as park rangers to kill off the ferral goats. The park service never did like—and perhaps still does not like—the deputized park ranger program mandated by the Congress for elk reduction at Grand Teton National Park. With Congresswoman Patsy Mink I went to Hawaii to get the ferral goat reduction program underway. When I left, the program fizzled. Out of sight, out of mind.

The role of fire in park management was another contentious recommendation of the Leopold Report.

In 1974, Laurance Rockefeller invited me to attend a meeting of the board of directors of the Jackson Hole Preserve in Grand Teton National Park. Horace Albright, a co-founder and second director of the park service, was one of the board members.

Lightning had recently set a fire in the park. In accordance with the new Leopold recommendations to let wild fires burn (unless they endangered human life and property), the superintendent was letting the fire take its course. It was not a pretty sight: smoke hanging in the valley and on the charred slopes of those majestic mountains. It was too much for Horace. He introduced a resolution that would have the board condemn such heresy. Laurance, graciously, asked me if I would like to speak to the subject and I did, explaining the basis of the policy as articulated by the Leopold committee.

Horace was much loved by all of us as a founding patriarch of the park service and that love was fully reciprocated by him. While muttering his doubts about this new found wisdom, he withdrew his motion. Old habits die hard and many a fine park ranger and superintendent did not jump with joy to embrace the new policy.

*   *   *

Communication is a tough and tedious, never ending, essential task, especially for an organization in change and transition.

I initiated an employee newsletter; instituted a system in which any employee could write me personally—by way of a blue envelope—on any subject desired; scheduled a face-to-face meeting with every superintendent at least once each year; and held a regional directors meeting every three months.

To insure that the blue envelope system did not become a sanctuary for backbiting, I imposed several conditions. Every communication had to be signed, had to be shared with the appropriate regional director having responsibility for the affected program, and had to be answered. And there were absolutely *no repercussions*, even if the employee was wrong in perception or reality, and especially not if the employee was right! This raised a few hackles until the workings of the system were understood and its integrity established.

I arranged to bring every superintendent face-to-face with the regional director at least once each year. In the early stages of the program we allowed no more than twelve superintendents at any meeting. There were no staff, no agenda and no minutes.

Decisions that required communication to staff were recorded by the regional director on a pink-colored memorandum and distributed to the appropriate office. The purpose of the meeting was to see and be seen; to listen and heed; and to explain, explain, explain.

We convened on Friday evening with a social hour and dinner together, met all day Saturday and again Sunday morning. We adjourned at noon.

For our meetings we sat around a common table. I would open on Saturday morning with a brief status report on budget forecasts, appropriation bills, legislation and the new management system of secretarial objectives, park service goals, program and personal performance standards. The superintendents were then encouraged to share with the regional director and me their problems, questions and concerns. We wanted an informal, freewheeling exchange: what's working, what's not. If it's broke, lets fix it *together*, if it ain't broke, let's roll it!

That first Saturday morning was draggy; they were not sure this was for real. After lunch, during which the regional director had salted the meeting with a couple of rough questions, the tempo of the discussion picked up. By Sunday morning the questions and problems began to boil up like drano in a stopped up pipe. We were still going strong when it was time to adjourn at noon.

They all went home and got on the telephone to their buddies who were yet to attend the meetings. Yes, they reported, you really could discuss your problems and get them resolved. The second and succeeding meetings began at full-speed.

After I had completed the first round of these meetings, I encouraged the superintendents to bring their spouses. In most park environments, the support of one's spouse is critical to accomplishing the mission of the service. Spouses did not attend the sessions with the superintendents. I met separately with them. Occasionally, I found them to be even more candid than the superintendents in laying out their common concerns about what we were doing and why. It was a real partnership-building experience.

Shortly after I became director, I went to Omaha to attend the retirement party of George Baggley. George was the first college-educated chief ranger of Yellowstone. There he met and charmed Herma, one of the first women naturalists in the National Park Service. They married and together had a great career in the service. In my remarks the evening of his retirement party, I noted all of this and applauded Herma's great contributions to George's career and to the National Park Service, concluding by saying, "The smartest thing George ever did was to marry Herma."

But George had the last word. In his remarks, after noting

with appreciation, my compliment to Herma and to him, he
went on to say, "I agree with what George said about my
marrying Herma. I know his wife, Helen, and I can say to
him that marrying her was the smartest thing he ever did."
Then, he paused and slowly continuing he added, "Now that I
have reflected on it, I think that is probably the *only* smart
thing he has ever done."

Long before the National Park Service was established in
1916, the wives of park employees had toiled and sacrificed
alongside their husbands in protecting the early parks, such
as Yellowstone, Yosemite, Sequoia, Mount Rainier and
others. In such remote areas, their service—unpaid and
often unsung—was essential to the functioning of the parks.
This noble tradition was treasured and nurtured by all directors of the Natioal Park Service—beginning with its co-
founders Mather and Albright. Many times I have heard
Horace Albright say he would never appoint a park superintendent until he had met his wife. In the closed society existing in many of the isolated rural western environments of
the early parks, the superintendent's wife was the park host-
ess, welcoming and entertaining visiting congressional committees, foreign dignitaries, state and local officials and
other prominent persons from the media and the public and
private sectors whose support was essential to the survival
and growth of the National Park System. She was counselor
and comforter to many a city girl newly married to a wilderness ranger; she was the ambassador to the neighboring
wives of ranchers, farmers and small businessmen nestled
along the park boundaries.

One night in Alaska when taking the secretary's advisory
board from Camp Denali to the McKinley Hotel, the bus
broke down. Isolated and tired, we were stranded not too far
from the house of the outpost ranger and his family at
Wonder Lake. The ranger's wife opened her home, warmly
and graciously greeting a troupe of people she had never seen
before. Counting board members, spouses and accompanying
staff, the group numbered thirty or more. She rustled up hot

drinks and refreshments. Her two small preschool children had been put to bed, but with the commotion were soon up to greet and entertain these strange, new people. Such examples of service, hospitality and support have been multiplied by the thousands over the years.

One of the more colorful rangers, Matt Ryan, then stationed in Death Valley National Monument, said of his bride, Rosemary:

> We have seasonal ranger help six months during the winter season and the rest of the time my wife and I are alone at the Emigrant Ranger Station, but the people don't stop coming. We have rather brisk traffic across the monument all summer —people taking a short cut from Beatty to Lone Pine—and they pass in front of our house at the head of a nine-mile grade, and there's a lot of need for public service. I can't be there all the time and Rosemary fills in at the information desk; she handles communications; she has learned to cool a car expertly and add water without burning herself; she has done very well with first-aid; she makes a doggone good jug of lemonade; and without her I just don't think the public would be served as well. And she loves to do this. She likes people very much; she is just a good average person who has a lot of interest in other people's problems.

Matt's bride, may be a *good average person* but, like most park wives, possesses an uncommon touch of class and talent. Rosemary, for example, is a writer whose work has been published in *Woman's Day*. Others are artists, sculptors, potters, weavers and photographers whose creative interpretations of native crafts and the natural scene have enriched our cultural legacy. They are teachers and scientists, whose works have advanced the knowledge and understanding of our natural and cultural heritage. Uniquely, the park wives have been equal partners with their husbands in holding aloft the standard of service which survives as the hallmark of the National Park Service.

The fabric of this rich tradition of service by park women

has been strengthened, nourished and expanded over the years—especially in the last two decades—as more and more women have sought careers in the National Park Service at every vocation from ranger to top administrator.

Operations evaluation is different from auditing. I wanted to know that internal controls were in place as required by the laws enacted by the Congress and the regulations promulgated by the General Accounting Office, the Office of Management and Budget and the secretary for accountability for money and property. I had an assistant director for administration to oversee these functions. But I wanted to know more.

The National Park Service is in the park resource preservation and people-serving business. You can have a clean bill of health from the auditors that tells you that no one went south with anything of value. But it does not tell you how well you accomplished the mission. I established an operations evaluation unit to answer that question. It was small; two clerical workers and four senior executives, with experience in legislation and regulations, budget and appropriations, personnel management, and field operations (either concessions, park, or regional management). Their reports, plus visitor comments, enabled me to see the operation through the eyes of the public—the ultimate bosses of all government business.

All operations evaluation reports were sent directly to me in blue envelopes. I sent a copy to the regional director. We scheduled a meeting in thirty days to review the report together. This gave him enough time to do any checking he wished to do.

The first one of these reports set off quite a storm. It had been made by the executive who had a background in personnel management. He reported eight or ten things below standard in the park, ranging from dirty restrooms and shoddy-looking signs to seasonal personnel who either through improper training or indifference, were not doing the job very well.

Without even checking out the report, the regional director called me on the telephone in an absolute snit. The park involved was one in which he had not too long previously served as superintendent.

"What the hell can he know about park operations?" he demanded. "He is a personnel man."

"Maybe so," I replied, "but he's not blind. If you like, I will go to the park with you for the review." I tried to calm him down.

"No," he replied, "I'll check it myself and call you."

A couple of weeks passed. One day, sheepishly he called me. "I hate to admit it," he began, "but he's right. I got things squared around and it won't happen in my region again."

This program had another beneficial impact. These four executives traveled extensively among parks in many regions. New initiatives and management improvements implemented by an innovative superintendent at one park could be shared quickly among all regions and parks. Operations evaluation looked not only at what was below standard, but also at what was being done better to accomplish our mission. Thus, it became a positive force for improvement.

In 1972 a management consulting firm retained by Secretary Caspar (Cap) Weinberger—then secretary of Health, Education and Welfare—reported on its evaluation of the management of federal government agencies delivering onsite services to the public. The report concluded that the National Park Service was one of the five best-managed such agencies in the federal government.

VIII

WORKING THE HILL

On the campaign trail in his run against Dick Jefferies, Colonel Pearcy often told a story that was enormously helpful to me in understanding and working with the remarkable people in the Congress. A farmer had an only son of whom he was very proud. The boy had made it clear he did not want to be a farmer but he could not make up his mind what career to follow. Finally, unbeknownst to the boy, the father decided to test him.

He set up a table in the living room and put a silver dollar, a Bible and a bottle of whiskey on it. Then the father hid in the corner behind a screen.

When the boy comes in—if he takes the silver dollar, he is
going to be a financier;
—if he takes the Bible he is going to be a preacher;
—if he takes the whiskey he is going to be a drunkard.

In a few minutes the boy walked in, saw the table—went over,
—picked up the silver dollar and put it in his pocket;

—picked up the Bible and put it
under his arm;
—picked up the whiskey, pulled the
cork out and took a swig.
The old man, in his excitement, jumped out from behind the
screen waiving his arms and yelling,
"Faith and bejesus, he is going
to be a politician!!!!

The Constitution assigns to the Congress the authority and
the responsibility for establishing the public land policy of
the United States. The executive branch (the president) may
propose, but it is the Congress that disposes.

The first of my goals was to expand the National Park System. If I was to succeed, it would only be with the active
support and interest of the Congress. I set about, methodi-
cally and relentlessly, to get it—a great learning experience.

Most of the substantive work of the Congress is accomplished by committees of both house and senate members.
Each body is organized into standing committees, select committees and special committees.

Special and select committees are established, usually, for
investigative—rather than legislative—purposes and, generally, are not permanent.

Standing committees are permanent committees of the
House and Senate, having jurisdiction over policy and program matters that closely parallel the organizational structure of the executive branch. For example, the House and
Senate Agriculture committees have jurisdiction over the Department of Agriculture. These standing committees not only
consider legislation to authorize or prohibit activities in the
program areas over which they have jurisdiction, but also
have the responsibility to oversee the implementation of legislation by the executive departments and agencies under
their jurisdiction. These dual responsibilities (legislation and
oversight) are a part of the checks and balances provided in

the Constitution between the executive branch (the president) and the legislative branch (the Congress).

The Congress through its oversight function has a check on the president in how well the law is administered. This function is exercised not only by congressional investigations, the taking of testimony from the public and the executive officers of the government in hearings and, if need be, enacting further legislation but also, importantly, by either appropriating or declining to appropriate money for expenditure by the executive departments.

Soon after Great Smoky Mountains National Park was established, some of the members of the Congress (particularly Senator Kenneth McKellar of Tennessee) were upset with the way the National Park Service was managing the park. After challenging its management without the desired results, Senator McKellar, who was the chairman of the Senate Appropriations Committee, simply curtailed appropriations for the park.

When the Mississippi congressional delegation became disillusioned at the rate of construction of the Natchez Trace Parkway, Congressman Jamie Whitten (a senior member of the House Appropriations Committee) had the needed construction money added to the president's budget.

Most standing committees are organized into subcommittees with jurisdiction over the policies and programs of a particular bureau of a department, such as the Park and Recreation Subcommittee of the House Interior and Insular Affairs Committee which has jurisdiction over *most* of the activities of the National Park Service.

It is in the subcommittee that the nitty-gritty work on most park legislation occurs. A park bill—whether proposed by an individual member of Congress (or a group of them) or by the president—is first considered in the subcommittee. The subcommittee takes testimony from those supporting and opposing the legislation. After hearings, the subcommittee marks-up the bill (reviews the bill and considers amendments and revisions) and reports it to the full Committee on

Interior and Insular Affairs. Generally, only bills approved by the full committee may be considered by the House, unless in a rare instance a majority of the members of the House sign a petition to discharge the committee from further consideration of the bill. The full committee may further mark-up a bill reported by the subcommittee.

Notwithstanding all that one may have read about the legislative process, legislation is only part process. The other part is people, and the people part is more important. Each body of the Congress (the House and the Senate) makes its own rules and when it chooses it can change them—and even on occasion suspend them. For example, in the waning days of the 99th Congress, Representative Joseph McDade of Scranton, Pennsylvania, a very senior member of the House Appropriations Committee, succeeded in amending the Omnibus Appropriations Bill (H.J.Res. 738, Public Law 99-500). The amendment established Steamtown National Historic Site in Scranton, authorized appropriations ($20,000,000) for its administration, and, appropriated $8,000,000 for its planning and management in the 1987 fiscal year. The amendment bypassed the National Park Service's planning process for recommending the establishment of national parks including National Historic Sites, and the president's administration report setting forth his views and recommendations on the proposal. Moreover, Mr. McDade's amendment bypassed the lengthy hearing process of the Interior and Insular Affairs Committee usually observed in congressional consideration of new park proposals. However, once the bill was enacted by the Congress and signed by the president, Steamtown became as much a part of the National Park System as is Yellowstone.

In getting legislation it is not only important to know the process; it is imperative to get to know the members of Congress and their staff.

The preponderance of the programs of the National Park Service involve the House Interior and Insular Affairs Committee, the House Public Works Committee and the House Appropriations Committee and their counterpart committees in the Senate. However, success is dependent from time to time, on the other committees on the District of Columbia, Administration, Government Operations and Rules, including their Senate counterparts. Thus, I established a regular routine by which my congressional liaison, legislative assistant or I maintained regular contact with each committee, and its staff.

The foundations of a successful congressional liaison program are the staff members of the committees and of the representatives in the House and the senators. The staffs see and talk with the senators and representatives every day. If the staffs understand and believe in your programs, they can support them when you cannot be there.

Soon after my arrival in Washington in 1963, I paid a courtesy call on Congressman O'Brien from New York, the ranking Democrat on the House Interior and Insular Affairs Committee. He said to me, "I don't know why you have called on me because I really have no interest in your program. But, I reckon you called on me because I am responsible for Wayne Aspinall's election." Wayne Aspinall of Colorado was the chairman of the House Interior and Insular Affairs Committee. In addition to the park service, the Interior Committee also had jurisdiction over the Bureau of Reclamation in the Department of the Interior. Irrigation water impounded by the Bureau of Reclamation is crucial to the agricultural economy of Colorado.

Continuing, O'Brien said, "Every election year I go out to Colorado to campaign for Wayne. I say to those folks out there, you'd better reelect Wayne and return him to the Congress; otherwise, I am going to be your chairman. And being from New York, I don't know what a weir is (a device for letting in and shutting out water from an irrigation ditch). It's always successful, they always return Wayne; they don't want me as their chairman," he concluded.

As I came to learn, he was not being facetious; he was

making two very useful points. First, the importance of seniority on the committees involved in the legislative process; and, secondly, the lack of widespread interest among the members of Congress in the National Park System. I could take advantage of this first point and I resolved to change the second one.

In getting acquainted with the members of the Congress and staff, my top priority was to pay courtesy calls on the members of the Interior and Insular Affairs committees, the Roads and Public Buildings Subcommittees of Public Works and the Appropriations Subcommittees that handled National Park Service appropriations.

Except for the chairman and the ranking minority member of each committee and subcommittee, I did not make appointments. I simply stopped by the office, introduced myself to the receptionist and explained the purpose of my visit. If the representative or the senator was available I was usually introduced. If they were not in the office, I simply left my card and departed. Upon my return to the office, I always wrote a letter. If I had seen the member, I expressed my appreciation for the opportunity of the visit and advised of my readiness to be of service. If the member was not available, the letter stated that I had stopped by to pay my respects and to advise that I was available to serve when needed. Later, one of the members who was not available, but who had received my letter, said to me, "I really appreciated that letter more than I would have your visit. I am too busy to take up my time with bureaucrats when I have nothing of concern to my constituents. It's good to know, however, that you are aware of the importance of my constituents and me to your program."

Moreover, I encouraged each superintendent coming to Washington on park business to schedule time for a courtesy call on the representative in whose district the superintendent's park was situated and the two senators from that state. Like we did in Washington with our courtesy calls, the superintendent did not have to see the member—just leave a card with the receptionist and say, "I stopped by to pay my respects and tell you I am available to be of service."

In visiting with me after my appointment as director, Horace Albright told me that the National Capital Park System in metropolitan Washington is a microcosm of the nation-wide park system. In the National Capital Park System are large natural areas, such as Rock Creek Park; historical areas, such as the Mall, the White House and the Washington, Jefferson and Lincoln Memorials; and recreation areas, such as Catoctin, Greenbelt and Prince William Forest Parks. Moreover, the management problems in the National Capital Parks are similar to those encountered in the parks nationwide.

Horace said that one of the programs he had always wanted implemented was "Show-Me" tours of the National Capital Parks for members of Congress, their spouses and staff, pointing out that few of them had the time or the opportunity to visit the parks of the nationwide system. He believed that such a program would increase awareness and understanding of our programs. I heartily agreed with him, but the director of the National Park Service has no "representation allowance" from which to finance such a program. The Congress, however, had authorized donations to the National Park Service in support of its programs.

If I wished to initiate such "Show-Me" tours, Horace offered to approach Laurance Rockefeller to make a contribution to support the work. Horace was a personal friend of Mr. Rockefeller and for several decades had been closely allied with him and his late father, John D. Rockefeller, Jr., in their park and conservation philanthropy. Mr. Rockefeller agreed and donated the money.

The program involved taking our guests via chartered bus on a tour of selected parks in the metropolitan Washington area usually in the spring when Washington is at its most beautiful. After the tour, usually beginning in the early afternoon, in alternate years we would take them by boat to Mt. Vernon or by mule-drawn barge to a picnic area on the C & O Canal for supper: prepackaged individual boxes of fried chicken, cole slaw, rolls and fruit. We had the buses take half the group to the site of the supper with the other half taking the barge or boat; and then we reversed the travel arrangements for the return trip to Washington.

I sent the invitations to the member's Washington residence, inviting both the member and spouse. The staff members of our committees were always invited. Frequently, if the member was too busy, the spouse accepted. This was eminently satisfactory to me. The congressional spouses were the eyes and ears of the members and my message got through. The program was a tremendous success in educating the members and the staff to the programs and the problems of the National Park System.

Early on, I learned that the most important thing in the life of a member of the Congress, whether in the House or the Senate, is a constituent. A great deal of their constituent service is in writing.

Many members I talked with explained the importance of getting answers promptly to their mail from constituents.

I installed a centralized control system in which every congressional letter was acknowledged within 24 hours of receipt. The acknowledgement letter simply said, we have received your letter and will reply shortly. The letter was then suspensed for ten days. If in ten days we did not have the information requested, another letter went to the member, saying the information is still not available but as soon as it is we will advise you. The important thing about the acknowledgment letter was that it gave the member an opportunity to communicate with his/her constituent that he/she was doing something promptly about the matter in which the constituent was interested. From my standpoint, the letter communicated to the member that I was aware of the significance of the member's interest. No promises were made in the acknowledgement letter about whether the decision would be favorable to the constituent.

During my courtesy calls several members emphasized the importance of advance preparation when testifying at a hearing on legislation. As one congressman explained, the hearing is to listen to what the director has to say; the director should answer the questions, not state he'll put the answers in the record. The purpose of a hearing is to get information, not for the opportunity to read the record.

Senator Bible, the chairman of the Senate National Parks Subcommittee, felt so strongly about this matter that he would not allow the lead witness for the service to testify on a bill unless the witness had personally visited the area.

Being prepared meant also having your supporters organized and briefed for the hearing. This lesson was driven home with great clarity at the field hearings on the Prairie National Park proposal in Kansas.

Normally, the subcommittees of both the House and the Senate hold hearings on each park proposal both in Washington and in the vicinity of the proposed park. The field hearing offers the members of Congress an opportunity to inspect the proposed park and to hear the views of the local citizens without putting them to the expense of traveling to Washington to testify.

Legislation had been introduced in the Congress to establish a tall grass prairie park near Topeka, Kansas. The park proposal was highly controversial. On one inspection trip in 1962, a shotgun-toting rancher ran Secretary Udall and Director Wirth off property involved in the proposal.

The Senate Park Subcommittee scheduled field hearings on the proposal in 1963. As the newly appointed associate director, I was sent out. I gathered with the staff the night before the hearing to review our local support and how many would be at the hearing. Assured that our support would be significant even though less extensive than the opposition, I was stunned by the events of the next day. The testimony of the few witnesses appearing in support of the proposal was unfocused, uncoordinated and ineffective. The National Park Service proposal was demolished and I was never again able to breathe new life into it—no member of Congress from Kansas would touch it.

This disaster was in marked contrast to our success at the Ozarks—an equally contentious proposal. Based on these contrasting experiences, one of the first changes I made in our legislative program when I became director was to designate one keyman in the field and one in the Washington office for every legislative proposal. The job of the keyman in the field was to seek out and organize grass roots support as I had done in the Ozarks. In Washington, the keyman was responsible for assembling all professional reports, maps and other data to support the legislative proposal at congressional hearings.

I tried never to take a congressional member by surprise; that is the last thing a politician can stand. Before initiating a change in course or a new program, I talked it over with the local congressman and senators or their staffs.

The Fire-fall in Yosemite Valley was an anachronism. It had been started by David Curry who developed Camp Curry in 1898. Though he had long since departed, the lodging area he first developed still bore his name as did the name of the successor concessioner—the Yosemite Park & Curry Company. When I became director in 1964 his Fire-fall still operated. An employee would build a fire at the top of Glacier Point, 3500 feet above the Valley floor. After dark, when the fire had burned down to red hot embers, another employee below Glacier Point at Camp Curry would start playing a recording of the song Indian Love Call and then yell, "Let the fire fall." The employee at the top of the point would push the embers over the edge and they would cascade to a ledge blow. It was a spectacular sight, but as appropriate to the majesty of Yosemite Valley as horns on a rabbit. I resolved to eliminate it. I remembered that another director, Newton Drury, had tried to eliminate it and the resulting uproar from the concessioner and the local California congressional delegation was such that he had to let it remain.

The campgrounds in Yosemite Valley were overrun with campers; the use greatly exceeded the designed capacity of the campgrounds, spilling over into the surrounding meadows. Moreover, it seemed that at every location the campers built a campfire producing mostly camp smoke because they didn't know how to lay up a campfire. Every evening a pall of smoke hung over the Valley. Correcting this condition was a long-range project; my immediate objective was to eliminate the Fire-fall.

My instincts told me that restrictions on camping would be much more sensitive to the Californians—the heaviest users of the Valley—than would the elimination of the Fire-fall.

I decided, therefore, to issue orders eliminating the Fire-fall, restricting camping to designated spaces and prohibiting campfires outside of the developed campgrounds. I first cleared it with the secretary—he was a politician after all, and my boss. With his approval, I visited the local congressman and the two senators to advise them of my plan. I took the precaution of advising them in advance that if the issue got too hot I was prepared to back off on the camping. They were not too sure that they could support me, but agreed that I should proceed. I then arranged a meeting with the president of the concession company. In my visit I learned that the Fire-fall had become an expensive operation for him because the company had to forage further and further away to collect the red cedar bark—the ideal fuel for the Fire-fall. The smoke in the Valley was a nuisance for his guests, so its elimination appealed to him.

Bases touched, I announced the program. The response was instant and vociferous. As I had suspected, the preponderance of the correspondence to the congressman, the senators and the secretary complained about the camping restrictions. When I was sure we had reached the crest of the protests I compromised on the camping restrictions and the Fire-fall was gone!

Joe Skubitz, a Republican congressman from Kansas, never lost interest in the possibility of having a prairie national park in his state. Joe was a cautious, conservative Kansan; he loved his state and its people. He was a warm, companionable man as open, honest and friendly as the plains from which he came.

Not too long after I entered private law practice in 1973, Joe called and asked me to come up to see him. The purpose of the visit was to tell me that he did not intend to stay in the Congress much longer—he was going to retire. But first he wanted to establish a prairie national park. He had been quietly discussing his idea with the ranchers in his district, many of whom had wreaked havoc on our initial park proposal; discussions had reached the point where they had agreed to sit down with him and look at a draft proposal. He asked if I would draft the proposal. By now, Joe had become ranking minority member of the full Interior Committee.

He outlined on a map what he wanted. His proposed park would certainly be no Yellowstone II; but it was a park and for that I admired his vision. Moreover, knowing the ferocity of the opposition we had encountered ten years previously, I admired his courage and willingness to begin the process again.

Happily, I agreed to draft his bill.

After several sessions I got a draft that satisfied his requirements. He scheduled a trip home to begin discussions.

In the meantime, the park service announced that it was sending a team of planners to Kansas to have another look at a prairie park. Joe was taken by surprise.

He immediately called the director who was not available. So he told one of his associates that he wanted the planning mission cancelled; he did not apprise him of his own efforts. Joe had assured his constituents that he would take no overt action without first discussing it with them; his scheduled trip and the planning mission might lead them to believe he had violated their trust. He made it clear that park service planners going into the area at this time would be politically embarrassing to him. The NPS refused to cancel the trip, saying it didn't take politics into account in its park planning.

Joe's anger radiated through the telephone when he called me later. He said, "I have just torn that park bill into a thousand pieces and they will never get a park as long as I am in the Congress."

How sad that the young bureaucrat with whom Joe spoke did not understand that politics is the medium through which the people exercise their sovereignty to establish their parks. Of what value is a professionally well-planned park, such as prairie, if the people, through their Congress, will not breathe life into it by legislation?

Joe Skubitz is now retired from the Congress. Regrettably, the nation still does not have its prairie national park.

Generally, the committees of the Congress will not hold hearings on a bill until they get an administration report setting forth the president's views on the proposal. Since the president has the power to approve or veto all legislation enacted by the Congress, advance knowledge of his position is important to the committee. Seldom does the Congress seek to consider legislation to which the president is opposed.

Our administration reports were drafted by the Interior Department and submitted, in draft, to the Bureau of the Budget (now Office of Management and Budget). They coordinated the draft with other affected departments and approved the final report in the name of the president. The report was then sent to the Congress by the Interior Department. Interior also provided the lead administration witness to testify before the congressional committee. Getting an administration report can sometimes be a sticky and frustrating business.

In the 1930s the Congress authorized the National Park Trust Fund Board to accept donations for the benefit of the programs of the National Park Service. The trustees of the fund were the secretary of the treasury, the secretary of the interior and the attorney general. The fund was managed by the Treasury Department and all donations were reduced to cash upon receipt, and invested in U.S. government bonds.

The investment was secure enough but the return was minimal. The fund never prospered. As a result my predecessor employed a consultant to study the situation and make recommendations on how to improve the program.

The consultant concluded that the fund was ineffective because people were reluctant to give to the government after having paid their taxes; and, even if inclined to give they were reluctant to see their gifts such as stocks or bonds reduced to cash without regard to the timeliness of such sales. He recommended that the trust fund be replaced with a foundation, managed by an independent board of directors authorized to conserve and manage assets for both growth and return. The foundation would have two government employees among its directors—secretary of the interior as the chairman of the board, and the director of the National Park Service as the secretary of the board.

Secretary Udall approved the recommendations and bills were introduced in the Congress to establish the National Park Foundation, transfer to it the monies of the National Park Trust Fund Board and abolish the board.

The draft administration report had to be coordinated with the Justice Department (attorney general) and the Treasury Department. All issues raised by the Justice Department were quickly resolved. The Treasury Department, however, was another matter. Their basic objection was to the new structure which would remove their control over the new organization. This, of course, was a nonnegotiable point—if they won, the legislation was dead. The Bureau of the Budget would not choose between the positions of Treasury and Interior and resolve the matter.

VIII. Working the Hill

I realized that if I was to get the legislation I would have to go elsewhere for a resolution. I had the support of the house and senate committees for the basic concept of the legislation but I had to get an administration report to move it through the Congress.

Henry (Joe) Fowler was then secretary of the treasury. I had not been able to get the matter above the assistant secretary level for consideration by him. But I knew that Secretary Fowler and Senator Harry Byrd, Sr. were great personal friends. Moreover, Senator Byrd was chairman of the Senate Finance Committee with oversight of the Treasury Department.

Senator Byrd was governor of Virginia at the time of the election of President Franklin D. Roosevelt. Through his friendship with the president, great things were accomplished for the National Park System. Senator Byrd was the father of the Shenandoah National Park and a moving force in the creation of the Blue Ridge Parkway connecting Shenandoah and Great Smoky Mountains National parks. He donated the money to build the "Byrd's Nests" along the Appalachian Trail. His love of the parks was as legendary as was his political power. I called him for help.

At 10:30 a.m. one morning I began to explain my problem to him and solicit his help. He interrupted. "Joe Fowler is coming to see me at 11:00. Go out there (in an adjoining office) and visit with Peaches [his administrative assistant]. I will call you in when Joe arrives."

In a few minutes the buzzer went off in Peaches's office and the senator told us to come in. He introduced me to the secretary and told me to relate my story to him. When I finished the senator said, "Joe, I'm very much interested in this matter and I would appreciate your looking into it." I was excused and left.

About 2 o'clock that afternoon I got a call from the Bureau of the Budget advising that the administration report favoring Interior's position had been cleared by Treasury for the Hill. The legislation passed and the foundation established.

* * *

While legislation was being considered by the Congress to establish Sleeping Bear Dunes National Lakeshore in Michigan, one of our most articulate and talented opponents was Mrs. Charlotte Reed, the congresswoman from Illinois. She and her family owned a summer cottage within the area proposed for the lakeshore. She loved the area and its people very much. She was convinced that the local residents could protect the area adequately. I had visited with her on several occasions trying my best to find a solution that would be satisfactory to her—to no avail. Finally, it became apparent that the subcommittee was going to have to face her opposition and either vote the bill up or down. The bill was called for subcommittee consideration.

In the meantime, I had been to see every subcommittee member. From these visits I knew that I had enough support in the subcommittee to win. The morning arrived to vote on the bill: Roy Taylor, the National Parks Subcommittee chairman, John Saylor, the ranking Republican member on the full committee (House Interior and Insular Affairs), Joe Skubitz, the ranking Republican member on the subcommittee, Wayne Aspinall, chairman of the full committee were all there early. They were each supporting the bill. At the appointed hour, Mrs. Reed came in with four or five of her colleagues that I knew were going to support her. A few additional members of the subcommittee wandered in until a quorum was reached. Roy Taylor announced the presence of a quorum and began the session. Almost immediately, several of my supporters who had appeared to make a quorum, got up and left. There were only a couple of minor things the subcommittee was going to change in the draft bill. They were quickly agreed to. Roy was ready to call for the vote on the bill. My supporters had not returned and I realized that Mrs. Reed had the votes.

John Saylor quickly sized up the situation and realized that we were going to lose the bill. If he voted for it and we lost, it would have been over for that Congress. Normally, a bill is considered only once in a Congress. So, when it came his turn to vote, he voted against the bill. This allowed him to ask for its reconsideration in another session of the subcommittee.

As soon as the meeting was over, I hotfooted it around to the various House offices to contact the members of the subcommittee who had told me that they were in support of the bill. I asked the first member I found if he had changed his support. "No," he said, "I support the measure."

"If you were for me, why weren't you there this morning?" I asked.

"Well, now, George," he said, "that's a different matter. I told you that I'm for you, but after I visited with you yesterday, Charlotte Reed called me, and asked me if I would stay away. Now, this way I can do a favor for Charlotte and not abandon my position." That was the story I got from every single one of them; so, I went back to see Wayne Aspinall, John Saylor, Roy Taylor and Joe Skubitz and reported. They called each of the members and told them that another session of the subcommittee was going to be scheduled and they would appreciate their presence. They came. John Saylor moved for reconsideration of the bill and it was passed out of the subcommittee. Subsequently it was enacted by the Congress.

The charming, gracious, gentlelady of Illinois, Mrs. Reed, had taught me a valuable lesson in how to count noses.

Congressman William (Bill) Colmer of Pascagoula, Mississippi was a tall, spare man with a happy, friendly countenance always about ready to break into a smile. His courtly, courteous manner belied a native shrewdness honed by decades of deep South and congressional politics. He was a great storyteller and he enjoyed your story as well—one in particular I remember:

A country boy, Luke, raised chickens and came to town every Saturday to sell them. He kept them, wings tied to-

gether, in a big wooden barrel. One Saturday as he was winding up for the day he had one old hen left. A lady came along
and wanted a hen, so with much ado, Luke reached down in
the bottom of the barrel and pulled out his last old hen—after
being handled all day she was pretty beat up. Luke turned her
over a couple of times, brushed down her feathers, flipped her
up on her right side and said that'll be $1.50.

Well, said the lady, I wanted one a little larger. Do you have
any more?

Luke, put the hen back in the barrel, rolled her over a couple of times, fluffed up her feathers, pulled her out and flipped
her over on the other side and the lady thought she looked a
little larger.

How much for this one, she asked.

Be $1.95, Luke replied.

Fine, said the lady, I'll take them both!

Bob McConnell, Secretary Udall's congressional liaison,
advised me that Congressman Colmer, who was then chairman of the House Rules Committee, wanted to see me. Before
I called him, I checked with our planners to see if we had
anything in Congressman Colmer's district that involved the
National Park System.

In a few hours, one of the staff brought me a study of Fort
Massachusetts that had been made by the National Park Service in 1935. Fort Massachusetts is one of the perimeter
Forts built after the War of 1812. The federal government
started to build it on Ship Island in 1857. It was not completed when Mississippi seceded from the Union and the Con-
federacy took it over. In September, 1861, they abandoned it
when the union gunboat Massachusetts occupied the Sound.
Between 1863 and 1865 the Corps of Engineers completed
the Fort. For several years the military listed it simply as the
"Fort on Ship Island"; later it was named for the gunboat
Massachusetts which had recaptured it during the Civil War.

I read the park service report which, in substance, concluded that the Fort was not of sufficient national significance to be included in the National Park System. I called

VIII. Working the Hill

Congressman Colmer's administrative assistant, a young man named Trent Lott who succeeded Congressman Colmer when he retired, and he made the appointment.

Colmer was cordial and gracious. When I sat down he opened his desk drawer and offered me a cigar. We each took one, cut the ends off and lit up. Then he said to me in his slow southern drawl, "Mr. Di'rector, I would like for you to go down to Pascagoula with me during the Easter recess. We can do a little shellcracker fishing, a little sheepshead fishing, spend two or three days and meet some of the local people. They need some help with a project down there—Fort Massachusetts."

I said, "Well, Mr. Chairman, I checked our files and found that we did a study on Fort Massachusetts in 1935. I have commitments over the Easter recess that make it inconvenient for me to go down at that time. However, I'd be delighted to send a team down there to update that report. Perhaps I could even get the study team down there while you are at home during the Easter recess."

The congressman leaned back in his chair, took a puff on his cigar, and said, "You know, Mr. Di'rector, I started out my career as a judge. I observed in that assignment that the jury usually brought in the verdict in accordance with the instructions from the judge. Now Bob McConnell tells me that you're a lawyer, and a pretty good one. Do you agree with my observation?"

I said, "Yes, sir, I certainly do."

"Well, then Mr. Di'rector," he asked, "when are you and I going down to see Fort Massachusetts?"

I knew then I had been had by a real pro.

"Mr. Chairman," I said, "I am going down there at your convenience. When would you like to go?"

"During the Easter recess," he replied.

So, I went down during the Easter recess and joined Congressman Colmer and his constituents at Pascagoula and Biloxi. We had two days of fishing and a glorious time together.

During our tour we had an opportunity to view many of

the beautiful barrier islands. There is a circle of them beginning with the Chandeliers in Louisiana, Cat, Ship, Horn and Petit Bois in Mississippi, Dauphin Island in Alabama and Santa Rosa in Florida. Santa Rosa had once been in the National Park System.

It became obvious during the visit that the chairman had already committed himself to do something to preserve Fort Massachusetts, and the National Park Service was the chosen instrument for this purpose.

I realized that with Congressman Colmer's influence I was going to get Fort Massachusetts. It was then that I broached an idea to him: "Why don't we really do something great down here while we are at it. Why don't we include all of those magnificent islands in one outstanding seashore?"

"Well," he said, "that includes a lot of other congressmen."

Of course it did. It involved Congressman Hebert, of Louisiana, Congressman Bob Jones of Alabama, and Congressman Bob Sikes of Florida, a close-knit powerhouse in the Congress.

Shortly after returning to Washington, Chairman Colmer called me to get something moving on Fort Massachusetts. I went up again to see him. I said, "Mr. Chairman, you're in the fort business and I'm in the park business; now why don't we merge our businesses and have a great seashore down there?"

"Well," he said, "that's not a bad idea and I'll look into it."

Gulf Islands National Seashore (Mississippi-Florida) was authorized January 8, 1971.

If the local congressman is in active opposition to your legislation you are not likely to get it passed.

Shortly after the Ozark National Scenic Riverways (Missouri) legislation was enacted, the administration proposed that the Buffalo in Arkansas be saved as a national river. With the pattern on hunting pioneered in the Ozarks, we had considerably more support for the Buffalo proposal. The Buffalo is larger than either the Current or the Jack's Fork (the

Ozarks of Missouri). It is a wild, magnificent smallmouth bass fishery.

The Army Corps of Engineers had proposed a flood control dam for the Buffalo. Their cost/benefit ratio supported its economic feasibility. Moreover, they had sold the natives on the employment opportunities that would be created by the construction of the dam.

In my judgment, the cost/benefit economic ratio for resource development projects is one of the greatest scams ever foisted on the unsuspecting taxpayer. The formula proves the old saw: figures don't lie, but liars figure. For example, almost invariably, a significant part of the alleged "benefit" is the "recreational value" assigned to the artificial reservoir to be created by flooding thousands of acres of productive land and ruining one of God's greatest treasures—a free-flowing wild river. In most instances, moreover, the alleged benefits —if ever realized—do not accrue to the taxpayers who footed almost all of the project cost but to the speculators whose shore lands are now made safe for development. The idiocy of it is enough to turn a strong man's stomach.

However, the local congressman, Judge Trimble, was convinced that the Buffalo should be dammed. He was adamant and outspoken in his opposition to making it a national river. Wayne Aspinall told me flat-out that he was not going to run over him.

I tried to get the legislation moving in the Senate, but I had no real support from the state's two senators. Senator McClellan and Senator Fullbright viewed their role pretty much as "ambassadors" for whatever the local congressman from that district in Arkansas wanted.

All of my dealings with Judge Trimble were friendly and courteous. He explained his position: he had given his word to the Corps of Engineers and their local advocates to support the dam and he was not going to change his mind. In short, Mr. Trimble did not want a national river—he wanted a dam. Senator McClellan and Senator Fulbright didn't give a damn.

In that case there was nothing to do but wait on either the Lord or Mr. Trimble's constituents to act and to watch to make sure I was not end-runned by the Public Works Committee authorizing the dam. Finally, his constituents acted—Congressman Trimble was defeated. The Congress authorized the Buffalo National River in 1972.

Sometimes even when you have done your homework with the Congress, you can lose for unexpected reasons from unexpected sources.

A part of the Summer in the Parks program was to provide camping opportunities at Prince William Forest Park to underprivileged children of Washington, D.C. Prince William Forest Park is located off of I-95, about 40 miles south of Washington. It was acquired in the 1930s as a recreation demonstration area. The authority for its acquisition was a New Deal program to acquire worn-out farm lands and develop them as recreation areas. When this program was discontinued at the beginning of World War II, all of these areas were transferred to the states as state parks except for two: Prince William Forest Park in Virginia, and Catoctin Mountain Park in Maryland which also includes the presidential retreat, now known as Camp David (originally designated by President Roosevelt as Shangrila).

During World War II, about 4500 acres of Prince William Forest were placed under the administration of the navy for use by the marines as a part of their training area at Quantico. The condition of this transfer was that the navy would obtain the money to buy the remaining privately owned land needed to round out Prince William Forest Park. By the late 1960s, the navy had done nothing to acquire these lands.

With the opening of I-95 it became obvious that unless we moved immediately to acquire these largely undeveloped lands around the park, most being occupied by modest farm dwellings whose occupants no longer farmed, the whole area was going to be lost to intensive commercial development. Since the transfer of these lands to the navy for administration was based entirely on the war effort, the National Park Service, through the secretary had made several attempts over the years to have the land returned to its administration so that they could be developed for public use. Always, these requests were rejected in the interest of national defense.

I decided to go to Prince William Forest one weekend and check the matter out for myself. The National Park Service had a house on the lake at Prince William Forest which we reserved for use by the secretary's staff and the White House staff—the house was for rent, not for free.

Helen, our three children and I went to Prince William Forest for the weekend. On Sunday I had arranged for the superintendent to take me onto the military administered portion of Prince William Forest. We drove through an open gate and into the heart of the acreage where we found a magnificent lake. The navy had dammed the stream and created a great trout fishery. Signs were posted all around the lake: "Reserved for Officer Use Only." In other words, no enlisted men may fish in these waters. I had my camera along and was busily taking photographs of these signs, the lake and the surrounding terrain, to demonstrate my point that the land was seldom, if ever, used for military purposes but, in fact, was an officer recreation enclave. After about 45 minutes, a Jeep arrived with two military police who wanted to know who we were and what we were doing in the "Restricted Area." We presented our Interior Department identification cards. They recognized the official government identification, but told us to get the hell out, in no uncertain terms. They did not, however, raise any question about my camera, so I got out with all of my photographs.

I knew from what I had seen at Prince William Forest that we were in for a fight if I expected to succeed in getting back jurisdiction of the land transferred to the navy, to make it available for public use. I went up to see Mendel Rivers, congressman from my home district in South Carolina and chairman of the House Armed Services Committee, explained the situation to him, and told him that I was prepared to compromise for a portion of the land which would allow public access to the now reserved officer fishery resource. I showed him the photographs and told him that I had not come to ask him to get in the middle of the fight or support me; I had come simply to tell him about the situation and ask him if he would stay out of it so that the navy could not end run me.

Mendel agreed he would stay out of the argument.

I called Assistant Secretary Frank Sanders and asked for a meeting explaining what I had in mind. He suggested that we should go to Quantico and meet with the base commander. I arrived on the lawn at the Pentagon to be taken by helicopter with Sanders to Quantico where we were met with all courtesy and respect that the military can extend to its civilian leadership. We were ushered into the base operations office. The conversation proceeded for a good half-hour with the officers going through a series of charts and maps explaining to me the importance of these lands to the military effort, how essential they were for its training, and repeated at length all of the arguments that had been made over the years for why the land could not be returned to the jurisdiction of the National Park Service. After listening to this while maintaining great control, I opened up my brief case and took out two albums of photographs. I gave one to Frank and the other to the military officer presiding at the meeting, sitting behind the desk. Secretary Sanders started turning the pages of his, showing the beautifully landscaped lake. I had put all of the scenic photographs first; then I had inserted the photographs of the signs, "Reserved for Officer Use Only." When he had seen two or three of the photographs, he suggested that, perhaps, they should take another look at the matter. The meeting adjourned and we returned to Washington.

Later, Assistant Secretary Sanders and I agreed on my original proposal: a small portion of the land adjacent to the public road would be returned to the National Park Service for administration; the visitors, and especially the groups of youngsters who camped at Prince William Forest would have access to fish in the lake on the Quantico portion of Prince William Forest Park; and the navy department would support the Interior Department's proposal for an authorization of ten million dollars to buy the remaining lands around Prince William Forest Park.

This proposal was presented to the Office of Management and Budget which immediately opposed it because it gave additional authorization of land acquisition money to the National Park Service. In the meantime, the proposal was leaked and one of the conservation groups in Northern Virginia opposed it because we were not getting back *all* of the land from the navy. The conservationists' objections justified OMB's actions to kill the proposal—which they did.

When I returned to the National Park Service in 1963, I knew 9 members of the Congress. When I left at the end of 1972 I knew over 300, and was on a "howdyin' basis" with most of the balance.

The first of my three goals as director had been to expand the National Park System. With the support of the Congress, significant progress had been achieved.

In nine years, the National Park System had been extended to every state in the union except Delaware. Sixty-nine new parks had been added to the system—nearly three-fourths as many as had been added in the preceding thirty years. With the Bible Amendment (Section 17(d)(2) to the Alaska Native Claims Settlement Act of 1971) we had assured the addition of millions of acres of pristine lands and cultural sites to the National Park System in Alaska. When the dust settled in 1980, the Congress had added 43,600,000 acres to the system in Alaska—an increase of more than 150% in the system as it existed in the lower 48.

We expanded the National Park System to preserve and interpret our cultural heritage: Wolf Trap Farm Park for the Performing Arts, Saugus Iron Works National Historic Site, and others.

We completed and published a National Park System plan identifying the themes of our natural, cultural and historic heritage that should be represented in the system.

The Congress had established a National Wilderness Preservation System (1964); a National Trails System (1968); and a Wild and Scenic Rivers System (1968).

With the Historic Preservation Act of 1966, we had obtained a matching grants program for the states and the National Trust for Historic Preservation to strengthen the preservation of our historic and cultural heritage by the states, local governments and private citizens and organizations.

Moreover, the National Park Service had designated a national landmark in private, state or local government ownership, commemorating either an historical event, a natural environment or a nationally significant educational study resource, in every one of the then existing 435 congressional districts.

Never again would a member of Congress be able to say to a director of the National Park Service what Congressman O'Brien had said to me: "I really have no interest in your program!"

IX

MOTHER'S MILK: APPROPRIATIONS

The late Jesse Unruh, Speaker of the California House of Representatives and State Treasurer, once said: money is the mother's milk of politics. He was right. Money follows policy and is the cornerstone for implementing programs.

Appropriation Acts originate in the House of Representatives. For the National Park Service that means the Subcommittee for the Interior Department and Related Agencies of the Appropriations Committee of the House.

The Honorable Julia Butler Hanson (Democrat, Washington), was the chairman of our Appropriations Subcommittee. She and I always sat down together before she began to make changes in marking up the National Park Service portion of the appropriations bill, to discuss any items that may have surfaced during the hearing that were of further concern to her or members of the subcommittee. When I arrived for our meeting, she angrily informed me that the land acquisition money for Herbert Hoover National Historic Site was going to be eliminated.

Congressman Fred Schwengel, Republican of Iowa, in

whose district the Herbert Hoover National Historic Site was located, had made a speech on the floor of the Congress that Mrs. Hanson had resented. That year, included in the president's budget was the balance of the authorized funds to acquire the remainder of the privately-owned lands at the Hoover Site. We already had options for some of the land.

I vigorously protested her decision to delete the monies, pointing out that with the escalation in prices, the fact that we already had some of the property under option, and that if we didn't get the money that year, we were going to have to go back and get the appropriations ceiling lifted by the authorizing committee.

"Do it!" she snapped, "because I am going to teach Fred Schwengel a lesson." And she did.

She taught me another lesson: there are really two Congresses—the House Appropriations Committee and the balance of the Congress.

Before coming to the Congress, Mrs. Hanson had served for many years in the state legislature. There she learned well the source of legislative power: money and seniority. She had both, appreciated them and knew very well how to use them. A tough and savvy politician, she, nevertheless, was first and always a lady. Attractive and thoughtful, she ruled with an iron fist in a velvet glove.

She very much resented the bland, inanimate designation, chair. She was *the chairman*. Her only concession to gender was "Madam Chairman."

Mrs. Hanson had a great interest in the programs of the National Park Service. Without staff from the committee or the park service, she and her family spent many weekends traveling to parks in and around the metropolitan Washington area. With her staff, she visited a great many other parks outside the metropolitan area. On those trips I usually accompanied her.

One summer weekend she went down to Jamestown-Yorktown, arriving at about 5:00 p.m. Just as she pulled her car up, the ranger walked out of the entrance station and closed the gate, announcing that visitation had ended for the day. When she returned to Washington, she called me first thing on Monday morning to come over to her office *immediately.* Unless she was upset, such a request was not usually made personally and, certainly, did not require an immediate appearance. I figured I was in trouble. When I got there, she was in a fine fettle about what had happened the previous day.

I reminded her that on several occasions I had invited her to let me know when she was planning her trips, so that I could call ahead and have the superintendent or a ranger meet her to facilitate her visit. She had always refused saying she could not very well go around checking up on how well I was doing things if she let me know in advance. "Then," she said, "you will have everything spit and polish; what I want is to find out what the average visitor receives and I just found that out this weekend!"

I agreed to instruct the field that during daylight saving hours, the gates would not be closed until dark—never mind when 5:00 o'clock came. Also, I succeeded in getting her to agree to let me know when she was going to visit park areas. "If you do not cooperate with me on this matter I intend to circulate your photograph to every superintendent in the field and make it a matter of duty for him and his entrance station rangers to memorize it so that they will recognize you on the spot." That was too much for her!

As I traveled around the city of Washington, I noticed that we had many parks, but the children always seemed to be playing in the streets. I began to pressure the National Capital Region to develop a program that would get children off the streets and into the parks. This ultimately resulted in the highly successful program, Summer in the Parks. It would never have happened, however, had it not been for Mrs. Hanson.

One day I took her to lunch with the understanding that afterwards we would go for a tour of some programs that were part of Mrs. Johnson's beautification efforts. At first,

Mrs. Hanson was not very much impressed with some of the projects. Finally, I said to our driver, "Take us down by Lincoln Park." As we entered this area east of the Capitol, the park was desolate and we saw children all over the streets. I said to her, "What would you think about doing something about this?"

She replied, "George, I think this is where you should be putting your money." As a result she added money to the budget to begin the program, Summer in the Parks.

It became apparent early on that for the program to be fully effective, we were going to have to transport some of these youngsters from the neighborhoods where they lived to where the parks were, such as the C & O Canal and Prince William Forest. Mrs. Hanson authorized me to use some of the appropriation for transporting the youngsters. It was tremendously popular. The next year I asked her if she would extend this authority nationwide. She said that would require substantive legislation and that I should have Wayne Aspinall authorize it. The bill was introduced and referred to the House Interior and Insular Affairs Committee. This was at the time that school busing was still a highly charged issue. Congressman Joe Skubitz (Republican, Kansas) very much opposed the program because, to him, it smacked of school busing. His opposition was so substantial that Wayne Aspinall told me that he was not going to handle the bill because he didn't want to get into a fight with Joe Skubitz. Once I reported this to Mrs. Hanson, she inserted language in the appropriations bill to permit me to transport children throughout the nation to the parks.

As soon as I got that authorization I called Fred Fagergren, who was our regional director in Omaha. Kansas was in that region as was Fort Scott, a park in Joe Skubitz's district in which he had a great interest and took deep personal pride. I asked Fred to go into Joe Skubitz's district, find the largest school system not too far from the fort and make a deal with the school superintendent for the National Park

Service to subsidize the transportation of the children from his school system to Fort Scott in the summer. The school system was delighted to accept. Fred reported that the school superintendent wanted to write and tell me how much he appreciated the program. I told Fred, "Don't let him do that. Tell him to get on the telephone instead and call Joe Skubitz and tell him how great the program is and how much he appreciates *Joe* making it possible."

Several weeks later I made a courtesy call on Joe Skubitz. When I entered his reception room I noticed that the door to his office was open and he was sitting at his desk. I asked his receptionist in a voice loud enough for him to hear, "Is the Congressman available?" Joe Skubitz got up from behind the desk, came quickly to the door and said, "Yes, I'm here and I want to see you." I went in and he pulled the door shut behind us. He began, "You son-o-bitch, you really did me in."

In mock surprise, I said, "Joe, I don't have any earthly idea what you're talking about."

"Well," he said, "several days ago I'm sitting at my desk and the 'phone rings." He identified the caller as the superintendent of the school system that had participated in the Fort Scott program. He quoted the superintendent: "Joe, I simply wanted to call you and tell you about one of the finest programs that we've had for our children this summer." He went on to describe the program and added, "The park service tells me that you're responsible for this and I want you to know that I think it is one of the best things you have ever done; we all really appreciate it."

Joe said to me, "As I'm sitting here listening to this, I can't figure out what he is talking about and why he is expressing all of this gratitude to me because I don't recall doing anything about such a program."

The school superintendent went into more detail about how they transported the children in the otherwise idle school buses with the National Park Service paying for the gas and the driver. Then Joe said, "All of a sudden it dawned on me and I thought to myself, that bastard Hartzog, he's had me." Concluding, he said, "If you want the damn legislation tell Wayne to go ahead."

In one of my visits with Mrs. Hanson about programs for children in the metropolitan Washington area, she suggested the idea of a children's farm. I explored the matter with the National Capital Region and discovered the old Oxon Hill Farm, which for decades had been owned and operated by St. Elizabeth's Hospital (a government operated facility for mental patients) to supply fresh produce for the hospital. When other sources of supply became available more economically, the farm was declared surplus and transferred to the National Capital Park System. The farm had been allowed to remain fallow, slowly returning to nature. In a short while, we had reclaimed a portion of the land for farming, growing such things as corn and millet.

The regional staff sought the cooperation of the Department of Agriculture's Research Station at Beltsville in stocking the farm. They provided us with, among other animals, a huge steer which the children named "Big Red," a pregnant sow, a few hens and a rooster.

As soon as word of the farm got around, people responded with gifts of more chickens, ducks, geese, a barnyard cat and more.

A farmer donated a wagon and a team of horses. We used the wagon and team to give children a ride from the parking lot to the barns, corrals and chicken yards. It was a smashing success. Mrs. Hanson enjoyed going there and watching these excited youngsters who, in some instances, were learning for the first time where milk came from. The sows farrowed, the hens and ducks hatched off their broods and that first summer, the place rocked with squeals of delight as the youngsters saw the young piglets, baby chicks, and ducklings.

The ranger uniform was blue denim shirt and bib overalls. The farm crew was enthusiastic.

New or innovative programs attract government auditors like honey does bears. Soon they descended on Oxon Hill.

IX. Mother's Milk: Appropriations

Experts at straining out gnats and swallowing camels, their focus was not whether we should be running a children's farm—*but what we were doing with surplus eggs and pigs.*

Surplus property was handled by the General Services Administration (GSA). After first circulating its availability among a whole list of congressionally-approved agencies and organizations if not claimed, would be advertised for sale to the highest bidder. Imagine selling fresh eggs this way!

As reported to me, the ranger-cum-farmer in charge responded to the auditor's question:

"We run a closed circuit farm here—we feed the surplus eggs and chickens to the pigs—we kill and grind up the pigs and feed them to the chickens!"

Subsequently, to avoid such questions in the future, the Congress authorized the National Park Service to sell the produce from living history operations and reimburse the appropriation which supported the activity.

Those successful experiments in living history interpretation convinced me that we should do this elsewhere in the National Park System. I got little to no support in the field. The superintendents, by and large, were not amenable to changing their routine operations, particularly when there was no new money to be had from it. As a result, I got the permission of Mrs. Hanson and Senator Bible to withhold a small reserve from the management appropriation of the National Park System. This reserve was to be used for program innovations, such as living history. When I had established the reserve, I told the superintendents that if they developed an acceptable living history program, I would finance it out of the reserve fund during its experimental first year and if it was successful, the next fiscal year I would add that money to their budgets. Well, they stampeded me! We had to be very selective about the programs approved.

Many innovative programs were approved—firing of historic firearms and cannon, cooking hard-tack, a bread that was a staple of the Confederate soldier, horse farms, artists in the parks and many others. We brought music to the parks by subsidizing summer programs by several symphony orchestras. Al Banton, the imaginative superintendent of the Lincoln Boyhood Home in Indiana made lye soap, the mainstay of poor America before octagon soap. My mother used to make it and it was all we had to bathe with and wash clothes. It is made first by burning hardwood—usually oak—to ashes; then leaching the ashes producing a strong alkaline liquid to which one adds hog fat; boiling the concoction until the fat dissolves then allowing it to cool to cut into bars or slices. A few baths in that and you looked old before your time. It always amazed me that visitors to the Lincoln Boyhood Home would pay twenty-five cents for a razor-thin slice of lye soap! I still wonder what they ever did with it. At any rate, it gave them a better understanding of rural America and the hard life of its poor.

While we were working with Eero Saarinen on the plans for the Jefferson National Expansion Memorial, I asked him to design the Museum of Westward Expansion. He declined, saying that he would not design a National Park Museum because all the park service was interested in were "glass cases and rusty nails."

This episode with Eero had convinced me that something should be done to make our museums more interesting. The first opportunity I had to do this after becoming director involved Hubbell Trading Post, Ganado, Arizona. Our staff had proposed the acquisition of this historic trading post and had recommended that it be frozen in time and filled with the artifacts of Hubbell's day.

I said, "Absolutely no way. If we are going to preserve a trading post, we are going to have an operating trading post, carrying on the historic work of Hubbell and the Navajos. The government doesn't have to operate it. The Southwest Monuments Association can operate it; they are a nonprofit cooperating association that supports the interpretive programs of the National Park Service.

But the Southwest Monuments Association would not do it

because they were convinced that it would be a loss operation.

I called Les Scott who was then the president and chief executive officer of Fred Harvey. Harvey had the concessions operations at Grand Canyon and Petrified Forest. I told Les that I wanted him to take over the operation of a living trading post at Hubbell. He wanted no part of it. I had some leverage however because of his concession contract, and I used it. He agreed he would operate Hubbell.

When the concessioner agreed to operate it, Southwest Monuments Association changed its mind. They decided that they would like to operate it. Since that was my preference all along I approved the proposal. The association was fortunate in being able to hire Bill Young as their general manager, an Indian trader on the Navajo reservation for many years before his retirement and move to Flagstaff, Arizona. Bill came back and put the trading post in operation in 1965.

Bill restocked the grocery store, and opened the sales room for buying and selling Navajo handcrafts, especially their magnificent rugs. He acquired a loom and had teams of Navajos weaving on site for the education and delight of visitors. In the spring he bought lambs and wool in the historic tradition of the Indian trader. The purpose of the operation was to give the visitor a living three dimensional understanding of Indian life on the reservation. An equally important emphasis of the program was to assist the Indians. Wisely, Bill, with the approval of the association, bought the Indians' crafts, lambs and wool for about 10% more than other traders offered; and, in turn, sold the merchandise for about 10% less than the regular commercial market. Even though the trading post was located off the highly traveled tourist highways, word of its operation spread rapidly and business boomed.

* * *

147

Michael J. (Mike) Kirwan (Democrat of Ohio) was one of the most senior members of the House Appropriations Committee. At the time I became director, he was chairman of the Interior Appropriations Subcommittee. Soon thereafter he went on to be chairman of a more affluent subcommittee. However, he remained as the ranking majority member on the Interior Subcommittee. He could be testy—even arrogant at times—but for the most part he was friendly and supportive of the park programs. You knew, however, when his patience was exhausted with procrastination and delay.

Early in 1966, I received a telephone call from Mike, saying that the National Park Service had a statue of the Irish poet and patriot, Robert Emmett, which he had been trying to get erected in Washington for some time without success. He had arranged a dedication ceremony for the statue on March 17, to which he had invited Mendell Rivers (the congressman from my home district in South Carolina) and John McCormack (Massachusetts) to be participants in the ceremony.

This obviously was no request—it was a decision. My budget had not yet cleared his subcommittee. He would never be so crass as to suggest any linkage, but the tone of his voice and the tenor of the conversation focused my attention on his problem. I said to him, "Mr. Chairman, I don't know anything about that statue, or where it is to be erected, but I'll find out."

He replied "You do that and let me know."

I hung up and called Sutton Jett, regional director of the National Capital Region. "Sutton, Chairman Kirwan wants Robert Emmett's statue erected for dedication on March 17. Do we have such a statue?"

"Yes," he said, "we do; it is in the warehouse."

"What's the problem?" I asked.

He answered, "George, it's where he wants the statue. He wants it on Massachusetts Avenue near the British Embassy. The planning commission doesn't want it there and Connie (Wirth) never thought we ought to try to push it through."

IX. Mother's Milk: Appropriations

The statue had been accepted by the Smithsonian Institution on behalf of the United States in 1916. It seemed to me that fifty years was long enough to find a location for its erection.

I suggested that Sutton find a suitable location on Massachusetts Avenue and start digging a foundation so that we could mount the statue and have it ready for dedication on March 17th. Somewhat incredulous, he asked, "What are we going to do about the planning commission?"

I replied "We're not going to ask them; we'll let them discover it."

Sutton found a beautiful triangle on Massachusetts Avenue between the British Embassy and the Irish Embassy but closer to the Irish Embassy. Mike was happy.

We erected Robert Emmett's statue. We didn't make March 17, but we did have a great dedication ceremony on April 22, after which Mendell Rivers, Mike Kirwan, John McCormack, Sutton Jett and I went to lunch at the Irish Embassy where I was introduced to Irish whiskey and Irish coffee.

I never did hear from the planning commission—but Mike never forgot!

Mrs. Bolton, Republican congresswoman from Ohio and the regent of Mt. Vernon, was the moving force in establishing Piscataway Park to preserve the Maryland overview across the Potomac River from Mt. Vernon. However, she and Mike Kirwan did not see eye to eye and Mike, when chairman, would never appropriate the money necessary to complete the park as authorized by the Congress. Even after he left the chairmanship of the Interior Subcommittee, Mrs. Hanson out of deference to Mike, would never put the item in the House bill. However, Senator Alan Bible, who was chairman of the Senate Appropriations Subcommittee, did put the money in the Senate bill for several years. Invariably he lost the money in the conference committee because of Mike's objection.

Even though all money (appropriation) bills originate in the House, both bodies (the House and the Senate) through their respective appropriations committees, consider the president's budget independently. The appropriate subcommittee of both the House and the Senate appropriations hold separate hearings on the budget and pass separate appropriations bills. Thus, an item in the president's budget that is reduced or eliminated, for example, in the House subcommittee may be increased or added back in the Senate appropriations bills. Moreover, as frequently happens, each subcommittee may include items not in the president's budget, but which are of particular importance to a member of either the House or the Senate. Not surprisingly, often the bills passed by the House and the Senate are significantly different from each other. These differences are resolved in a Conference Committee.

After several losses in the Conference Committee, Senator Bible said to me, "I'm not going to include any more money for land acquisition at Piscataway Park until you get an agreement out of Mike Kirwan that he is not going to object to it in Conference; otherwise it is a useless exercise."

I called Mr. Kirwan's secretary and asked if I could see him. He graciously agreed to see me. I explained what the problem was: we still had some critical acquisitions to make in Piscataway, the land was escalating in value and, soon, if we did not get the appropriations we were going to be out of authorization, and would have to go back and get new authorization from the Interior and Insular Affairs Committee to acquire the land. I told him that I understood his problem with the item and that I really was not asking him to vote for it; I simply was asking him not to actively oppose it. "If I can get an agreement out of you not to oppose it," I said, "Senator Bible will put it in the Senate bill; otherwise, Senator Bible has advised me that he is not going to put it back in the bill inasmuch as he does not intend to go through any more useless exercises."

Congressman Kirwan leaned back in his chair, folded his hands across the top of his stomach and said to me, "Now you know, George, I am not going to make any such an agreement as that."

I said, "Mr. Chairman, if you can't make any agreement can you give me a glimmer of hope—so that I have some reasonable basis for going back to Senator Bible?"

He replied with a twinkle in his Irish eyes. "Why don't you do this: go tell Alan that I will not make any commitment to you as you've asked, but why doesn't he go ahead and put the money back in the bill?"

I reported this to Senator Bible, and sure enough he put it in the Senate bill. It was near the top of the list of differences between the appropriation bills passed by the House and the Senate as they went to Conference.

Mrs. Hanson, chairman of the House Appropriations Subcommittee, served as chairman of the Conference Committee. Senator Bible, chairman of the Senate Appropriations Subcommittee, led the Senate delegation to the Conference Committee. Mike was a member of the House delegation to the Conference Committee.

One of the staff who attended the Conference related the events. Mrs. Hanson read off item one. It was resolved. She then read off Piscataway Park and announced, "The House recedes" which meant, of course, that they would leave in the money that the Senate had put in the bill for Piscataway Park.

Mike Kirwan was sitting beside Mrs. Hanson with his eyes closed, his head down on his chest and his hands folded across the top of his stomach without a sound. Mrs. Hanson assuming that he hadn't heard her, said, "Piscataway Park, the House recedes." Not a sound. Finally a third time, she said in a louder voice, "Piscataway Park, the House recedes."

Mike Kirwan lifted his head, opened his eyes, turned his head toward her and said, "Madam Chairman, what's item three?"

We got the money!

* * *

With the exploding growth of the National Park System from 1963–72 (an average of nine new parks each year), and the escalating costs of the Vietnam War, our operating budget came under increasing pressure. We initiated a series of evaluations of our overhead (Washington and regional offices) to see how we could redeploy our resources to maintain field operations. Some wag dubbed the program Ratchet and the name stuck.

These reviews disturbed a lot of "comfort zones." For example, both in the regions and in the Washington office we had divisions of ranger activities. Now, the rangers are the cornerstone of every park organization and they are extremely talented, versatile people. One day they pack mules; the next fight forest fires; another keep law and order; and so on during the week, trapping and removing recalcitrant bears, comforting lost children, manning entrance stations. Whatever is not assigned specifically to someone else is done by the rangers. Every superintendent has used the phrase "Have the rangers do it," thousands of times. A park would not be a park without a ranger.

But what, pray tell does a ranger do in a regional office in Omaha or Philadelphia or in the director's office in Washington, D.C.? It was illogical, unnecessary and uneconomical so I abolished those divisions and reassigned the personnel to productive work.

But I wasn't finished yet.

The National Park Service had the most educated, talented, innovative cadre of people I have ever known—in or out of government—embracing seventeen identifiable professional disciplines in the social, physical and environmental sciences ranging from architects to zoologists. Within the bounds of approved congressional/secretarial policies and objectives I wanted to turn them loose. I told the regional directors that I thought the handbooks which, for the most part, told you how to do the job were stifling our field people. They disagreed; so I appointed a committee of them to look at the situation and make recommendations. Soon, the committee reported the handbooks were needed to insure uniformity. That did it!

My objective was not uniformity but creativity and productivity. I abolished fifty-six volumes of handbooks, including the three I had written, and substituted instead objectives, goals, program and personal performance standards. Man-o-life did I catch hell, one would have thought I had repudiated the King James version of the Holy Scriptures!

These changes produced some lively reactions from the field: poems predicting dire consequences, such as Dirge, 1965, and letters relating uncomplimentary remarks poured into my office.

DIRGE, 1965

Behind closed doors in Washington, in a locked and guarded room,
There meets a small, selected group—the harbingers of doom.
One man alone controls the key—he keeps them out of touch—
And his only words that are overheard are "Thank you very much."

From the grim gray halls of Washington to sunny Santa Fe,
In 'Frisco, Richmond, Omaha and Philadelph-i-ay
The vassals of this overlord all know that they're in Dutch.
They await their fate, and they fear to hear the "Thank you very much."

Retirement pay is figured close, RIF points are counted up—
Each night the drink is stiffer in the after-hours cup—
Morale is low, and around each heart dread, icy fingers clutch—
For there's little doubt some will be out, with a "Thank you very much."

Mid-management's the dirty word—some offices will close—
Or will they shrink? The active brain behind that lengthy nose
Coldly prescribes efficiency; no "family problems" crutch
Can change his plan—if you're the man, it's "Thank you very much."

His key unlocks that guarded door—was that a muffled shriek?
And then, unblinking, from on high, with barely parted beak,

BATTLING FOR THE NATIONAL PARKS

The eagle swoops upon us rabbits in our hutch—
The talons bite—through pain and fright rings "Thank you very much!"

Bob Borrel

When President Johnson sent the 1969 fiscal year (July 1, 1968–June 30, 1969) budget to the Congress, there was not enough money included in it for the National Park System to continue field operations at acceptable levels of preservation and visitor use. During the preparation of the budget, I had protested to Secretary Udall, explaining that unless the money was increased we faced some very difficult choices: permit deterioration of the resources and visitor services; close some parks entirely; or curtail operations at all of the parks for a portion of each week or year. My pleas fell on deaf ears at the Bureau of the Budget.

When the bill was under consideration by the Congress I communicated the same message to the House and Senate Appropriations Subcommittees.

There is always a cat and mouse game between the president and the Congress about budgets. The administration invariably cuts where it has strong reason to suspect the Congress will increase and the Congress reciprocates by cutting the president's favorite programs that it believes are excessively funded and increasing the ones he cut. For example, one year the Bureau of the Budget cut out all fish hatcheries —a favorite of Mrs. Hanson's. As a general rule, the whole process levels itself out.

The 1969 fiscal year budget proved to be an exception. The Congress *did not increase* funding for the operation of the National Park System. After the bill was enacted, I called a meeting of the regional directors to explore our options. There was no unanimity as to how to approach the problem so I decided to spread the pain, inflicting as little as possible at any one area. I recommended to the secretary that he approve a nine-point program to curtail operations to fit the appropriation. This included cutting hours, closing seasonal facilities out-of-season, and closing some areas altogether.

Before implementing the plan, I briefed the appropriate members of the subcommittees.

There was a loud outcry when I put the plan into operation. It was soon quelled in the Congress by both Mrs. Hanson and Senator Bible strongly supporting the action I had taken. That is not to say, however, that everyone was happy with the decision.

This program, also, was assigned a name—a newspaper man in Washington dubbed it the Washington Monument Syndrome. The popular memorial was one of the areas put on a reduced operating schedule.

Senator Joseph Montoya of New Mexico prevailed on the Chamber of Commerce at Carlsbad to advance the money needed to restore full operations at Carlsbad Caverns National Park.

Senator Clifford Hansen of Wyoming took a different approach. He and his staff almost inundated us with telephone calls and letters demanding the most minute details of my management, from the need for an employees' newsletter to snow plowing.

The parks were operating on this reduced schedule when Secretary Hickel arrived. I briefed him. He had no way of knowing at that time whether I had acted properly in ordering the reduced schedule of operations. He made it clear, however, that my job was on the line, if, in his judgment, he found evidence that my decision was not fully supported by the facts.

One of the first chores assigned Dr. Leslie Glasgow when he was sworn in as assistant secretary for Fish, Wildlife and Parks was to evaluate the merits of what I had done. Glasgow had been a university professor. He was an astute, scholarly, shy, and considerate gentleman. He undertook this assignment with diligence. We were required to lay out the whole record for him and his staff. As a result of his investigation, he recommended, and the secretary approved, a supplemental appropriation for the National Park Service of $17,000,000 to put the park system back on a normal, operating schedule for the balance of the fiscal year ending June 30, 1969. The Congress appropriated the money and operations were restored to a normal schedule.

P. J. Ryan, a former employee of Petrified Forest National Park, wrote of this episode in the *Thunderbear* publication:

Now that I have described the futility of a strike [of the NPS] one might still ask if a strike or withholding of services was ever attempted in the NPS?

Surprisingly enough, the answer is yes.

The incident occurred during the reign of George B. (Wizard George) Hartzog. Mr. Hartzog was a man of many facets. He was perhaps the most formidable agency chief since John Wesley Powell. In a department not exactly known for shrinking violets, only the Bureau of Reclamations Floyd Dominy could cross swords with him in any hope of success.

A fourteen hour a day workaholic as well as the cigar industry's answer to aerobics, Mr. Hartzog worked with an endless, exhausting zeal that was almost supernatural. Indeed, he was almost scary. Congress vaguely realized that if they did anything to antagonize Wizard George, something bad might happen; exactly what, no one knew. Since fear of the unknown is exceeded only by curiosity of the unknown and since it was unlikely that he could turn all of them into frogs, Congress decided to provoke the Wizard.

It withheld funds.

Retribution was sure and quick in coming. The Wizard spun around three times, changed himself into a labor leader and ordered two national parks out on strike.

Now, technically this wasn't a strike, it was more like "a withholding of services and closure to protect the resource due to lack of funds." The two parks chosen for this action, Petrified Forest and Carlsbad Caverns, both possessed unusually complete control of access. In addition, both parks were near chambers of commerce that took a deep and abiding interest in the welfare of travelers passing by.

Your kindly editor was assigned to Petrified Forest at that

time and was on hand to greet the first of the throng that was not going to see one of Nature's Wonderlands that day.

As there was nothing specific in our job descriptions about being torn limb from limb, it was considered wise and prudent that we wear old clothes and paint the entrance station. In addition to old clothes, I added a Norweigian accent as everybody likes Norweigians.

OPEN THAT GATE!

"Ay yust bane day painter, Moom, Ay don't hav' day kay."

WHOSE IN CHARGE AROUND HERE?

"Vell, vy don't you try tose fellers in Vashington, Ay yust bane paintin'."

A few hearty souls tried to push down the gates with their cars to the detriment of their cars. Judging from cartridge cases, one frustrated visitor had emptied the family Luger at one of our best locks during the night.

Meanwhile, at Carlsbad, the locals were offering to pay the wages of the park staff if only the golden cornucopia of visitors would flow again. People were also writing letters.

After about three weeks of this, Congress asked if something could not be done to lift the Curse. The Wizard told them of the magic word, MONEY. It was spoken, and all was as before. There was some talk of reprimanding the Wizard, but it died away. After all, no one wants to be turned into a pumpkin.

With enthusiastic bipartisan support of the Congress for innovative programs, such as living history, Summer in the Parks and others, we made the parks relevant to millions of our citizens: number two of my three goals.

In the first year of Summer in the Parks in the Washington metropolitan area, we introduced tens of thousands of youngsters to the parks of their nation's Capital. And we did it without adding a single new acre of parkland. Working with local governments, school districts and numerous volunteer groups, such as the Boy and Girl Scouts, Campfire Girls and others, we brought the children in from the streets and away from their isolation in dreary environments of concrete, crime and chaos. With games, music, fishing, camping and just plain quiet time in God's great out-of-doors and among

the nation's monuments, memorials and museums, we lifted
—if, indeed, only briefly —their painful burdens of despair.

The National Park Service administers more urban parkland than any agency of any government at any level—long
silent battlefields (Richmond, Virginia), forts (Charleston,
S.C., Savannah, Ga.), open squares (Washington, Philadelphia, St. Louis) and many, many other lands associated with
our national history. The talented field people of the park
service adapted the successful Washington programs to their
local urban parks in countless communities across the land.
We shared these program innovations with numerous state
and local government park systems to enrich their programs.

Great new urban parks were established in New York/New
Jersey (Gateway National Recreation Area) and at San Francisco (Golden Gate National Recreation Area) to bring parks
to people who otherwise may never have had the opportunity
to delight in the renewing and re-creating experience in such
remote national parks as Yellowstone, Glacier, Big Bend and
other national parks set aside to preserve the pristine lands
of our natural inheritance.

X

BUREAUCRATIC TURF

Competitiveness among federal agencies for mission and turf is as intense as any in private enterprise for product and market share. A Washington classic in the annals of such bureaucratic conflict is that between the U.S. Forest Service and the National Park Service.

Gifford Pinchot, the first forest service chief, fiercely opposed the establishment of the National Park Service in 1916 believing that the new agency posed a threat to his national forest turf. He was correct. Many of the great Western parks, such as Grand Canyon, Grand Teton, Bryce Canyon and others, were carved in whole or in large part from the national forests.

The intensity of the bureaucratic rivalries of the two bureaus escalated over the years, reaching a crescendo of bitterness in 1950 over the establishment of Grand Teton National Park in Wyoming. Though somewhat more civilized after the twenty-five year Grand Teton fight was over in the fifties, the controversies over turf were still seething when the Kennedy Administration arrived in Washington.

At the beginning of his administration in 1961, President Kennedy appointed two able and resourceful politicians to lead the Departments of Agriculture and Interior. Orville

Freeman, former governor of Minnesota, was appointed secretary of agriculture, the department that includes the forest
service. Stewart Udall, a former congressman from Arizona
(Tuscon), was appointed secretary of the interior, the department that includes the National Park Service.

The Outdoor Recreation Resources Review Commission
made its report to President Kennedy early in his administration. One of its principal recommendations was that there
be a new federal bureau to coordinate the federal effort in
outdoor recreation; to develop a nationwide outdoor recreation plan; and, to administer a federal-state matching
grants program for the acquisition of land and development
of outdoor recreation facilities.

In 1936 the Congress had authorized the National Park
Service to perform many of the functions that the commission
now recommended be vested in a new bureau. Utilizing his
general authority to organize and manage the programs of
the department, Udall, in 1962, created the new Bureau of
Outdoor Recreation (BOR), by secretarial order. He vested in
it the recreation planning and coordination functions of the
National Park Service. Later the Congress confirmed the secretary's action when it gave the new bureau a legislative
charter and expanded its functions to include administration
of the newly enacted Land and Water Conservation Fund.

To head the new bureau, Udall appointed Dr. Edward
Crafts, a deputy chief of the U.S. Forest Service. Crafts had a
Ph.D. in forestry. As cold and calculating as an Alaska gray-
ling, he was a brilliant, skilled career bureaucrat. His superior performance in organizing, staffing and managing the
mega-million dollar grants program of the Land and Water
Conservation Fund without one whiff of scandal or allegation
of mismanagement, earned him a Rockefeller public service
award from Princeton University. Crafts enjoyed the confidence of both Udall and Freeman.

One of Crafts's charges from Udall and Freeman was to
cool the long-running bureaucratic/jurisdictional conflict between the National Park Service and the U.S. Forest Service.

X. Bureaucratic Turf

Two such conflicts were then in progress: the management of recreation on the Bureau of Reclamation's Flaming Gorge reservoir on the Green River in Wyoming and Utah, and the question of carving a national park from the national forests of the North Cascades.

In a long-standing agreement between the National Park Service and the Bureau of Reclamation, the National Park Service administered the recreation programs on reclamation's reservoirs, unless the reservoirs were wholly within a national forest which was administered by the forest service. Flaming Gorge was unique; it was divided approximately equally between lands within the national forest and lands outside the national forest.

Crafts drafted an agreement to govern the relationships between the park service and the forest service for Flaming Gorge and the North Cascades. Udall and Freeman approved. In bureaucratic circles the agreement became known as the Treaty of the Potomac.

Solomon-like, the agreement decreed that each agency manage one-half of Flaming Gorge National Recreation Area. A joint Interior/Agriculture study team would be appointed to resolve the issue of whether to make the North Cascades a national park. Crafts would be chairman of the study team and each secretary would appoint two members, one each from the park service and the forest service and one each from the secretarial staffs or the general public. This agreement was in place when I returned to the National Park Service as associate director in February, 1963. The two secretaries had implemented the Flaming Gorge arrangement and legislation to confirm the arrangement had been introduced in the Congress. Udall designated me as the departmental witness to support the arrangement.

Alan Bible, chairman of the National Parks Subcommittee of the Senate Interior and Insular Affairs Committee, believed in visiting every area proposed for legislation. He had scheduled an inspection trip to Flaming Gorge that included a little leisurely fishing. As the designated departmental witness, I went along. During the trip I fished with Senator Len Jordan of Idaho, who was the ranking minority member on the subcommittee. A forest service ranger was our guide and boat operator. While we were placidly fishing away, the ranger's radio crackled with news of a boating accident down the lake. Within a matter of minutes a National Park Service boat went at full throttle down the lake, followed within seconds by another boat from the U.S. Forest Service. That puzzled me, but I didn't comment about it until we landed, when I asked the superintendent, "How serious was that boating accident?"

"Oh," he said, "it wasn't all that serious. Some guy stood up in a boat and fell out." I remarked that I thought it was catastrophic because they called out both the park service and the forest service. He said, "That's routine."

I replied, "That's a tremendous waste."

"Yes, I know it is," he said, "but that's the way it operates."

When I returned to Washington, I went to see the secretary. "Stewart," I said, "you told me that I am to be the departmental witness on Flaming Gorge. One of the questions that Alan Bible is going to ask me is about the efficiency of this operation. I am going to have to tell him the truth—that this isn't efficient at all." I related the boating incident to him and concluded, "In my judgment, we're wasting $100,000 a year in duplicative services."

Stewart asked what I thought we should do about it, and I replied, "I think we ought to have the regional directors of the park service, the forest service and the Bureau of Outdoor Recreation take a look at it because I don't want to get trapped into a situation where I have to blow the bill out of the water."

Udall called Orville Freeman and told him of my concerns and suggested the study I had proposed. Freeman agreed. They appointed the regional directors of the forest service, the park service, and BOR to have a look at it and find out if there was any duplication, and if so, how much.

Their study confirmed my suspicions. We were wasting a

bundle. The forest service was adamant in holding onto its half of the area. It looked like we were headed for the fighting mat again.

I began visiting with Senator Jackson's staff. Senator Jackson was the chairman of the Interior and Insular Affairs Committee and the junior senator from the state of Washington in which the North Cascades is located. When nominated for president, John Kennedy had named Senator Jackson as chairman of the National Democratic Committee.

In line with Senator Jackson's orders to remain rigorously objective pending completion of the study, his staff was discreetly silent about the senator's views on what should be done in the North Cascades. But you can learn as much sometimes by what you don't hear as you can by what you are told. I got a feeling that Senator Jackson wanted a national park in the North Cascades. If he did, he was going to get one; and if he got one, of course, I had one. Certainly I would rather have a horse of a park than a rabbit of a recreation area around an artificial lake. I decided to take the gamble.

The park service withdrew from Flaming Gorge and turned it over to the forest service. They had their rabbit!

In the meantime, the North Cascades study team had been formed with Crafts as chairman, Art Greeley, associate chief of the forest service, me to represent the National Park Service, and two secretarial appointees, one each from Agriculture and Interior.

From the outset of our study of the North Cascades, the team members deferred to Crafts's leadership. After all, if the departmental team members could not rise above their parochial, bureaucratic interests to view the public interest, Crafts was the vote needed to achieve bureaucratic victory.

At the first working session of the team I insisted that we confront and resolve an old saw of the forest service: that they could manage the resource as well as the park service. I had always believed such an argument demeaned both agencies and begged the question of each agency's mission. Both agencies recruited their rangers from the same schools. We got as many bright ones as did the forest service and vice versa. They were a talented, able, devoted lot. Only the agency mission separated them. In the field—the parks and the forests—they were friends, neighbors and comrades-in-arms fighting their common enemies of pestilence, both man-caused and the natural calamities of fire, flood and earthquake. Moreover, they hired each other's children during the summer to earn money for college. The bureaucratic battles were in Washington.

Continuing, I argued that our sole criterion for decision-making should be the highest and best use of the resource. If it should be preserved as park and recreation land, it should be managed by the park service; if it was land that should be available for consumptive resource utilization, it should be managed by the forest service.

Art Greeley, the forest service's associate chief was a warm, sensitive, reserved and cautious man. A second generation career forest service employee, his father was a former chief of the forest service. Art may have become chief had he not taken early retirement to enter Wesley Theological Seminary and become a Methodist minister. He conceded the merit of my argument about setting aside the discredited competency issue. He was not sure that at the beginning of the study we should decide the philosophical question of management according to primary mission because the forest service was, also, in the business of managing recreation lands.

After hearing us both out, Crafts came down on my side. The land would be classified on the basis of its highest and best use and allocated between the two agencies according to primary mission: preservation/outdoor recreation to the National Park Service; consumptive resource utilization to the U.S. Forest Service.

This was a decision of enormous strategic importance to me. The North Cascades is the last place in the lower 48 where the Lord put His hand on the land to make it a thing

of majesty and beauty. There was certainly a park there—all
that remained was to identify it.

The study team had a small staff, reporting to Crafts. Its
job was to classify the land, keep records of the proceedings
and draft the report.

Crafts decreed a two-pronged approach to the study: on-
site inspection of the resources; and public hearings throughout the study area, most of the state of Washington. Support
to the team in the field would be shared by the forest service
and the park service. It was to be a civilized, cooperative effort—no bushwhacking! That was a tall order, but for the
most part it worked that way.

The field staffs of the forest service and the park service
did a commendable job in organizing the on-site inspection
trips by the study team. By boat, bus and aircraft we surveyed all of the North Cascades in Washington. Each agency
was given the opportunity to show off its programs and articulate its management philosophy. Both agencies were on
their best behavior, putting their best foot forward.

The clear-cutting policy of the forest service in these majestic mountains had brought the wrath of the conservationists down upon its head. Their policy permitted a logger to
cut every tree in a huge stand of virgin Douglas fir. These
plots ranged up to 100 acres or more. The resulting scar,
especially when viewed from the road by the sightseeing mo-
torist, was an obscenity to the landscape. A primary justifi-
cation for the clear-cutting policy was the need for full
sunlight to encourage regeneration. Notwithstanding this
silvi-cultural argument, the forest service had decided that it
had to make some modification in the policy to blunt the
public outcry. It settled on a two part approach: reduce the
size of the clear-cut plots and shield the clear-cuts from the
roadsides by establishing a landscape zone along the road
corridors. One morning, Herb Stone, the regional forester,
took the team and a contingent of observers by bus to see the
results of the new policy in operation.

We had traveled several miles along a dirt road in the forest with magnificent trees hugging the ditch-lines. No clear-cuts were visible. Herb was waxing eloquent about the efficacy of the new policy. As we rounded a curve our bus braked to a sudden stop. Dead ahead was an eighteen-wheel logging truck parked in the ditch, below a scene of utter devastation. The logger had skinned the hillside down to the ditch-line. Poor Herb trying to explain his way out of the fiasco reminded me of the Ozark farmer:

> One bright fall morning a traveling salesman stopped by a farmer's house in the Ozarks and asked the small boy playing with the old hound dog in the front yard if his mother and father were home.
> "Yep," said the boy.
> "Can I see them?" the salesman asked.
> "Nope," said the boy.
> "Why?" asked the salesman.
> "Well it's like this," said the boy, "Paw sleeps in a short nite shirt. Last night he heard a noise in the hen house. He got his shot gun and went out there and old Rover here followed him. When Paw got in the hen house, old Rover put his cold nose up Paw's nite shirt and they been pickin' chickens since 3 o'clock."

For the public hearings the forest service mobilized its special interest constituencies—loggers, grazers, sports hunters, water users, local governments with which it shared receipts from forest uses, state conservation agencies involved in wildlife habitat management and cooperative forestry research and management. It was a formidable army.

Unlike many times in years past, the park service now had an army too—the national conservation organizations, several of which had large concentrations of members in the Pacific-Northwest, especially around the Seattle area. They were professors, students, mountain climbers, campers, hikers and a host of others determined to save their North Cascades. Well organized, in fighting trim, they were the green berets of our smaller army. Moreover, our army was better generaled by the creative leadership of the North Cascades coalition. You could count on them at every hearing to discomfit the special interests with their well-researched, articulate documentation about the resources of the region and their values both economic and environmental.

Crafts carefully led the team through the combat zone of the public hearings. He produced a report which was unanimously agreed to by the study team and approved by the two secretaries. The report recommended a North Cascades National Park, a Lake Chelan National Recreation Area and a Ross Lake National Recreation Area—all three to be managed by the National Park Service. Senator Jackson promptly introduced legislation to implement the recommendations. On October 2, 1968, the president signed the law establishing three new park areas. I had my horse!

XI

THE REDWOOD
NATIONAL PARK

A Redwood National Park to preserve a vignette of the coast redwood forests of California was a haunting dream of all who had been privileged to experience the majesty of these towering giants.

Except for a few thousand acres preserved in California's state parks, largely as the result of private philanthropy engineered by the Save-the-Redwoods League, the virgin stands were owned by four large timber companies—Miller Redwood, Simpson, Arcata and Georgia-Pacific—and by the United States in an experimental forest administered by the U.S. Forest Service.

By the decade of the fifties a Redwood National Park had become a matter of urgent concern to many conservationists. The remaining old growth stands were being harvested at a rapid rate. Unless something was done soon, the best that remained of these magnificent groves would be lost forever.

Thus, it was, that in the late 1950s, at the urging of its president, Mel Grovesnor, and Connie Wirth, then director of the National Park Service and a trustee of the National Geographic Society, the society financed a study of the coast Red-woods of Northern California. The study was to inventory the redwoods and identify those areas suitable for park purposes.

Most of the remaining virgin stands were located in Del Norte and Humboldt counties in the Mill Creek (Del Norte) and Redwood Creek (Humboldt) watersheds. Redwoods are shallow-rooted trees, highly susceptible to loss by flooding. Of those set aside in the state parks, hundreds downstream on their watersheds had been lost to floods over the years. Natural watershed protection to control flooding was an important consideration to any further preservation efforts.

The Geographic study resulted in a brilliant report that confirmed the long-held belief of concerned conservationists: time was of the essence if the nation was to have the Redwood National Park of its dream. The report concluded that the tallest and most extensive remaining groves were in Redwood Creek—a lengthy and large watershed prone to flooding; groves of lesser size and extent but still of park-quality were in Mill Creek, a smaller watershed which permitted greater protection against destruction by flooding.

The Geographic report laid the scientific foundation for a park. But there were other vexing and difficult issues to be resolved.

There was no agreement between the Sierra Club and the Save-the-Redwoods League—the two premier conservation organizations concerned with redwood preservation—of where the park should be located. The Sierra Club demanded a very large park encompassing the finest groves in the Redwood Creek Watershed. The Save-the-Redwoods League, mindful of the destructive impact of flooding, wanted the park in the Mill Creek Watershed.

The Del Norte-Humboldt economies were heavily dependent upon harvesting the old growth redwoods.

Miller's ownership was limited pretty much to Mill Creek —a large park there would likely put its California operations out of business. Arcata's ownership was concentrated in

Redwood Creek. A large park carved from its holdings would likely put it out of business.

The redwoods in federal ownership in the experimental forest managed by the forest service were not of park-quality.

The capacity of the four companies to harvest old growth was in delicate balance with the remaining inventory. A reasonably sized national park, even if spread among the holdings of all of the companies, would likely put one or more of them out of business unless they could, in return, acquire the experimental forest already in federal ownership.

Finally, the forest service was determined not to surrender its lands in order to create a park.

At the outset of the process to develop a park proposal, Udall made several strategic decisions which proved to be of enormous importance to our final victory.

First he enlisted the interest and support of Mrs. Johnson in the effort to establish a Redwood National Park.

Then he designated Ed Crafts, director of the Bureau of Outdoor Recreation, to be point-man in assessing the resource (timber) values involved. Crafts was highly respected by the timber companies. Moreover, through his long service in Washington he had become close friends with Phillip S. (Sam) Hughes, the deputy director of President Johnson's Bureau of the Budget. The final recommendations to the Congress for a park would need approval of the Bureau of the Budget.

Finally, Udall designated Fred Smith, an associate of Laurance Rockefeller, as an "ambassador without portfolio" to the Redwood industry.

Fred was a highly successful businessman who joined Rockefeller's personal staff after he retired from business. He was a member of the secretary's Advisory Board on National Parks with a long time interest in conservation issues. A warm and engaging man, he wore the mantle of elder statesman with dignity and style. Tall, gray-haired, of gentle countenance, he had learned well the art of listening. He was an ideal choice for the role Udall assigned him.

Countless hours were consumed in studies of alternate locations, shapes and sizes for the proposed park; the economic consequences of a park on the local area; and the cost to the government of acquiring the park. Dozens of meetings were held with all affected interest groups. Three crucial factors stood out. First, the cost of buying an entire watershed was deemed to be too high. Second, with the inclusion of the existing California redwood state parks in the region within the national park, additional private land acquisition could be minimized. And third, it was essential that the experimental forest be made available in exchange for redwood lands acquired from the timber companies for the national park.

We initiated negotiations with then Governor Reagan for inclusion of three of the state parks. In exchange for federally-owned, surplus beach property, the governor would recommend that the legislature authorize the transfer of three redwood state parks to the federal government for inclusion in the national park.

Sam Hughes took the experimental forest issue to President Johnson. The president directed that the forest be offered to the timber companies as part consideration of lands acquired from them for the park.

These issues resolved, a park proposal was formulated: a portion of the park would be in Redwood Creek and a portion of it would be in Mill Creek. Three redwood state parks would be included in the national park. The federally-owned lands of the experimental forest would be authorized for exchange with the timber companies whose lands were to be acquired for the park.

With great fanfare President Johnson called a news conference to unveil the park proposal. With Mrs. Johnson at his side he announced that he was sending a bill to the Congress to establish a Redwood National Park. Dozens of people who had worked long and hard in shaping the proposal were invited to the White House to share this happy occasion with President and Mrs. Johnson. It was the pep rally before the battle.

Great wealth makes for great fights. The Redwood National Park proposal was destined to be a bitter, bruising battle; if established, the park would be the most costly in history.

The timber companies retained batteries of brilliant, high-priced lawyers and lobbyists in Washington and elsewhere around the country.

The Sierra Club activated its large, enthusiastic and influential membership. It reached out to the other conservation organizations to network an amazingly effective fighting force of concerned citizens across the land.

Nothing illuminates the ferocity of the fight more dramatically than the high price the Sierra Club paid for its valiant work in behalf of the park. At the height of the fray, the Internal Revenue Service revoked the Sierra Club's tax exemption, contending it had exceeded the permissible bounds of lobbying by tax-exempt organizations. It was a jolting blow. Wounded, but undeterred the club pursued the fight with increased intensity.

The local congressman, Don Clausen, who was a member of the National Parks Subcommittee, was caught in the middle. His district extended along the coast from the Oregon line to within a few miles of San Francisco. His big moneyed supporters in the redwood country to the north wanted no park. His growing conservation constituency in the south wanted a large park.

Responding to the pressures of Don Clausen, the House passed a bill for a very small park. It was unacceptable. In the meantime, with the support of Senator Kuchel of California, the ranking minority member of the Senate Interior and Insular Affairs Committee, the Senate passed a bill pretty much in line with the administration proposal. The difference had to be resolved in a Conference Committee.

Senator Jackson was named as the chairman of the Senate delegation to the Conference Committee on the Redwood National Park. Wayne Aspinall was the chairman of the House delegation. In the case of extremely controversial legislation, the conferees sometimes designate their respective chairmen/women to resolve the differences for further consideration by all of the committee membership.

Patiently and skillfully, in frequent consultation with their committee colleagues, Jackson and Aspinall negotiated a compromise. The final bill did not provide for a perfect park, but it was greatly improved over the House version.

Senator Jackson showed me the outline of the final park he and Wayne Aspinall had agreed on. I was ecstatic. At last the dream was to be reality!

In my enthusiasm I immediately placed a call to Newton Drury in California. Newton was a founder of the Save-the-Redwoods League. His leadership in saving California's magnificent redwoods is legendary. I was sure that he would be as delighted as I that we were going to have a Redwood National Park.

Excitedly, I told him of my meeting with Senator Jackson, describing in some detail the areas to be included in the park. Far from being elated, he laid the wood to me. The park was too small, we had lost some of the most valuable stands, we had accepted areas that could not be protected from floods, etc. He was right on all counts. He was not mollified by my explanations of why these compromises were necessary. Finally, I ended the conversation with a reminder.

"Newton, the first time I ever met you, you recounted your dream for a Redwood National Park. Tonight, I have one. If it's not right, my successor can fix it—but never again will we have an argument about whether we are going to have one."

Compromise is the essence of the legislative art. Thus, legislation is seldom perfect. Happily, it is never permanent.

Years later, under the leadership of Congressman Phil Burton of California, the Congress did fix the original park

XI. The Redwood National Park

by greatly expanding its boundaries to include most of the Redwood Creek Watershed. When all the bills are paid it is estimated that the cost of the expanded park may be as much as one-billion dollars—and worth every cent of it!

XII

TRAVELING WITH
MRS. JOHNSON

Mrs. Johnson took a great interest in our work in the National Park Service and, as a result, under her inspiration and counsel to the president, the National Park System flourished.

With a little tea at the White House, Mrs. Johnson did wonders to convince doubting congressmen of the merits of our park proposals. Gracious, enthusiastic, articulate, always charming even when exhausted she was our premier traveling saleslady. The head of steam she helped us build up for new parks continued the momentum of the program for years after she left the White House.

Her living legacy of new parks and her efforts to awaken the national consciousness to natural beauty continues to enrich the daily lives of all Americans. With her Beautification Committee, she garlanded the city of Washington with a profusion of flowers and bedecked it with hundreds of ornamental and shade trees.

Her work for the National Park System has been commemorated in the establishment of Lady Bird Johnson Park on the banks of the Potomac River (Virginia) and the naming in her honor of a magnificent grove of towering redwoods in Redwood National Park (California).

With her effervescent, talented and delightfully witty assistant, Liz Carpenter, we traveled to a great many national parks—Redwood, Point Reyes, Rocky Mountain, Grand Teton, Yellowstone, Big Bend, the Blue Ridge, Shenandoah, Statue of Liberty, Virgin Islands, Padre Island, Fort Smith and many of the parks in the metropolitan Washington area.

In the five years of our travels together to the national parks we never had a planned ceremony for Mrs. Johnson ruined by rain, fog or other inclement weather. We did have some close calls, however.

California fog is notorious. Early on the morning of the dedication ceremony at Point Reyes, the superintendent and I went out to the dedication site. You could not cut the fog with a knife. Mrs. Johnson and her party were scheduled to arrive by helicopter. We had about despaired that she would make it when the sun broke through, burned off the fog and we had the most beautiful day I ever encountered at Point Reyes. After the ceremony, an old-timer came up to me and said, "Mister, I want to shake your hand because you must be the luckiest fella in the world. I been living here all my life and I ain't seen a half a dozen days like this one."

We scheduled a trip to Big Bend National Park, Texas, for the spring of 1966. At that time, the desert blossoms with a profusion of wild flowers, including magnificent cactus, and the weather is moderate.

I am the world's least qualified photographer and its worst mechanic. Knowing these limitations, I asked our chief photographer, Woodie Williams to loan me the simplest, surefire, no-frills camera he had, load it and provide some extra rolls of film. For once, I wanted to be prepared, personally, for whatever unique photo opportunities we might encounter.

In the park, the party stayed at the lodging facilities up in the mountains of the Chisos Basin. During our visit, a barbecue had been arranged at a picnic area down on the Rio Grande. Mrs. Carpenter invited me to ride to the affair in the car with her and Mrs. Johnson. Mrs. Johnson was radiant in a bright red dress. I took along my camera. Just as we came off the mountain we passed a magnificent cactus in full bloom. I had never seen one with such a profusion of blossoms. Instantly, Liz said, "Stop the car. George, get a photograph of Mrs. Johnson and that cactus so we can give copies to the members of the traveling party."

Liz posed Mrs. Johnson next to the plant on several different sides. A unique opportunity and I was lucky enough to have it all to myself. I shot the whole roll of twelve exposures and sent a ranger to Marathon to have it developed immediately. Late that night the young man returned with my pictures. "Mr. Hartzog," he said, "I don't think you are going to like these."

"Why," I asked, "didn't they come out?"

"Oh, yeah," he said, "they came out real nice—in black and white!"

The candelilla plant, native to northern Mexico and the Big Bend region of Texas produces a valued ingredient for making fine polishes, varnishes, etc. In Mexico at the time, the export of candelilla wax was controlled by a government sponsored marketing cartel. The local producers found it to be much more profitable to haul their wax across the Rio Grande and market it in the United States. With the preservation of the native plant life in the park, the largest supply of the plant was then in Big Bend National Park. A flourishing trade in candelilla wax developed in the vicinity of the park with the traffic moving in both directions. Poachers would harvest the plant in the park, pack it across the river which is not very deep or wide, boil off the wax in Mexico then pack the wax back across the river to the wholesalers. It was a pesky problem; and the operation was difficult to control because of the differing views of the United States and Mexico about the subject. The sale of the wax in the United States was legal and the U.S. authorities could care less about where it came from; only the harvesting of our park plants was illegal. The production of the wax in Mexico was legal and their authorities could care less about where the plants came from. Only the exporting of the wax through other than the government cartel was illegal.

We had planned a float trip on the river as a part of the First Lady's visit to the park. I was with one of the rangers and a secret service agent in the lead boat. As we came around a bend in the river we noticed smoke rising on the Mexico side of the river. "Boiling wax," the ranger said. As we came out of the mouth of the canyon, we noticed five men standing around a fifty-five gallon drum elevated on stones with a fire blazing away underneath it. Leaning up beside a tree nearby was a double barreled shotgun. To our left in the park was a thoroughly cleared patch from a lush stand of candelilla plants. The secret service agent and I were concerned and we so expressed ourselves to the ranger. "Oh, they won't bother us," he said, "just wave at them and stay on course. They'll be back tonight peddling their wax!"

We did as the ranger instructed and so did those in all the other boats and, in turn, we were greeted warmly by our Mexican neighbors!

I received only one complaint about any of Mrs. Johnson's efforts to restore beauty to America. As a part of her itinerary for her trip to the Blue Ridge Parkway, a visit was scheduled by the Bureau of Public Roads and the Virginia Department of Highways and Transportation to Interstate 81. She and her Beautification Committee had been active in trying to get the highway departments to landscape their road corridors. The purpose of her visit to Interstate 81 was to plant some multi-flora roses as the beginning of a project by the state to landscape the median strip of the newly constructed highway. Multi-flora roses are hardy plants that produce an abundance of small beautiful blossoms in the spring. In the fall, they head up and the seed are a source of food for the wild birds.

Several years after her visit, I had occasion to speak at a meeting in the Shenandoah Valley, where Interstate 81 is located. To establish rapport with the audience, I related my earlier visit in the area with Mrs. Johnson when she initiated the plantings in the median of Interstate 81. After the talk, a gentleman came up to me and said, "So you're the fellow that ruined my pasture." With some amazement, I allowed as how I didn't know what he was talking about. He continued. "Well, them birds have scattered the damn multiflora rose seeds all over my pasture—and I now got more roses than the highway department!"

After Mrs. Johnson's visit to the Statue of Liberty, she, Liz, Helen and I had been invited by Mr. and Mrs. Laurance Rockefeller to visit with them at their Pocantico Hills Estate on the Hudson River. During our visit, the Rockefellers took us on a tour of the Sleepy Hollow Restoration, one of a great many projects to which the Rockefellers have contributed generously to preserve America's natural and cultural heritage. As a part of our tour, we stopped at a local fair where many artisans, craftsmen and farmers were demonstrating their skills as practiced in the 18th and 19th centuries. One exhibit was sheep shearing by hand—not with power clippers. In her exuberant way, Liz, said, "George, you're a country boy. Why don't you shear the sheep and let's get a picture of you and Mrs. Johnson." The shearer was happy enough to surrender his shears. Dressed in the only dark suit I had taken along on the trip, I kneeled down, put one knee against the back of the ram and started shearing away. By the time I finished one side Liz had enough pictures, so I got up and returned the shears. I also discovered that I had kneeled down in fresh sheep manure. It was a right smart smelly ride back to Pocantico Hills.

XIII

REAPPOINTED
DIRECTOR

Early in his term as governor of Alaska, I went to Juneau, the state capitol, to meet with Walter Hickel and brief him on the national park programs in Alaska. We had a pleasant, constructive visit. At the meeting I also met his assistant, Dr. Carl McMurray. When Hickel came to Washington as secretary of the interior he brought Carl McMurray with him to be his executive assistant. As a result of my visit to Alaska I was one of the fortunate few in the Washington Office of Interior who knew them.

With the change of administration in Washington in 1969 there was a real movement afoot to fire me. One of the leaders in this effort was Senator Clifford Hansen of Wyoming.

In any new administration it takes awhile to get a hold on all the levers of power and process. One of the procedures in the Interior Department was centralized control of congressional mail. When congressional mail arrived in the secretary's mailroom, it was logged in for control purposes and sent to the bureau head responsible to prepare a draft reply for the secretary's signature.

The letter from Senator Hansen recommending to the secretary that I be fired was sent to me for reply.

I was out of town so my secretary opened the blue envelope (used to route confidential mail internally to an addressee) in which the letter arrived from the mailroom. When she read the letter, she was petrified. Realizing that I would be returning the next day, she locked the letter up in her desk. When I returned to the office, she came in, her hands trembling and her face ashen white, saying, "Mr. Hartzog, we have the most awful letter here." I took it from her nervous hand and read it. I was greatly amused, not about its contents, but how it got to me, with a big red slip on the front of it saying: PLEASE PREPARE REPLY. I immediately picked up the telephone and called Carl McMurray. "Carl, you got a minute? I'd like to read you a letter from Senator Clifford Hansen of Wyoming, addressed to the secretary."

As you know, our people throughout the nation are concerned and disappointed over limitation of visitor services in our national parks.

Mr. Udall's action represented his approval of recommendations by the Director of the National Park Service, George Hartzog. After careful study of this situation, it is my considered opinion that the actions to make park opening dates uncertain and to cut service to a five-day week in many cases were unwarranted.

Further, it appears that the National Park Service leadership made these recommendations in a deliberate effort to force modification of the requirements of the Revenue and Expenditure Control Act of 1968. The recommendations, to severely limit these very important services in an area most likely to irritate the public, were made following a personnel reduction of less than three per cent.

This represents either poor management or a deliberate attempt to bring public pressure against the law which the Congress saw fit to impose.

In either case, I can only conclude that it would be in the best interest of all to have new leadership in the National Park Service.

I do not believe that Director Hartzog should be continued in office.

When I finished reading the letter, there was stunned silence at the other end of the telephone. He said, "How the hell did you get that?"

I said, "From your mail room with instructions to please prepare reply. I am calling for guidance on what kind of reply the secretary wants to make."

He said, "Send me that damn letter."

I said, "Carl, I'll be happy to do that just as soon as I make seventeen copies of it because I don't want this one to get misplaced anywhere." So I sent my secretary around to the mail room and photographed the letter and then had her take the original to Carl McMurray.

Mendacity is not unknown in politics. Senator Hansen, in his letter cites a "reduction of less than three per cent." Conveniently, he ignored the earlier reductions amounting to more than twelve per cent. Together, the total reduction was fifteen per cent.

For several weeks after Hickel was sworn in as secretary, I received no indication from him as to whether I was going to be retained as director.

In the meantime, I learned that the White House had offered my job to William Penn Mott, Jr., then the director of California State Parks. Bill not only declined the job, but endorsed my continuing in the job. (Bill was appointed director of the National Park Service in 1985). I had also received a copy of a letter of March 17, 1969, from Nathaniel Reed to Hickel declining the job. A copy of the letter had been inadvertently sent to one of the staff members in my congressional liaison office.

This incident illustrates the difficulty of keeping secrets in government.

The drumbeat for my dismissal continued. I called my friend, former Congressman Tom Curtis, (Republican from St. Louis) and asked for his advice. I told him that a rumor had come to me that Congressman Johnny Rhodes of Arizona had asked that I be replaced. He told me that he knew Johnny Rhodes very well, that he was a man of great integrity and candor, and that if he had done such a thing he would tell me. Tom suggested that I go see him. I told him that I did not know Mr. Rhodes that well, and asked Tom if he would make me an appointment.

Johnny Rhodes, as Tom had indicated, was candid. He came straight to the point. "Yes, I did ask the president to replace you because some of my friends had asked me to do it. But then the White House said to me, 'Who do you want appointed?' So I asked my friends for replacements. None of the people they suggested were as qualified as you, so I told the president I was not interested in seeing you replaced. I believe, however, that you may have a problem with Gordon Allott."

Gordon Allott was the senior senator from Colorado. With the retirement of Senator Kuchel of California, Allott had recently become the ranking minority member of the Senate Interior and Insular Affairs Committee. He was also a close personal friend of Senator Clifford Hansen of Wyoming who had asked Secretary Hickel to fire me. With the Senate in the control of the Democrats, the White House in the control of the Republicans, the ranking minority member of a major standing committee of the Senate usually has great clout at the White House. I knew that if I did have a problem with Gordon Allott I was, indeed, in great jeopardy.

Senator Allott is a lawyer by training; cordial, but reserved and formal, certainly not inclined to indulge in chit-chat.

I asked for an appointment with the senator and he agreed to see me.

I related to him my conversation with Congressman Rhodes and bluntly asked, "Do I have a problem with you?"

He began by saying he really didn't know me; he had heard me testify but he knew nothing about my work. He said he had not asked the president to fire me.

It fell far short of a ringing endorsement and I knew I had a problem—if only one of indifference.

I told him that the reason I had not been in frequent contact with him on our programs was because he had not been the ranking minority member on either the full committee or the National Parks Subcommittee and that under the rules of the game (seniority) as I understood them it was expected that I should work through the ranking senator. I told him that I thought I had performed satisfactorily in this regard and that I would hope he would check it out. Moreover, I told him that now that he was ranking I certainly expected to work closely with him as I had with Senator Kuchel.

I concluded by telling him, frankly, that without his endorsement, I doubted that I would survive.

He agreed to think over the matter and call me.

Immediately upon my return to the office, I called Dr. Robert (Bob) Stearns in Denver, the father-in-law of Supreme Court Justice Byron White. Dr. Stearns, a former president of the University of Colorado, was a member of the secretary's Advisory Board on National Parks. He was a brilliant, cultured, witty man. He and his wife were delightful traveling companions during the board's annual inspection trips. During these travels, I had learned that Bob Stearns was instrumental in obtaining Gordon Allott's nomination by the Republicans for the Senate Seat he then occupied.

I reported to Bob my conversation with Senator Allott. He promised to contact Gordon.

In a few days I received a call to visit Senator Allott. He had talked with several of his friends in Colorado and with Wayne (Aspinall, chairman of the House Interior and Insular Affairs Committee, also from Colorado) and he had called the president to ask him to keep me.

Some days after my visit with Senator Allott, the secretary called me to come up and visit with him. He told me that he had decided to retain me as the director of the NPS. I expressed my appreciation and told him that I would do my very best to operate the service to achieve his goals. I also told him that if at any time he changed his mind, that all he had to do was to let me know, and I would leave without causing him any embarrassment.

He then said to me, "Well, now you know, this is conditional upon us checking you out."

I said, "What do you mean, checking me out?"

"Well," he said, "we have to find out whether you're acceptable to the Republicans; we have to find out whether you are a Republican."

"Oh," I said, "Mr. Secretary, if you expect to find out whether I am a Republican, you must believe I'm too stupid to be director and you really shouldn't reappoint me. Since I entered the National Park Service I've never registered, except as an Independent. But let me ask you a question. I'm from South Carolina and Strom Thurmond is our Republican senator. Do you really believe that there are enough Republicans in South Carolina to elect Strom Thurmond?" A flash of astonishment rushed across his face, and he said to me, "Get the hell out of here!" That's the last time Wally Hickel and I ever discussed partisan politics.

Wally Hickel was fired as secretary in the fall of 1970. The president named Rogers C. B. Morton of Maryland to succeed him. I was elated with the appointment.

Morton was a native of Kentucky from which his brother, Thruston, served as United States Senator. Rogers had moved to the eastern shore of Maryland; he had been elected to the Congress from this district. He served on the National Parks Subcommittee of the House Interior and Insular Affairs Committee. We had worked together closely when he sponsored the legislation to save Assateague Island National Seashore (Maryland and Virginia). He was a strong supporter of the park programs and over the years we had become good friends. With him in charge, I had no fear of continuing as director.

XIII. Reappointed Director

I briefed the new secretary on the programs of the National Park Service, including reviewing with him the policy/objectives that had been established by Secretary Hickel. He approved of them.

After the briefing, Morton dismissed the staff and said he wanted to talk with me privately. He began by saying, "I would like for you to be a part of my administration."

I said, "Rogers, I am a part of your administration."

"No," he said, "I want you to be assistant secretary for Fish, Wildlife and Parks." Assistant Secretary Glasgow had been fired at the same time as Wally Hickel.

I said, "Well, Rogers, frankly I don't have a great hankering to be an assistant secretary."

"Well," he said, "I want you and Pecora (then director of Geological Survey) to be a part of my administration and I'm going to make Pecora an assistant secretary too." As a matter of fact, he replaced under secretary Fred Russell with Bill Pecora. The conversation ended by my telling him that if he insisted on switching me, certainly I would accept his decision but if I had a choice I would rather stay as director. Several days went by and he called me again. "Come up here and let's talk about that job." So I went up to his office and he said, "I really want you to take that assistant secretary's job."

I replied, "Rogers, I'll do anything for you." But again I reiterated, "If you're asking me my 'druthers,' I'd 'druther' stay where I am. If you're ordering me to take it, I'll accept it."

"No," he said, "I'm not going to order you to take it. The White House wants me to appoint a Californian and I don't want him. Do you know any young Republican that might fill that job?"

I said, "I think that I might know two or three; the one I know best is a young fellow I've been working with for several years in Florida. He is an assistant to the governor. His name is Nat Reed. His father developed Hobe Sound in Florida. His mother is a Pryor from St. Louis. They are an extremely fine, wealthy, Republican family."

He said, "I don't know Nat Reed."

"Well," I said, "you're going down to Florida to the Everglades this weekend, why don't I call Joe Brown who is my state director down there and who is going to be your escort, and have him invite Nat Reed to join you on that trip to the Everglades?"

"Why don't you do that," he said.

Rogers Morton made the trip and Nat Reed joined him. When Rogers returned he called me to ask, "You get along with him alright?"

I said, "I've gotten along with him perfectly fine."

"Well," he said, "He's my man." So Nat Reed was appointed assistant secretary for Fish, Wildlife and Parks to replace Dr. Glasgow who had been purged along with Hickel.

XIV

LBJ

After President Johnson left office in January, 1969, and returned to his Texas ranch, he took a great interest in seeing that the LBJ National Historic Site was established. Legislation had been introduced into the Congress to authorize the site on his ranch along the Pedernales River. He and Mrs. Johnson were going to donate the property, reserving a life estate. At the same time this legislation was pending there were also bills to enlarge the area of the Eisenhower Farm in Gettysburg and to establish the President Taft National Historic Site in Ohio.

I was concerned that the LBJ bill might get sidetracked in light of the opposition that he had encountered near the end of his presidency. I discussed the matter with Wayne Aspinall, the chairman of the House Interior and Insular Affairs Committee, and he agreed. He suggested that he handle the bills as a package. They would all be considered at the same time and add mutual support to each other.

After this agreement was reached, I received a call early one morning from President Johnson. He wanted to know what the progress was on the LBJ legislation. I told him that it was going to be marked up shortly in the subcommittee and that it was going to pass. He asked, "How do you know that?"

I said, "Well, Mr. President, I have talked with every member of the subcommittee and every one of them is going to vote for it. Moreover, Wayne Aspinall and I have an agreement that your bill, the Taft Bill and the Eisenhower Bill are going to be handled at the same time as a package."

He said, "I'll be damned; I wish I had known you when I was president," and hung up. I accepted this as a real compliment.

A few days later I was on the Hill visiting with Wayne Aspinall, and he said to me, "I understand you talked with President Johnson the other day."

I said, "Yes, sir, I did. He was inquiring about his bill, and he seemed to be pleased with the progress."

"Well," he said, "immediately after he talked with you, he called me."

I commented, "That's interesting, why?"

Wayne said the president started the conversation, "I'm sure you know this guy Hartzog." Wayne said he allowed as how he did. The president then asked, "What kind of fella is he?" Wayne said he replied he's a pretty nice guy. The president asked, "Can you believe him?" And Wayne replied that he had found that he could always believe me. The president then said, "Well, he told me the damndest story this morning. He said that you and he have a deal to handle my bill, the Taft Bill, and the Eisenhower Bill all at the same time as a package, is that right?" Wayne said that this was right. To which the president responded, "I'll be damned," and hung up.

In considering the proposal to establish a National Historic Site on his ranch, President Johnson was very much interested to know how President Eisenhower had handled his farm. So he and Mrs. Johnson arranged for a visit with Mrs. Eisenhower at Gettysburg. On the way, they stopped in Charlottesville, Virginia, to visit their daughter Linda and Chuck Robb. Chuck was then in law school at the University of Virginia. It was during this visit that President Johnson suffered his second heart attack and we had to cancel out the Eisenhower trip.

Several days after his hospitalization, I received a call from Mrs. Johnson asking me if I could come down to Charlottesville and visit with the president to discuss the area to be included within the National Historic Site. I was pleased to do so. I gathered up my maps and went to Charlottesville.

At the hospital, I was warmly greeted by Mrs. Johnson, and promptly ushered into the president's room. He was wired up with every kind of gadget you can imagine with a doctor standing beside him at the head of the bed.

I had brought along an easel for the map so that the president could see it while still lying in bed. I put the map mounted on a board on the easel and started to explain the proposed boundaries to him whereupon he said, "Give me that map." I took it off the easel and handed it to him. He propped the map up on the top of his stomach and asked for a pencil. I gave him one and he started drawing on the map. "You can't have this, but what you really ought to have is this. You ought to include this over here which your people haven't done," and he continued to revise the map. In a few minutes, Mrs. Johnson came back into the room to say, "Lyndon, Billy Graham is outside waiting to see you." He responded, "Tell, him to wait. I'll be through here in a few minutes," and he continued to draw the boundaries that he wanted on the historic site, explaining why he had made each change.

When he finished, I said to him, "Mr. President, this is probably the only national park in the system that will have been planned by a president. Since this is now your plan, why don't you initial it." And he did.

During the time we were studying the LBJ Historic Site, the president and Mrs. Johnson invited Helen and me, on two or three occasions, down to the ranch. On our last visit there, he had started smoking cigarettes again. One afternoon he decided to take us for a tour of the ranch in his famous white

Lincoln Continental. The secret service were following in a station wagon. The president drove over the ranch roads and sometimes over the open pasture. Obviously, he loved the land a great deal. We had been out for about a half an hour, when he said to me, "George, would you like a drink?"

I said, "Well, I would, Mr. President if you would like one."

He said, "Yeah, I think it's time for one," it now being around five o'clock in the afternoon. He stopped his car. A secret service agent came up to it, and the president ordered drinks for us. With drinks in hand, he proceeded on down the road. He had not gone very far, when he realized that he had smoked his last cigarette, and he said to me, "George, you smoke?" I said, "Yes, sir."

"You have any cigarettes?"

"Yes, sir," and with that I reached in my pocket and took out a new pack of Parliaments, opened them and passed them up to him. He took one out, lit it and threw the pack up on the dash board.

"You don't smoke much, do you."

"Well, Mr. President, Helen thinks that I smoke too much."

"Well," he said, "I don't know why she should worry, there ain't any damn tobacco in these things."

When President and Mrs. Eisenhower donated their farm at Gettysburg to be a part of the Gettysburg National Military Park, I suggested to their attorney that it might be wise for them to reserve a life estate. He reported back that they did not wish to do so, since Mrs. Eisenhower did not expect to live there after the general passed away.

Shortly after the general's death, her attorney called me and asked for a meeting. Mrs. Eisenhower had changed her mind and now wished to remain on the property. We worked out a special use permit which allowed her to stay there. It was not clear to me at the time, however, what brought about this dramatic change in her attitude. When visiting with President Johnson at the ranch he told me this story: apparently, the reason the life estate had not been reserved was that Mrs. Eisenhower was afraid to stay in the house all alone. When this word reached President Johnson, he decided that something should be done about it. After consultation with the Congress, he authorized secret service protection to be continued for her. It was at that point she then decided she would like to stay on at the farm after the general's death.

I will never forget the last party Helen and I attended at the White House while LBJ was president. Mel Grovesnor and I were standing behind the president while he was chatting with a small group of guests. Observing the president's broad, muscular back, his weaving head and waving hand— for whether engaged in conversation or making a speech his whole, huge frame was involved—Mel remarked: "George, an era is passing. It will be a long time before we have another one as big in size or vision." As I came to know the president after he returned to his beloved ranch, I often reflected on Mel's comment—and still do. I agree.

XV

A HERITAGE ENRICHED

The park philanthropy of the Rockefellers is legendary. Three generations of this family have supported park and conservation programs at all levels of government.

John D. Rockefeller, Jr. gave the nation Acadia National Park. He contributed critically needed funds to match those of Tennessee for the acquisition of Great Smoky Mountains National Park. His son, Laurance Rockefeller donated the Virgin Islands National Park. Father and son have given tens of thousands of acres for Grand Teton National Park.

In countless other ways through gifts of money and artifacts they have supported the land acquisition, museum and interpretive programs at a long list of national parks.

Laurance inaugurated the program of the National Park Foundation in 1968 with a grant of one million dollars in "seed money."

Not so well known is the park philanthropy of the Mellon family. Paul Mellon and his father are renowned for their gift to the United States of its world class National Gallery of Art and many priceless art treasures. The Mellons have been devoted to the National Park System, as well. They joined with North Carolina in acquiring Cape Hatteras National Seashore, America's first national seashore. They financed the

National Seashore Study which sparked action to save the remainder of the nation's undeveloped seashores, most of which were authorized and acquired in the 1960s and '70s. Mrs. Mellon established the Rose Garden at the White House and redesigned and landscaped Lafayette Park in front of the White House.

Early in March of 1970, I received a telephone call from the secretary of Paul Mellon telling me that Mr. Mellon would like to have me for lunch at his home in Washington on March 17, which is my birthday. She did not know the purpose of the luncheon but I accepted with pleasure.

During the week or so until the luncheon I reviewed the gifts of the Mellons to the National Park System wondering what project he may be interested in discussing. I was not prepared for the magnificent birthday surprise that awaited me.

On March 17 I arrived a few minutes before twelve, and was shown into the drawing room by the butler, who offered me a glass of sherry, which I declined. A few minutes later, a distinguished looking gentleman, gray hair, ruddy cheeks, his whole bearing and demeanor exuding success, entered the room. I arose to meet him and he introduced himself as Stoddard Stevens, Mr. Mellon's lawyer. The butler returned immediately with two glasses of sherry for Mr. Stevens and me. In a few minutes Mr. Mellon arrived and was served a glass of sherry. The three of us proceeded into the dining room. Seated for luncheon, we made small talk still giving me no idea of the purpose of the luncheon. During this conversation I learned that Mr. Stevens was a senior partner in the law firm of Sullivan and Cromwell in New York, and also a trustee of the National Gallery of Art. Mr. Mellon was chairman of the board of trustees of the National Gallery. A few minutes into luncheon Mr. Stevens turned the conversation abruptly, by saying to me, "How would you like to have Cumberland Island?"

I was floored by his question, but I immediately responded, "I can't think of anything in the world I would rather have than Cumberland Island." Cumberland Island is, perhaps, the most magnificent of all the off-shore islands along the coast of the Southeastern part of the United States.

Decades ago, it was acquired by Andrew Carnegie, who kept it in its natural condition during his lifetime, except for agricultural pursuits. It was inherited by his five children who could never agree how to divide the island among themselves. The point of disagreement involved alleged mineral values in commercial quantities in one-half of the island. The matter dragged through the courts for years. Some of the children had died and their children had succeeded to their parent's portion of the inheritance. It was rapidly becoming an extremely complex partition suit. Finally, the court settled on an ingenious solution.

It divided the island in half, a northern half and a southern half, and the Judge divided each half into five parts, and each group of heirs, by lot, got a northern fifth and a southern fifth of the island.

Immediately after the partition, one group of heirs sold their fifth to Charles Fraser, the developer of Hilton Head Island. Fraser is a sensitive, talented entrepeneur, who had done some extremely fine development on Hilton Head. The National Park Service, however, had been particularly eager to prevent the development of Cumberland Island. We had explored several approaches to preserving it. In the absence of legislation authorizing the expenditure of federal money, however, we had had no success. Thus, this offer from Stoddard Stevens was welcome news.

He continued. "Assuming that you can agree to the conditions that we would like to discuss with you, Mr. Mellon is prepared to buy the island and give it to the National Park Service." The conditions were that the National Park Service would assign a land acquisition officer to negotiate for the property; Charles Fraser's property would be acquired first to forestall development; each purchase contract would have to be reviewed by Mr. Stevens and, if approved, the purchase price would be paid by Mr. Mellon; and that title must be taken in the name of a tax-exempt organization which would, in turn, donate the land to the United States when the Congress authorized the acquisition of the island.

We had the perfect instrument in the congressionally chartered National Park Foundation. The foundation was chartered by the Congress to accept gifts for the benefit of the programs of the National Park Service. The Congress had authorized the park service to utilize the services of federal employees in carrying out the work of the foundation.

I laid this suggestion before Messrs. Mellon and Stevens and they thought it was an ideal approach.

During our discussion, it was obvious that Mr. Stevens knew a great deal about Cumberland Island, but I did not know how he came by this extensive knowledge. When I returned to the office after lunch, I called my friend, Alfred (Bill) Jones at Sea Island, Georgia to tell him the good news. Bill and Kitt Jones, owners and developers of Sea Island, were great friends of the National Park Service. Bill Jones had devoted a lot of time and money to the development of Fort Fredericka, which is on the adjacent island of St. Simon. Bill was delighted and he told me how Stoddard Stevens knew so much about Cumberland Island.

Mr. and Mrs. Stoddard Stevens vacationed each February at Sea Island. Over the years they had become close friends of Bill and Kitt Jones. When Cumberland Island had been divided and Charles Fraser had acquired one-fifth of it, it was obvious to Bill that the island would now be developed. Charles Fraser had started development immediately by building an air strip and a caretaker's house on the island. Concerned that we were faced with the last opportunity to save the island, Bill had suggested to Stoddard Stevens in February of 1970 during his visit to Sea Island, that he would like to take him for a picnic and a drive on Cumberland Island. Mr. Stevens agreed and Bill made arrangements with Lucy Ferguson, one of the Carnegie daughters who still lived and farmed on the island, to provide them with a jeep so that they might see the island. There is a dirt road the full length of the island (fortified with seashells through the muddy lowlands). Except for this utility road, there was no significant development. Stoddard Stevens was so impressed with the beauty and magnificence of the island, that upon his return to New York he told Mr. Mellon of the danger it faced, prompting the call to me for lunch.

Mr. Mellon provided over $7½ million to acquire approximately seventy-five percent of the island before the Congress passed legislation to authorize the acquisition of the remainder with federal funds.

My good fortune in obtaining a performing arts park for the National Park System was just as unexpected as Cumberland Island. Secretary Udall called me to his office where a meeting was underway with Catherine Filene Shouse and her attorney. Mrs. Shouse, department store heiress and Washington arts patron, had just offered the secretary more than 100 acres of her Wolf Trap Farm in nearby Fairfax County, Virginia, as a park for the performing arts. She offered to donate more than $3 million to construct a performing arts facility, later named Filene Center. Her offers were accepted enthusiastically. The Congress concurred and on October 15, 1966, authorized the first national park for the performing arts. Wolf Trap Farm Park for the Performing Arts has been a huge success.

Saugus Iron Works National Historic Site (Massachusetts), authorized by the Congress on April 5, 1968, was another major donation to the National Park System. Donated by the First Iron Works Association, Inc., Saugus is a reconstruction of the first integrated ironworks in North America. It includes the ironworks, furnace, forge, and rolling and slitting mill, an important reminder of the beginning of the industrial revolution in the United States.

For more than one hundred years, tens of thousands of Americans have contributed to their national parks. With gifts of money, art and antiques from hundreds of donors, the elegance of the White House has been restored as the enduring symbol of the continuity of our democracy.

Park philanthropy has added lands, buildings and programs in dozens of national parks. But park philanthropy is more than money and materials; it is devoted men, women and children contributing, selflessly, of their time and talents. Their genius, creativity and downright hard work enrich the park experience of every visitor.

Hopefully, this tradition of park philanthropy will remain as enduring as the National Park System itself.

XVI

ALASKA

Late one afternoon I entered the "C" Street corridor, first floor of the Old Senate Office building (now the Russell building) to keep an appointment with Senator Alan Bible, a man who, more than any other in the Congress, held the keys to "life and death" for the National Park System. After a few steps into the dimly-lighted, block long corridor, I noticed that he turned the corner at the other end. As we approached each other, first, I could see his lips moving, but hear no sound. In a shuffling gait, the result of a muscular difficulty which induced his retirement from the Senate we approached each other in the deserted hall. As we neared, I could hear him saying, "I ain't a gonna do it, I ain't a gonna do it."

Within a few steps, I said, "Mr. Chairman, what ain't you gonna do?"

"I ain't a gonna make the whole United States a national park—not even for you."

Bible was the senior Senator from Nevada, the chairman of the National Parks Subcommittee of the Interior and Insular Affairs Committee and the chairman of the Subcommittee on Interior and Related Agencies of the Senate Appropriations Committee. I could run from him, but I could not hide because he controlled all of the legislation for the National Park System and all of its appropriations to implement such legislation.

Senator Bible was a modest, reserved man; he was no glad hander but was a cautious, thorough lawyer. Alan did everything well. He fished well, he presided well, he campaigned well, he represented his state and his nation with distinction. He and his bride, Loucille, were warm friends and delightful companions. Our relationship was such that on December 28, 1970, I was comfortable in sending him the following bill which had been given to me by the staff at our annual Christmas party:

A BILL

To facilitate the Expansion and Administration of the National Park System, and for other purposes.

Be it enacted by the Senate and House of Representatives of the United States of America in Congress assembled, That, within the National Park System, as now or as hereafter constituted, everything is hereby authorized.

Sec. 2. The Director of the National Park Service is hereby authorized to establish such units of the National Park System as he deems necessary: *Provided,* That no such units shall be established in any foreign country until prior consultation with the Secretary of State, or on the moon without prior consultation with the Administrator of N.A.S.A.: *Provided further,* That interpretive moon rockets shall be provided in accordance with the Concession Policy Act of 1965.

Sec. 3. All functions and duties of the Forest Service of the Department of Agriculture are hereby transferred to the Director of the National Park Service.

Sec. 4. The Corps of Engineers of the United States Army shall damn well do what the Director of the National Park Service tells them to.

Sec. 5. The Bureau of Land Management better watch its step.

Sec. 6. The National Park Service is hereby admitted to the Union as a Sovereign State, and the incumbent Director

thereof shall be the Representative and both Senators there-
from.

Sec. 7. The Director of the National Park Service is hereby
authorized to sign United States Government checks for any
amount he deems proper.

Long before the National Park Service was established,
many scientists and conservationists were studying the in-
credible rich storehouse of natural and cultural treasures of
Alaska. After numerous studies, surveys and reports, only
four Alaskan areas had been included in the National Park
System by 1964: Mount McKinley National Park (1917) and
Sitka (1910), Katmai (1918) and Glacier Bay (1925) National
Monuments.

With the blessing of the secretary, Stewart Udall, I had a
simple credo for expanding the National Park System: take it
now, warts and all. In other words, don't let boundaries and
adverse uses delay the process. If you try to solve all the
problems you may never get the park. Alaska was ripe for
the taking.

In 1964 I appointed a task force to evaluate the studies
that had been made, review the remaining park possibilities
available and prepare a blue print for a national park program in Alaska.

The task force consisted of Sigurd Olson, George Collins,
chairman, Doris Leonard, Robert Luntey and John Kauffmann. Sig Olson was a member of the secretary's Advisory
Board on National Parks, a distinguished scholar and author
and the chairman of the Wilderness Society. George Collins
had retired from a distinguished career in the National Park
Service and was a real authority on Alaska. Doris Leonard
was an intelligent, enthusiastic conservationist. Her husband, Dick Leonard, a distinguished San Francisco attorney,
for many years had been the president of the Sierra Club.
Bob Luntey, a landscape architect, and John Kauffmann, a
writer/editor, were active National Park Service employees.
Their landmark report—OPERATION GREAT LAND—be-

came the cornerstone of all of our subsequent studies in Alaska. The completion of the report in January, 1965, was fortuitous; in 1965, Dr. Melville Bell Grosvenor, editor of the National Geographic Journal had been elected by his colleagues as chairman of the Advisory Board on National Parks.

The Historic Sites Act of August 21, 1935, established the Advisory Board on National Parks, Historic Sites, Buildings and Monuments. The board had a strong influence on the development and management of the National Park System. It not only advised the secretary of the interior and the director of the National Park Service on policy, but it evaluated new areas proposed for addition to the system. Its eleven members served staggered terms of six years. From its inception to the advent of the Nixon regime, the membership of the board consisted of nationally and internationally recognized authorities in the fields of history, natural history, architecture, archeology, anthropology, journalism, publishing, other scholarly pursuits and business. Its illustrious chairmen have included, among others, Dr. Waldo Leland, Alfred A. Knopf, Frank Masland, Jr., Dr. Wallace E. Stegner, Nathaniel Owings, Dr. Stanley Cain and Dr. Emil Haury. The views of this prestigious board were always sought and considered by the Congress.

The patina of distinction covering the board which had been so carefully tended by each successive administration since its establishment in 1936 began to be washed away by Nixon's White House minions. One of their early appointees startled some of us at a reception one evening when, standing up drunk, he inquired of one board member, "How much did you pay for your seat?" Without shame he continued to prattle that he had paid $125,000 for his. It remained, however, for the ineffable James Watt to administer the coup de grace to whatever little distinction remained of the board. Some of his appointments scaled new heights of contempt for the "green weenies"—a term derisively applied by his compatriots to the leadership of the citizen led environmental organizations.

It is true, however, that there is a silver lining to every cloud. Watt's reign of environmental terror electrified and reinvigorated the environmental movement, thus insuring its survival as a continuing vital, vigilant force on the national political scene. He was, without question, the most successful spur to increased membership ever to serve the citizen conservation organizations. Their memberships skyrocketed while he was secretary of the interior.

During my tenure as director, the advisory board scheduled an annual field trip to inspect existing parks and to evaluate proposed areas. To facilitate communication between the board and the parks subcommittees of the House and Senate, I always invited the subcommittee members to join the board on its field trips.

Mel Grosvenor, his father, Dr. Gilbert Hovey Grosvenor and the National Geographic Society had long had an interest in Alaska. The Society had a strategic role in the preservation of the Valley of Ten Thousand Smokes in Katmai National Monument. Mel was overjoyed at the opportunity to take the board to Alaska in 1965 on its annual field trip. We were fortunate, also, when three members of the House National Parks Subcommittee, the chairman (Ralph Rivers of Alaska), the ranking majority member (Roy Taylor of North Carolina), and the ranking minority member (Joe Skubitz of Kansas) accepted our invitation to accompany the board. By rail, air and automotive transport they saw vast areas of the state and especially, many of the areas identified by the Alaska Task Force in its January report. In Fairbanks, Anchorage, Juneau and native villages along the way, the board had an opportunity to visit with civic leaders and public officials. Ralph Rivers, traveling with us, opened many doors. This trip gave great encouragement and impetus to the work of the staff then being assembled in Alaska by assistant director Theodor Swem for our great push forward.

And we had our lighter moments. Mel Grosvenor and I went fishing in Grosvenor Lake—named for his father—in Katmai. Normally a great fishery, try as hard as we could even with the ranger helping out we were skunked. Quite a distance from shore as the day was winding down, we decided to call it off. The ranger and I packed up our gear, deciding to let Mel drag his lure home. Slowly the ranger began to troll home. About a hundred yards from shore, Mel, yelled, "Stop, I'm hung up." The ranger cut the throttle, looked back to check the snag only to see Mel's line paying out as something was leaving for parts unknown. With a timely assist from the ranger, Mel reeled in a three-pound trout. Only a fish at the end of a line can turn a grown man into a little boy again!

During our visit to Glacier Bay we took a boat ride to the face of Muir Glacier to watch the great blocks of ice break away and plunge into the bay sending flumes of water hundreds of feet in the air. It is a spectacular show but one that must be watched from a distance lest the undertow created by these giant falling icebergs take the vessel down with the ice. On our return to dock, we stopped in the lake for a picnic lunch. All the party was assembled on the stern, except Mel. About the time I missed him one of the rangers came aft and whispered too loudly—for Mrs. Grosvenor heard it also—that Dr. Grosvenor was on an iceberg.

Icebergs can be unstable and survival in the frigid waters of the bay is problematical.

I rushed to the front of the boat followed closely by Dr. Grosvenor's bride, Ann. I was not prepared for the scene; the starboard side of the boat was rocking gently alongside an iceberg. Atop the iceberg was Dr. Grosvenor, inching along as though in search of something I had not yet spotted, wisps of gray hair blowing in the breeze. In a startled voice I would never have dreamed possible, I yelled, "What in hell are you doing over there?"

Calmly, without even looking at me, he said, "Getting a rock." About three feet in front of him on top of the iceberg was a black rock about the size of a football.

Ann, with fright in her voice, immediately ordered him back to the boat. She was less successful than I—he did not even respond to her.

I could see the headlines, "Director of NPS drowns National Geographic Chief."

But he had retrieved his stone, gingerly made his way back to the boat, handed me the rock and clambored aboard.

Upon his return to Washington he had it sliced up and sent each member of the party a slice with a note on back:

Slice of ice-rafted rock, rescued from oblivion by Mel Grosvenor in Glacier Bay, during Advisory Board visit to Alaska, July-Aug., 1965. Rock type: Schist. Cut by: Ariz. Bur. of Mines Culprit: Emil W. Haury.

Dr. Haury is a noted archeologist, former head of the Department of Archeology and Anthropology at the University of Arizona, Tuscon, and, in 1965, was a member of the Advisory Board on National Parks.

Brooks Camp, where the group stayed in Katmai, is located on the bank of the Brooks River, a great trout fishery and a spawning stream for salmon. Ralph Rivers decided that he wanted to introduce his lower-48 congressional friends to the cherished experience of Alaska fishing. One morning during our stay, shortly after daybreak, one of the rangers and I, accompanied by the National Geographic's chief photographer, Tony Stewart, set out along the bear trail through the grass for up-river fishing. First, we staked out the chairman, Ralph Rivers; further up, but out of sight, we posted Roy Taylor. Moving on up the river, we selected a spot for Joe Skubitz on a little point jutting out onto the stream. Tony Stewart lagged behind us photographing the congressman and the river. When we had posted Joe Skubitz, the ranger said to me, "One of my favorite spots is on up the river, a half mile or so." We set out for it.

The spot he had identified was screened from the bear trail by low brush along the river bank. I attached a fly to the rod. It was a once in a lifetime moment: air clear and crisp in the early dawn, the river rippling gently by. As the ranger parted the brush I had a clear view of the hole; to our complete surprise we had just intruded on three brown bears fishing in the same hole. I was ready to retreat quietly and unobtrusively as we had arrived. "No," counseled the ranger, "all we have to do is start clapping our hands and yelling and they will leave." Deferring to his superior knowledge I put down the fishing rod and joined with him in clapping and yelling. Sure enough the three bears began sloshing a retreat to the other side of the river. Just before arriving at the other shore, however, one decided he would return to our side of the river, but further downstream. His initial route indicated he would come ashore about where we had left off Congressman Joe Skubitz.

To have a brown Kodiak bear confront the congressman from the plains of Kansas was not my idea of how to improve my congressional relations. The ranger and I took off in a dead run to Skubitz, clapping our hands and yelling like maniacs. When we arrived at his station, Joe had not seen the bear. We then headed for Roy Taylor, more slowly because we didn't know whether the bear had come ashore or was still in the river. In a moment or two, dead ahead in the trail we saw the bear grass waving back and forth. "He's on the trail, headed our way," said the ranger. No sooner had he spoken, than we observed the grass moving in the opposite direction. The bear either had spotted us or scented us and turned around going ahead of us downriver. In the meantime, unbeknownst to us, Tony had finished photographing Roy Taylor and was proceeding upriver to Skubitz. It was inevitable that Tony and the bear would meet. We could not warn Tony for we didn't know where he was. The huge bear reared up on its hind legs in the trail shortly ahead of him. It scared the liver out of him. As soon as we spotted the up-raised bear, we began to clap our hands, and the bear dropped down on his front feet and ran off through the grass away from the river. We met a very shaken photographer.

I had had enough for one morning and continued on to the camp where the group was having breakfast.

I related the experiences of the morning to Mel. He grew more excited by the minute, exclaiming, "Oh, boy, Tony must have gotten some great pictures." Shortly, Tony and the rest of the fishermen arrived. Mel, said excitedly, "Gee, Tony, George told me about the bear. You must have some wonderful pictures."

Glumly, Tony responded, "No, not a one." Incredulously, Mel inquired why.

"Because I was too scared," Tony replied as he dug into his breakfast.

For several years after this watershed trip by the board, the Alaska land issues, state selections/native claims/federal reservations, steamed and blurped like a Yellowstone mudpot. The day of decision was rapidly approaching, however, when the House began serious work in 1969 on the legislation that, finally, became the Alaska Native Claims Settlement Act of December 18, 1971 (PL 92–203).

We all realized that this would be the last opportunity to preserve additional areas worthy of inclusion in the National Park System in Alaska. The OPERATION GREAT LAND task force report had developed proposals totalling approximately seventy-six million acres. John Saylor of Pennsylvania (then the ranking minority member of the House Interior and Insular Affairs Committee) and Congressman Morris Udall, Democrat of Arizona, also a committee member, were leading the support in the Congress for reserving these and other lands from selection by either the natives or the state of Alaska. This provision was lost in the House.

John Saylor called to inform me that our last opportunity would be in the Senate.

I immediately called Senator Scoop Jackson who was the chairman of the Senate Interior and Insular Affairs Committee and asked for an appointment. He was a powerful, creative leader for park preservation. His countless contributions have enshrined his memory forever in the annals of distinguished public service.

Senator Jackson listened to my presentation carefully, and said, "Of course, I am interested and I am willing to support the proposal. However, I have agreed that Alan Bible is going to have the principal responsibility for that legislation, so you need to talk to him."

I got my appointment with Senator Bible and explained what I had in mind. He said to me, "I have never been in Alaska. I don't know whether what you want to do up there is worthwhile or not. I'm going to be guided primarily by what the two Alaska senators tell me."

I knew that the two Alaska senators were not going to be very receptive to my expansive proposals. So I said to him, "Mr. Chairman, if you've never been to Alaska, why don't you come with me this summer?"

"No," he said, "I have my vacation plans. I'm going to take my vacation with my former law partner, Bob McDonald, and my lifelong friend, Dr. Fred Anderson. We are going to take our wives on a very leisurely vacation which we have not done for years."

"Senator," I said, "Alaska is one of the greatest places in the world to take that kind of vacation. If you'll just get them there, I'll see that every arrangement is made to show you Alaska. You will have a trip such as none of you has had anywhere."

"Well," he said, "I'll have to think about that and talk with them."

I left and was on pins and needles for ten days awaiting his decision. Finally, he called and said, "Yes, we'll go to Alaska."

We made the arrangements. Peggy and Ed Wayburn of the Sierra Club from San Francisco joined us for a portion of the trip sharing with the Bible party their extensive knowledge of the Alaska parklands. Celia Hunter and Ginnie Woods, owners and operators of Camp Donali, stirred us all with their vision and enthusiasm for the opportunities and challenges available in preserving vignettes of America's last frontier. With Vida Bartlett, widow of Alaska's beloved Senator Bob Bartlett, we renewed old friendships and received invaluable guidance to Alaska's political structure. Regional Director John Rutter and his intrepid crew organized the itinerary for a "show me" trip such as none of us ever had experienced. By air, rail, boat and bus, we took the party all over the state to look at all of our major proposals. Senator Bible and his friends were tremendously impressed.

At Glacier Bay National Monument, the Bible party caught a goodly number of salmon. We decided as a special treat, one of the park staff would smoke them and ship them to the party when they returned home.

One day I received a telephone call from an upset Superintendent. Just before the smoking was completed, bears broke into the smokehouse and feasted on Senator Bible's salmon. "Don't worry," I said, "just start fishing."

Near the windup of our trip in Alaska, Senator Bible and I decided that while we were there, it would only be appropriate to have the Fish and Wildlife Service and the forest service people meet with him and review what, if any, deficiencies there existed in their programs so that he could take care of them in the legislation. I arranged a coffee for their meeting with Senator Bible. Their plea was for some limited additional acreage to round out some of their units.

We had agreed that after the trip to Alaska, Helen and I would go back and visit with the Bibles at their home at Lake Tahoe. We had a joyous few days together. During that time he told me to give him some draft language to accomplish what I wanted to do in Alaska and he would insert it in the bill. That provision became Section 17(d)(2) of the Native Claims Act. It reserved eighty million acres to be identified by the secretary and withheld from selection by the natives and the state of Alaska. Senator Bible had increased my proposal by four million acres to accommodate the discussions we had in Alaska with the Fish and Wildlife Service and forest service people.

The act gave the secretary two years within which to make recommendations for apportioning the eighty million acres among the National Park Service, the U.S. Forest Service and the Fish and Wildlife Service and provided that Congress would have five years thereafter to pass the needed legislation.

Section 17(d)(1) of the act also authorized the secretary to withdraw additional lands until they could be studied and classified. His authority to protect the interests of all groups was not confined to 17(d)(2).

As the study group began to formulate its withdrawal proposals for consideration by the secretary, the special interest groups—the commercial hunters, the diggers and the cutters—zeroed in on Section 17(d)(2) and began to apply the heat to put much of the land into the forest system and the Fish and Wildlife Refuge System. It would be easier for them to get at it there in the future. My judgment was that their arguments, no matter how specious were falling on receptive ears in the study group. Finally, in frustration at the turn of events, on March 6, 1972, I wrote Rogers Morton a personal letter, saying:

> You will recall our conversation on the Native Claims Bill, following the trip Tom Flynn and I made to Alaska with Chairman Bible. After counseling with you, I provided Senator Bible with a draft of language which became Section 17(d)(2)(A) of that historic legislation.
>
> The purpose of that language...was to provide you the tool to reserve for a brief moment the discretionary authority of the administration and the Congress to protect, in perpetuity, 80,000,000 acres of the best of America's last frontier for this and future generations.
>
> ...for the most part, we have preserved our heritage—both natural and cultural—as residual values. In Alaska, we have the opportunity to reorder this priority.
>
> Shall we interpret the law to reserve the option to the people—through their Congress—to choose a "legacy" or an economic gain? Shall we strike boldly the anvil that must forge a

new "environmental ethic" for this age if we are to survive as a society? Rhetoric, yes! But real issues.

The reservation of 80,000,000 acres under 17(d)(2)(A) that possess *prima facie* value as pristine heritage lands, preserves the public's option to decide these issues...

...yours is the last clear chance to serve this enormous public interest.

On December 17, 1973, Morton made the administration's recommendations to the Congress. Overall, the proposals involved 83,470,000 acres—80,000,000 acres of (d)(2) lands and 3,470,000 acres from (d)(1) lands. Allocations were as follows:

National Park System	32,600,000 acres
National Wildlife Refuge System	31,590,000 acres
National Forest System	18,800,000 acres

The balance of the acreage was for the Wild and Scenic Rivers System.

My worst fears in 1972 had been confirmed—the exploiters carried the day.

In a comprehensive history of the Alaska Lands Issues, National Park Service historian, G. Frank Williss chronicles the nine-year struggle. Of Morton's recommendations Williss has this to say:

"The proposed 5,500,000-acre Wrangell National Forest on the flanks of Wrangell-Saint Elias National Park seemed to National Park Service planners to be a particularly obscene arrangement, leaving as it did, a park consisting primarily of 'rock and ice.' Equally galling to Alaska planners was the failure to include a strong regional planning provision, something which most involved felt would be essential for the future of the Alaska parks, and loss of wilderness designation for Gates of the Arctic National Park."

Moreover, the recommendations allowed for continued sport hunting in the proposed new national park units. This was a gross perversion of existing public policy that had prohibited sport hunting in national parks for more than one hundred years.

All hell broke loose when these "obscene" proposals arrived at the Congress.

The citizen conservation groups (the Wilderness Society, National Audubon Society, Friends of the Earth and the Sierra Club) were outraged. The Sierra Club and the Wilderness Society had been urging that 119,600,000 of the (d) (2) and (d) (1) lands be reserved from selection and settlement. Of this total, they had proposed that 62,000,000 acres be included in the National Park System.

Congressman James Haley (Democrat of Florida)—no friend of national parks—who succeeded Wayne Aspinall as Chairman of the House Interior and Insular Affairs Committee, introduced legislation incorporating the administration proposals.

Senator Jackson introduced legislation to withdraw 106,094,000 acres of which 43,200,000 acres would be preserved in the National Parks System. Congressman Morris Udall introduced a similar bill in the House. Predictably, Congressman Don Young and Senator Ted Stevens (both of Alaska) introduced legislation to withdraw 66,800,000 acres predominantly for multiple-use purposes—only 14,020,000 acres were proposed for the National Park System.

Numerous other bills were introduced by many members of Congress.

Not surprisingly, the Nixon/Ford administrations demonstrated only tepid interest in resolving the complex issues. Nixon had never shown any particular interest in national parks; Ford made much of the fact that he had been a seasonal park ranger at Yellowstone National Park, but I could never get any real help from him on our park legislation when he was a congressman. Just before he was defeated by Jimmy Carter, his long suppressed park interest was revived. Historian William C. Everhart, author of a history of the National Park Service tells the remarkable story:

XVI. Alaska

In the late summer of 1976 President Jerry Ford's reelection bid was in trouble. According to the polls, he was losing ground steadily to candidate Jimmy Carter. On a day in early August, Assistant Secretary of the Interior Nat Reed paid a visit to the White House campaign staff. One of the few administration officials with credibility to the conservation community, Reed suggested that the President was overlooking the political attractiveness of the national parks. Just about everyone, Reed pointed out, was lamenting the state of the parks during the Bicentennial year. Much of the criticism was being leveled at the Nixon-Ford administration for failing to provide adequate support. In June the House Government Operations Committee had issued a report, *The Degradation of Our National Parks*, that had received widespread publicity.

Reed offered a proposal: pick an appropriate time and place for the President to make a dramatic announcement of a program to rehabilitate the entire national park system as a Bicentennial gift to the nation. There was a flaw, Reed granted. This would constitute a rather abrupt reversal of the Nixon-Ford policy of cutting back on park funding; in both budgets Ford had submitted to Congress, he had asked for substantially less money than the Park Service had requested. And with the election only a few months off, the Democrats would assuredly accuse the President of playing politics with the parks. Still, the White House campaign experts judged, the program sounded like a surefire vote getter; Reed was asked to have the Park Service put the package together.

On August 29 Jerry Ford "returned home" to Yellowstone, where he had served as a park ranger during the summer of 1936. From a platform erected in front of Old Faithful (which performed on schedule at the climax of his speech), he called upon Congress to appropriate $2.5 billion for land acquisition, maintenance and rehabilitation of facilities, and increased staffing for the national parks and wildlife refuges. As Nat Reed had predicted, the Democrats fired back. An "election year flip-flop," charged Jimmy Carter. After being subjected to embarrassing questioning by the Senate Interior Committee, Interior Secretary Thomas Kleppe argued, with little effect, "The time frame makes it look like political hypocrisy, but I deny that."

While grateful for Ford's election-time conversion, Park Service people figured he did well to get through his speech with a straight face, considering that on several recent occasions he had refused to allow the Service to use the funds or fill the positions already provided by Congress. To hear him tell it, Ford had never forgotten that glorious season he had spent in Yellowstone forty years before, but in the memory of the oldest Park Service graybeard he had never turned a hand to help the parks during his entire career in the House of Representatives. Ford's ploy failed to turn his campaign around, but the parks profited despite his defeat: President Jimmy Carter endorsed the additional funding and Congress cooperated.

Lacking leadership by Nixon and Ford, the Congress let the Alaska proposals lie fallow from their submission to the Congress in 1973 until the end of Ford's term in January 1977. In the meantime, astounding and fortuitous change occured in the leadership of the House Interior and Insular Affairs Committee: Morris Udall of Arizona became committee chairman; John Seiberling (Ohio), scion of a tire fortune, was named as chairman of a Special Subcommittee on General Oversight and Alaska Lands; and, Seiberling chose Harry Crandell, formerly the Wilderness Society's director of Wilderness Reviews, to be his chief of staff.

On the first day of the 95th Congress, that convened in January, 1977, Udall, with seventy-five cosponsors, introduced legislation to withdraw and reserve 115,300,000 acres; 64,100,000 acres of the total would go to the National Park System. The bill would authorize the president to withdraw an additional 1,600,000 for inclusion in the Tongass and Chugach National Forests. A similar bill was introduced by Senator Jackson in the Senate. Moreover, both bills would prohibit sport hunting and mining in the proposed units of the National Park System. At last there was significant movement to add to the National Park System the substantial acreage I had proposed to Senator Bible when he incorporated the (d)(2) Amendment in the Alaska Native Claims Settlement Act of 1971.

These bills established the skirmish line for the last great park battle between the forces of today's greed and those that would preserve a heritage for future generations. The fight was protracted, arduous and brutal.

The 1971 Amendment (d)(2) had given the Congress five years within which to act after the administration submitted its recommendations for allocation of the reserved 80,000,000 acres. The recommendation had been submitted by Secretary Morton on December 18, 1973. That five-year period would expire with the adjournment of the 95th Congress at the end of 1978. Thereafter, if not otherwise protected, these reserved lands would become available for state selection and disposal. Delay became the handmaiden of the exploiters.

Both the House and Senate had passed legislation to allocate the (d)(2) lands. The bills differed in content; a conference committee of the two bodies struggled to resolve their differences as the deadline approached. Senator Mike Gravel (Alaska), obstinately and inexplicably, frustrated agreement with a series of demands unacceptable to the other Senate/House conferees. The state of Alaska sensing that Gravel would kill the legislation, which he did, on November 14, 1978, filed state selection applications for 41,000,000 acres, including 3,970,000 acres that had been reserved for proposed national parks and over 5,000,000 acres that had been reserved for proposed wildlife refuges.

Carter's secretary of the interior was Cecil D. Andrus, former governor of Idaho, with an established record of environmental leadership. He responded to Alaska's cynical action by withdrawing all of the (d)(2) lands and more under the general authority vested in him for the protection of the public lands. On November 16, 1978, Andrus withdrew from selection and settlement 110,750,000 acres pursuant to Section 204(e) of the Federal Land Policy and Management Act. President Carter, on December 1, 1978, utilized the authority of the 1906 Antiquities Act to establish seventeen national monuments in Alaska totalling 56,000,000 acres. Every president since 1906 had used the authority of this act to add new areas to the National Park System, usually in modest numbers and limited acreage. President Carter gave breathtaking new meaning to an old and reliable authority.

These brilliantly executed actions by Andrus and Carter had two salutary effects: first, they preserved the opportunity to renew the battle in the 96th Congress (1979–80), thus frustrating the sordid attempt of the exploiters to achieve victory in the quagmire of legislative delay; and secondly, it put the mark of Cain on them. If they hoped to achieve any of their aims they would have to return to the bargaining table in good faith.

Legislation similar to that considered by the 95th Congress was reintroduced in the 96th Congress when it convened in January, 1979. The renewed fighting had lost none of its intensity. Finally, as the 96th Congress was winding down at the end of 1980 a compromise was reached. On December 2, 1980, President Carter signed into law the Alaska National Interest Lands Conservation Act of 1980. That legislation added 43,600,000 acres to the National Park System; 53,720,000 acres to the National Wildlife System; 3,250,000 acres to the National Forest System; and created the Steese National Conservation Area and the White Mountains National Recreation Area (totalling 2,220,000 acres) to be administered by the Bureau of Land Management. The legislation preserved segments of 25 rivers in the Wild and Scenic Rivers System. Moreover, of the total reserved lands, 56,400,000 acres were designated as wilderness for addition to the National Wilderness System. Nobody was completely satisfied—but that is the nature of the legislative process. In asking the House to accept the final bill Morris Udall said, "Neither I nor those who support me consider this legislation to be a great victory for the cause." He was unduly harsh on himself and his valiant troops. They had achieved a significant victory best summarized by President Carter when he signed the bill. Carter said, "Never before have we seized the opportunity to preserve so much of America's natural and cultural heritage."

Many people rightfully can claim credit for the great treasures that have been preserved for all generations in Alaska, and quite properly they should get that credit for many hands were on the oars. But, the captains of the vessel that preserved the opportunity were Scoop Jackson and Alan Bible. Had it not been for them there would have been no work for the others in the years that followed the enactment of the Alaska Native Claims Settlement Act of 1971. This was vouched for in a letter to me of May 8, 1985 from three young lawyers, now in private practice in Washington. They were all assistants to Senator Jackson: Bill VanNess, formerly chief counsel of the Senate Interior and Insular Affairs Committee; Grenville Garside, formerly staff director of the committee; and Howard Feldman, formerly chief counsel of the Investigating Subcommittee of the Government Operations Committee which was headed by Senator Jackson. They wrote to me as follows:

> We equate you with the Redwoods, with the North Cascades and—though few know this—with being the architect of the Alaska National Interest Lands and Conservation Act. Together with Alan Bible and Scoop Jackson you wrote a chapter in the Park Service Book that reduces all other chapters—important as they are—to prologues and epilogues.

The great battle to establish the national parks in Alaska was over in 1980; but the war goes on.

The National Park Service is now embarked on preparing management plans for each of the new national parks. These plans will establish the administrative guidelines by which the parks are to be preserved. It is a contentious process fraught with many pitfalls in the seemingly endless debate over preservation vis-à-vis use.

Philip Shabecoff, writing an article in *The New York Times* titled "Alaskans are Deeply Divided on Federal Role in Land Use" reports:

> Among the more hotly argued issues are *use of fish and game* for subsistence, *access to parks* and preserves and the related issue of *tourist development*, the fate of *private property* on the protected lands, and *economic development, including mining and timbering*. (Emphasis supplied).

Other complaints noted by Shabecoff against the park service are its ban on commercial hunting in park wilderness and the use of off-road vehicles.

An oft-repeated shibboleth of park opponents is that Alaska is so different its resources must not be locked up in parks. Horse feathers! Substantially, the same argument has been advanced against every park carved from the public domain lands of the American West. This nation is not so impoverished (deficits and all) that it must consume the seed corn of our posterity.

From whom are the resources of the parks locked up? From the rape, ravish and run exploiter that would disrupt and destroy the biotic communities of life—yes. From the scientist, the photographer and those who would visit in harmony with the web of life of which we are all a part—no.

The park issues in Alaska are remarkably akin to those we have wrestled with for more than a hundred years in the lower 48: access, tourist development and the exploitive private interests (mining, logging, etc.) that would diminish the parks for all of the people.

To jeopardize, either for material gain or parochial, political expediency the unspoiled treasures that are America's national parks in Alaska would be an unpardonable obscenity.

Many of the problems now besetting our national parks in the lower 48 can be explained by lack of knowledge and understanding of the natural world about us and the urgency of building a new nation. No such rationale for exploitation exists in Alaska. As I wrote Morton in 1972, "For the most part, we have preserved our heritage—both natural and cultural—as residual values. In Alaska, we have the opportunity to reorder this priority."

Indeed we must.

XVII

WATER FOR THE
EVERGLADES

The Army Corps of Engineers is an anomaly among agencies of the federal government.

Every foot soldier whether in maneuvers or in battle has admired the remarkable achievements of its redoubtable combat engineers. Many of America's most distinguished military leaders first wore the gold bars as second lieutenants of engineers. Whether building or demolishing, the corps can do anything.

In addition to its role as a distinguished part of America's military might, it has domestic, civilian functions involving navigable rivers, harbors and flood control. The natural constituencies for these programs are the maritime industry, the barge operators, flood control districts and every local government and Chamber of Commerce that either has or aspires to have a harbor or waterway improvement to promote navigation. Many former officers of the Corps of Engineers find safe haven in retirement among these special interest groups.

In peacetime, a great deal of the energies of the able and

talented officers of the corps are devoted to these civilian pursuits of rivers, harbors and flood control. The slick and well executed lobbying of the corps in behalf of such public works projects makes it one of the single most powerful agencies in government. Its awesome power is derived from three little publicized sources: first, the lobbying might of the military establishment which coddles the Congress with every imaginable perk from medical attention for the sniffles to solo airplane junkets to South America; secondly, the well orchestrated grass roots lobbying of the network of special interest groups that climb aboard its annual pork barrel trains; and lastly, the favored financing of its wetland reclamation projects which masquerade as "flood control."

In 1902 the Congress established the Bureau of Reclamation to reclaim the arid lands of the West for productive purposes. The beneficiaries of its water projects must share in their cost, usually on a 50-50 basis with the federal government. On the other hand, if a Corps of Engineers's project involving wetlands can travel under the guise of flood control, the federal government picks up the tab for up to 100 percent of project costs. Is it any wonder, then, that the Bureau of Reclamation has now been eclipsed by the Army Corps of Engineers as the premier water management agency of the federal government? Nowhere is the perverseness of this public policy more evident than in South Florida.

Everglades National Park is located south of the Tamiami Trail. The trail, passing through the Miccosukee Indian Country, connects Miami on the East coast with Naples on the West coast of Florida.

The wonderland water environment of the park, supporting a variety of fish, alligators and small animals, is home to one of the world's greatest assortment of bird life. The park's estuaries are nursery grounds for the shrimp that flourish in the Gulf of Mexico. This fragile and delicate environment has been nourished and sustained for centuries by waters flowing down the River of Grass from Lake Okeechobee, north of the park. Much of the year, the park is covered by a slow-moving sheet of water. During this period an extraordinary mass and variety of plant and animal life is spawned to nourish one of the most diverse and largest food chains in the world.

To enhance the growing agricultural economy of South Florida, the south shores of Lake Okeechobee had been diked higher and higher over the years to restrain the waters of the lake.

A series of torrential rains breached the dikes, devastating man's agricultural intrusions and killing many people. Diking was proven to be an incomplete solution; the real answer was specially designed structures and devices to remove the water from its natural drainage to the ocean. Permanent structures offered other advantages; much more wetland could now be made safe for farming and development; and, secondly, as a "flood control project" the United States taxpayers would pay most of the costs.

In the meantime, in 1934 the Everglades National Park was authorized. Located at the end of the slow moving waters through the River of Grass, the park's survival depends upon an uninterrupted flow of water into the park.

Getting rid of as much water as quickly as possible took unfortunate priority over watering the park. As a result, the Army Corps of Engineers was drying up the Everglades National Park through the Central and Southern Florida Flood Control Project. They were sluicing most of the rainfall into the Atlantic Ocean before it could follow its normal flow down through the Everglades nourishing the unique natural environment. The National Park Service had been trying, without success, for several years to get the corps to change its procedures and release enough water into the Everglades to maintain the fragile environment.

I went to Miami once to make a speech on the subject. I explained that when the archeologists, years hence, unearthed Miami from the desert which was being created by the Army Corps of Engineers, they were going to wonder about the mentality of a generation that allowed such a magnificent heritage to be destroyed. All of my efforts were in vain. The corps gave lip service to the preservation of the Everglades while they continued to drain the water out to the Atlantic.

I concluded that I needed a superintendent who could play hardball with the corps while cultivating and mobilizing local support. I asked my regional directors to recommend somebody who had the necessary public relations skills and who was tough enough to deal with the Army Corps of Engineers. One of the names suggested to me was Roger Allin, then stationed in the Southwest regional office. I decided to make my second visit to Platt National Park (Oklahoma) and asked the regional director to send Roger along as my driver so that I would have a leisurely opportunity to interview him and size him up for the job I needed to have done. He was articulate, had a pleasing personality and was a career employee. He had served honorably as a pilot in World War II and had worked for the Fish and Wildlife Service before transferring to the National Park Service. I was impressed.

I explained to him the problems at Everglades and the program I had planned to deal with them, and then asked, "Roger, do you have the stomach for a fight?"

"Yep," he said, "I do." He was my man.

"How would you like to be superintendent of Everglades National Park?" I asked.

"I'd love it," he responded. So, I moved Roger Allin to the Everglades National Park as superintendent. He was supported by a brilliant staff of scientists and hydrologists, led by Manuel Morris, William Robertson, and Frank Nix.

Roger did a superb job, but I didn't know how well he was succeeding until one day I got a call from Senator Spessard Holland, the senior United States senator from Florida.

Senator Holland was widely acknowledged as the father of Everglades National Park when he served as governor before coming to the senate. Distinguished in appearance and bearing, he epitomized a U. S. senator. He was effective and constructive in his service to his state and nation. Moreover, his agreeable personality endeared him to a host of friends and his seniority placed him firmly in the circle of the reigning bulls of the senate. Unfortunately for me, however, he most often was found on the side of the Corps of Engineers in the continuing NPS/corps controversy over water for the Everglades.

The purpose of Senator Holland's call was to tell me that I had to, "Move this guy Allin out of the Everglades."

"Why," I asked the senator, "do I need to move Allin?"

"Because he is upsetting my constituents in South Florida."

I thought I knew who Allin was upsetting: the land speculators who, for the most part, were benefiting from having their wetlands reclaimed for development, in the name of flood control at the taxpayers' expense. Not to be churlish, however, I replied, "Senator if I have a superintendent down there who is working against the interests of the people of South Florida I will certainly straighten him out. Tell me what he is doing."

"He is going around criticizing the program of the Army Corps of Engineers, organizing the extremists with the challenge that they must do something to prevent the park from being dried up, making speeches and issuing press releases proclaiming the destruction of the park." Continuing, the senator complained, "You know I have a great interest in that park and take a lot of pride in its establishment."

I allowed as how important he was to the park, but declined to move Allin, saying to the senator that Allin was doing exactly what I had asked him to do. I did not endear myself to the senator.

In the meantime, I had convinced Secretary Udall and his solicitor, Ed Weinberg, that there was sufficient legal authority to require the corps to deliver water to the park. By legally defining the project as flood control, the waters being collected and flushed to the ocean were flood waters. In riparian water rights states, flood waters belong to whomever collects them; in this case that was the corps. The solicitor wrote an opinion agreeing. The army general counsel disputed his conclusions. So, the matter was presented to Ramsey Clark, then President Johnson's attorney general. The issue languished there for months. As the administration was winding down the secretary arranged a meeting with General Clark to try to persuade him to resolve the legal issue before he left office.

Ramsay Clark played the greatest game of dodge ball I have ever witnessed. Excuses floated through the air like balloons at a carnival—shortness of time, complexity, need for more information, coordination, etc. It was apparent to me that he had no stomach for this fight. He took a pass and the legal argument died.

My last hope of dealing with the corps on this issue was the Congress. There I had no support from Senator Holland. Nevertheless to the Hill I went to lay my burden before Senator Jackson (Washington), Senator Bible (Nevada), Senator Nelson (Wisconsin) and Senator Randolph (West Virginia). I was especially attentive to their staffs explaining the issues and the impending disaster to the park.

They championed the cause. As a result, a provision was included in the omnibus flood control legislation requiring the corps to deliver a minimum of 315,000 acre feet of water to the park annually. This was the minimum our scientists said was necessary for the park's survival.

When the committee reported this provision, I received a call from the Washington headquarters of the Corps of Engineers complaining that such drastic action was not necessary that, indeed, we could just agree and the corps would do it. I had learned the hard way that the results of my agreements with the corps about the Everglades had been very much like trading a bucket of coal for two buckets of ashes. I told my caller that I had agreed many times but nothing ever happened; and, now that I had the votes I thought I would proceed. Soon, thereafter, I received my expected call from Senator Holland. He did not like the provision and said so. Moreover, he said the corps didn't like it and he didn't see why the matter couldn't be worked out without legislation. I explained to him how many worthless agreements I had made with the corps and, in the meantime, the park was dying. He was not moved. Instead, he said he was going to have the provision removed on the Senate floor. I knew that he could. It was now time to play my last card.

I said, "Senator, I know if you stand up on the floor and oppose this provision it will be removed. If you do that, however, you will also have killed the park you fathered." He hung up without another word.

One of my legislative staff reported to me that when the bill was called, Senator Holland walked off the floor. The provision passed. (Sec. 2, Public law 91-282, dated June 19, 1970 (84 Stat. 310).

This was a landmark victory for posterity's heritage over this generation's greed.

To secure the survival of the park for all time, the Congress, in 1974, authorized the Big Cypress National Preserve north of the park. The preserve, encompassing tens of thousands of acres of wetlands, provides protection against further manmade intrusions in this fragile water environment.

Hopefully, the magnificent heritage of the Everglades National Park is secure at last.

XVIII

SEEKERS AFTER
SPECIAL PRIVILEGE

Every director must contend with the seekers after special privilege in America's national parks. For Steve Mather, the first director, one such an event involved a sawmill the Great Northern Railroad had been permitted to erect in Glacier National Park during the construction of the Many Glacier Hotel. When the permit for its operation expired, the sawmill was not removed as agreed. Thereupon, Mather, with thirteen well-primed charges of TNT, blew it up setting off a legal and political explosion of no mean proportions.

The tenure of Newton Drury, the fourth director of the National Park Service, came to an end in the cataclysmic battle over the proposed Echo Park Dam in Dinosaur National Monument.

My star-crossed encounter with a special use permittee began quietly one fall evening in 1971. Following a dinner party in the Cocolobo Club at Biscayne National Monument, Superintendent Joe Brown and I were bidding goodnight to Howard Bouterse, brother-in-law of C. G. (Bebe) Rebozo, a friend and confidant of President Nixon, when Joe said, "Howard wants to talk with you about his house." We agreed to meet for breakfast the next morning.

When Bouterse had departed, I inquired what it was about the house that Howard wanted to discuss. Joe replied, "Termites are in the house and there is danger of extremely great structural deterioration unless something is done immediately to remove the infestation and repair the damage."

Bouterse was a National Park Service employee and he occupied a house on the Cocolobo Club property recently purchased by the government.

The National Park Service is one of the few, if not the only civilian agency of the government that is authorized to operate a revolving quarters account for maintenance of employee housing. Park employees who are required to occupy housing within the park, pay a monthly quarters rent which goes into a revolving fund and remains in the park for expenditure to maintain the housing. Because there are many small areas within the National Park System that may not have adequate funds in any one year to finance needed repairs, we operated the account at that time on a regional basis. If, for example, Biscayne needed a housing repair job of $5,000 and there was only $500 in its quarters' account, the region could, on paper, loan the additional $4,500 from the Everglades if they had a surplus. Biscayne would repay the Everglades account from future quarters' rentals.

So I said to the superintendent, "Why don't you ask the region to loan you the money from the quarters account and go ahead and fix the house. Why do I have to get involved in it?"

"Bouterse is not on the quarters account," he replied. "He occupies the house under a special use permit."

The flip side of the revolving fund quarters account is that *all* National Park Service employees occupying park housing must be on the quarters account. Special use permits for the use of park housing are issued only to non-park service employees occupying such housing. Receipts from special use permits go directly into the miscellaneous receipts of the Treasury—not into the revolving fund quarters account. Realizing that the special use permit arrangement in this instance was not consistent with the regulations, I instructed the superintendent to cancel the permit, put Bouterse on the quarters account and ask the region for quarters money to repair the house.

At breakfast the next morning, I advised Howard that we were cancelling the special use permit, putting him on the quarters account and that the superintendent would soon begin repairs on the house he occupied. He seemed happy. I was happy; one more messy detail cleaned up.

A couple of weeks after my return to Washington, I was told that President Nixon and Mr. Rebozo were deeply offended with my action cancelling the special use permit.

"How could that be?" I asked. Since I had cancelled the special use permit, they no longer felt secure in landing at the small dock on Adams Key during their frequent boat trips on the bay. That was nonsense! The Secret Service guards the president every minute of every day. There was no way that this elite cadre of agents was going to allow a boatload of sightseers on that small dock when the president was docked there. I would doubt if the Secret Service would allow another boat to get within a hundred yards of the dock if the president were either in residence or on a boat docked there. I decided to check further, and uncovered the tale.

In 1968, the Congress authorized Biscayne National Monument consisting of several off-shore islands along the South Florida coast. One of the islands is Adams Key on which was located the Cocolobo Club.

Carl Fisher, who created Miami Beach out of a swampy peninsula, bought Adams key in 1917 from the Saunders family, the original settlers, and built the Cocolobo Club as a hideout for wealthy and influential invitees.

Membership dwindled after the 1929 stock market crash, and the troubles that accompanied the Great Depression of the 1930s. Fisher finally sold the club and all of Adams Key to Gar Wood, the wealthy inventor and speedboat racer. After a period of time, Wood disbanded the club and kept it as a private retreat until he sold it to a group which included U. S. Senator George Smathers, Thomas Wakefield, and Nixon confidant, Bebe Rebozo.

A number of presidents had been guests or members of the club, including Harding, Hoover, Johnson and Nixon. The club guestbook shows Warren Harding was there on February 11, 1921, along with Albert Fall, secretary of the interior, and friend Edward Doheny, who were involved in the Tea Pot Dome Scandal. William Amlong, who wrote an article for the *Miami Herald* on this topic, expressed the possibility that the oil deal may have been planned at the club during a fishing vacation.

When the Congress authorized Biscayne National Monument, the National Park Service did not have a land acquisition office in the Miami area, but the Army Corps of Engineers did. Accordingly, we made an arrangement with the corps to purchase the land for the National Park Service. One of the properties they purchased was the Cocolobo Club on Adams Key.

In a memorandum for the file of 24 June, 1969, A. E. H. Westcott, project manager, Real Estate Project Office of the corps, wrote:

> On 23 June, 1969, a further conversation was held with Thomas Wakefield one of the parties in ownership of the Adams Key Tract. Mr. Wakefield stated that he had discussed the government's suggestion regarding the donation of this property with Mr. Rebozo and Mr. McCrae. All parties agreed that they would be willing to sell to the government for the amount of the appraisal. They do not wish to donate the property.

In a letter to Mr. Westcott of June 27, 1969, Mr. Wakefield advised him that "at any time you or your representatives desire to visit the island they need only identify themselves to the resident caretaker, Mr. Howard Bouterse and he will be glad to show you around the premises."

By deed dated September 29, 1970, the government acquired the Cocolobo Club property of which Howard Bouterse was the resident caretaker. There is a provision in the Civil Service Code that permits the government to hire, without competitive examination, full-time employees whose livelihood depends upon the property acquired by the government. In this case, it was Howard Bouterse. The request for his employment as a caretaker was submitted to me and I approved it. As an employee required to live on the island he was entitled to live in government housing. He already occupied a house on the premises and he continued to occupy the same house at the time of my visit in 1971 when he wanted the government to repair the termite damage to the structure.

Soon after the Cocolobo Club property was acquired it was suggested that we should fix up an apartment in the clubhouse for President Nixon who frequently vacationed in South Florida. I approved the proposal and work was underway when I arrived there in the fall of 1971.

By letter to Mr. Westcott of April 17, 1970, Mr. Wakefield had made a request to reserve "for residential use for as long a period of time as can be permitted" the two-story cottage (presently the caretaker's cottage) located west/southwest of Casino, on Adams Key, Biscayne National Monument, together "with the right of ingress and egress to the cottage. . . ."

On January 28, 1971, the acting superintendent of Biscayne National Monument issued Mr. Wakefield a standard form revocable special use permit during the period from 30 September, 1970, to 29 September, 1975 for that "certain two-story cottage designated as the Caretaker's Cottage or guest house No. 2 . . . together with the right of ingress and egress." The annual rental fee was $350. This was the house occupied by Bouterse.

With this innocuous record it was difficult for me to understand why the president of the United States would be upset with the revocation of the special use permit. However, in government, things are not always the way they seem.

Upon further inquiry, I learned that "the right of ingress and egress" had been interpreted as exclusive use of the small dock on the island. Except for official parties, only those permitted by the caretaker could dock there. My field personnel told me that the dock was a favorite landing spot for the president and Mr. Rebozo on their frequent boating trips on the bay. Surely, with the extensive Secret Service protection surrounding the president at all times, cancellation of the special use permit did not jeopardize this activity. I kept on asking why. The soup got thicker.

Mr. Rebozo kept his houseboat tied up at the dock from which, according to the superintendent, his mother frequently fished. Damned cheap rent for housing, docking space and family recreation in the Miami area, I'd say.

To the best of my knowledge President Nixon never visited Adams Key again and never spent a night in the very nice apartment we had fixed for him in the Cocolobo Club. My informant had said, "The president and Mr. Rebozo were deeply offended with my action cancelling the special use permit."

The bell had begun to toll on my tenure as director.

XIX

FIRED

Now on that, take that park service, they've been screwing us for four years. Rogers Morton won't get rid of the son-of-a-bitch. But he's got to go," President Nixon exulted at Camp David following the November, 1972 election. (H. R. Haldeman, *THE ENDS OF POWER*.)

I first met Richard Nixon when he visited St. Louis in June, 1960. He was then vice president and running hard for the presidential nomination. His supporters among the local Republican leadership wanted to host a reception for him. After being turned down for a suitable space by the General Services Administration and the post office, they approached me through the JNEM Association. Quite a few of them were members of the association.

The Old Court House in St. Louis is a part of JNEM and was used as the administrative headquarters of the Memorial. It has a long and interesting history in the development of St. Louis and the west. It was the site of the "Manifest Destiny" speech of Senator Thomas Hart Benton. It was also the site of the Dred Scott trials. From its Fourth Street steps Mr. Joseph Pulitzer bought the St. Louis Post-Dispatch at public auction in 1878. The building has a magnificent center space, the rotunda, similar to, but smaller than that of the U. S. Capitol.

The president of the association asked if they could host a reception for Mr. Nixon in the rotunda. I agreed provided it was tied in with a tour of the area to cast the affair with an aura of officialdom. Subsequently, I called Howard Baker, my regional director in Omaha and told him what I had done and that the association had asked me to extend an invitation to him to attend. Howard was upset. He declined the invitation and chastised me for allowing a partisan political event to be held in the rotunda of the old courthouse. I agreed that certainly Richard Nixon was a partisan politician but I countered by saying that he was, also, the vice president of the United States; and that if the rotunda in the old courthouse could not be used to host the second highest official in the land I didn't know who else would be allowed to use it. At any rate, the reception took place; it was a delightful affair.

I did not see Mr. Nixon again until after he was elected president and took office in 1969. By then, I was the director of the National Park Service.

The director of the National Park Service, by presidential order, served as the chairman of the Committee for the Preservation of the White House. This committee was established first informally in the Kennedy administration, and then formalized in the Johnson administration to advise the curator, the chief usher, and the First Lady on the furnishings and decorations of the historic rooms of the White House that are on exhibition to the public. The director of the National Park Service is also a member of the board of directors of the White House Historical Association, which is a nonprofit cooperating association that publishes and sells the guide books of the White House. The association's revenues are used to support the acquisition and decoration programs of the historic rooms of the White House. Through the workings of these two organizations, I occasionally had the opportunity to shake hands with the president, but nothing more. I did, however, have a number of occasions to visit at length with Mrs. Nixon. She is gracious, charming, shy, and considerate.

The Second World Conference of National Parks was to be held in Yellowstone in September of 1972. This was a worldwide meeting of leaders from more than a hundred nations that have established national parks. Yellowstone was the world's first national park and a great celebration was planned there under the leadership of the National Park Centennial Commission which had been chartered by the Congress to celebrate the 100th anniversary of the establishment of Yellowstone National Park in 1872.

We, of course, had invited President Nixon to the ceremony. He declined and sent Mrs. Nixon. Shortly after her arrival, word was passed to me that I was not to appear with Mrs. Nixon for any picture taking sessions. This point was further clarified when I was told specifically by a representative of the secretary's office, that my presence would not be needed on the walk of Mrs. Nixon, Secretary Morton and Superintendent Jack Anderson when they went sightseeing around Old Faithful.

The rumors of my imminent firing were circulating like a fall prairie fire. Horace Albright, the second director and a cofounder of the National Park Service, took it upon himself to talk with the secretary, Rogers Morton, about the matter. Horace reported that the secretary was in full support of my continuing, but he was not sure that I was going to make it because I had some powerful enemies. Horace said he persisted: "Like who?"

Rogers responded, "Well, Bebe Rebozo for one." He was the only one, Horace said, that Morton chose to name.

Horace then began to quiz me about what I had done to offend Mr. Rebozo. I told him, "Beats me, I never met the man."

Then I remembered the special use permit at Biscayne National Monument. I related the story to him. "That's it," Horace said, "and you are in a lot of trouble, because Rogers was not very optimistic."

While Mrs. Nixon was in the park, we had scheduled an evening program at the junction of the Firehole and Gibbon Rivers, the legendary site of the Doane Expedition Campfire at which the park idea was born. The Doane Expedition explored the Yellowstone National Park region and wrote the report that was the basis for action by the Congress in preserving the magnificent resource.

A bounteous barbeque had been prepared for the evening. After the barbeque, Mrs. Nixon was to greet the delegates and light the campfire. Secretary Morton was to deliver the major address of the conference. About half-way finished with the barbeque, we could observe on the western horizon a tremendous thunderhead coming in. It was menacingly black, filled with thunder and lightning, and at that time of the year, with snow as well. I suggested to Mrs. Nixon's advance people, that instead of having her going through the line after the crowd had finished being served, meeting with the crew and having her dinner that, perhaps, we should dispense with the barbeque and proceed immediately to the program. We could arrange for her to have dinner back at Old Faithful Inn where she was staying. They would have no part of it. She had her barbeque, and met all of the staff. The program began just about the time the thunderhead arrived. The temperature dropped out of sight with gale winds blowing. Most people were ill-prepared for such a horrible night. Conspicuous among those ill-prepared was Mrs. Nixon. She was seated on the platform in the front row. Horace Albright, then in his eighties was seated behind her. I was sitting next to Horace. Mrs. Nixon brought her greetings and I presented Secretary Morton for the major address. We had written the first draft of the secretary's speech. The final speech was typed in big type on bond paper bound in a notebook so that he could read the speech and turn the pages without being intrusive.

Morton was a great extemporaneous speaker but a pedantic reader. His speech was a major statement of the meaning, values and policies of national parks and it was long. The

XIX. Fired

storm was now in full fury; on and on Rogers went. Horace and I, our arms exhausted, alternated holding umbrellas over Mrs. Nixon to try to protect her as much as possible from the snow. In the meantime, the secretary's text was getting wetter and wetter. Having been over the speech several times, I realized after quite a spell that he was only about two-thirds of the way through it. I wondered in silent pain how long he would go before he quit. As a participant in the program, I had removed my overcoat. He had not removed his. Fortunately, in another minute or two, the snow had become so heavy, that the final pages of the secretary's speech glued together and he simply had to stop. I quickly adjourned the meeting. Everybody fled for the Old Faithful Inn. Superintendent Anderson rode with Mrs. Nixon back to the inn. When they got in the car, she slipped her shoes off, and said to Jack Anderson, "Mr. Anderson, would you please rub my feet, they are about to drop off!" Jack Anderson massaged Mrs. Nixon's feet to try to get the blood circulating in them on the way back to the inn.

When we were critiquing the conference later, I was asked, "What was the biggest mistake you made?"

Without hesitation I responded, "Letting the secretary keep on his overcoat at the campfire ceremony."

Upon my return to Washington from the conference, I immersed myself in the legislative program. The Congress had caught the spirit of the Park Centennial Celebration; 1972 was a banner year in which thirteen new parks were added to the system—eight in October alone—including Cumberland Island National Seashore, Gateway National Recreation Area (New York/New Jersey) and Golden Gate National Recreation Area (California). Rumors of my firing persisted.

Senator Hansen of Wyoming had led the charge to have me dismissed in 1969; he was still around and I was concerned that he may try again.

I knew that my relationship with my boss, Secretary Rogers Morton, was solid. He had confirmed his support to Albright at Yellowstone. Nat Reed, the assistant secretary, my other boss, and I had been friends for years, so I had no worry there.

The White House is a unit of the National Park System. We maintain the grounds, provide all manner of support to the curator of the historic rooms, the art and antique collections of the mansion, and assist the office of the chief usher who is head of the permanent White House staff. The incumbent chief usher had previously served as assistant director of our National Capital Region. I had never received a complaint about any of the services we provided to the president and the First Lady.

My legislative accomplishments could hardly be faulted: twenty-six new parks had been added to the system in the first four years of Nixon's administration—eight more than had been added in the eight years of the Eisenhower administration.

Why, then, did these disconcerting rumors of my firing persist?

I called President Johnson who, in the presence of Billy Graham and me at the Redwood National Park, had told President Nixon what a good job I was doing and that he was fortunate to have me. I asked the president if he could find out what was going on. President Johnson reported back that he had asked John Connally to talk with President Nixon about retaining me and that Mr. Connally had advised Johnson that nothing could be done; the president's decision to fire me was final. Just after President Johnson's call, another friend who had been working in my behalf advised me that he was told that Rebozo had asked the president to fire me. Finally, yet a third friend told me that the condition of the president's reappointment of Morton as secretary was that he immediately fire me.

When Rogers Morton's reappointment was announced, I called to congratulate him and to ask if I could come up to see him. In the meantime, I had my secretary type out a termination of employment form which the department uses as a

XIX. Fired

notice of personnel action. The form must be signed by the supervisor of the person about whom the action is to be taken. I put the typed form in my pocket and went up to see the secretary.

Rogers C. B. Morton was a huge man, perhaps six feet, four or five inches; a handsome countenance, and a striking figure. He was sitting morosely behind his desk when I walked through the door; not until I got almost to the desk did he get up to shake hands with me. This was most unlike Rogers Morton who was an extroverted, gregarious, hand-shaking politician normally greeting everybody enthusiastically and immediately. I sat down in a chair beside his desk and said, "Rogers, I understand that your reappointment is conditioned upon firing me. I told you when you came over here that I never expected to be an embarrassment to you, and at any time you wanted me to go all you had to do was to tell me. I really meant that, so I brought along this form for you to sign." I took the termination notice out of my pocket and handed it to him.

After looking at it he handed it back and said, "I'm not going to sign it."

I said, "Well, Rogers, if you're not going to sign it, I'm not going to leave. I am too young for regular retirement. Unless I'm fired, I am not eligible for a reduced annuity and I am not going to walk out of this building without some retirement. I'm deeply in debt from borrowing money to stay in this job and I need that pension no matter what I do on the outside."

He said, "I'm not going to sign that form, because I'm having lunch tomorrow with the president, and I'm going to try to get him to let me keep you as my assistant secretary for Indian Affairs. Would you take that job?"

I replied, "Rogers, I have never thought about it, but, the Indian programs have always been very close to my heart, and I think that if I didn't have the job of the director of the National Park Service, the only other job in the government that I would consider would be the assistant secretary for

Indian Affairs because I believe that I could do something worthwhile working with the Indians."

Rogers responded: "I do too, and I'm going to talk with the president about it at lunch tomorrow."

I then told him that before making a definite commitment to him that I would have to talk it over with Helen, "Because she's involved importantly in my career."

"Well," he said, "you talk with her and call me in the morning before I go to the White House."

I came home that night and Helen and I sat up until two o'clock in the morning talking about whether I should go ahead and leave or agree to accept the assistant secretaryship of Indian Affairs if the president approved it. Her question to me was, "Why did you come back to Washington, after you left in the first place?"

I said, "To be the director of the National Park Service."

She said, "That's right. And that's the job we both love. If you can't have that, tell them you don't want any." On that we went to bed.

Early the next morning I called the secretary. He was in a meeting and didn't return my call before his secretary reported he had to go to the White House.

About three o'clock I got a call from the secretary's office asking me to come up and see him. I put my blue form back in my pocket and went back upstairs. When I walked in the secretary's office, his countenance was even more glum than it was the previous day. He blurted out, "Well, they won't do it."

I said, "Rogers don't let that bother you, because Helen said to tell you, 'No, we won't go,' so I reckon this is the end of the line. You need to sign this form which I brought back."

He took the form, signed it and handed it back to me.

I said, "You didn't date it. You've got to put a date on it."

He responded "I'm not going to put a date on it."

"Rogers, you have to put a date on it otherwise personnel won't process it."

"You put a date on it," he replied.

XIX. Fired

So, I put down December 31, 1972. He asked what date I had put down. I told him.

"Well," he said, "you can stay until the beginning of the next administration."

I did not stay.

Before I left the director's job on December 31, 1972, Ronald Walker, then the president's chief advance man working under Haldeman in the White House was appointed as my successor. Ron Walker came into government as an assistant to Wally Hickel, when Hickel was appointed secretary. Of all the people that Hickel brought in with him, I thought Ron Walker was among the most talented. With the secretary's concurrence I tried to recruit Ron for the operating chief of the National Park Foundation. In the meantime, however, Haldeman upped the ante and took Walker to the White House.

When his appointment was announced, I called to congratulate him and told him that Helen and I would like to give a reception for him and Mrs. Walker and introduce them to the senior management of the National Park Service and to the staff people of the various conservation and environmental groups with whom he would be working as the new director. A date was agreed on and the reception was organized. It was held in the dining room of the headquarters of the National Capital Region in East Potomac Park. We issued invitations to several of the White House staff, including Haldeman and Ehrlichman. Neither accepted. I was told by one of my friends that Mr. Ehrlichman's reaction to the invitation was, "What is that son-of-a-bitch trying to do to us now?"

At the reception I toasted Ron and Anne Walker, telling the group of my earlier effort to hire Ron. Continuing, however, I said, "I did not have my job in mind!"

Rogers and I never discussed the reason for my dismissal; he volunteered no reason and I asked for none.

Being fired was one way that my tenure as director could be ended. I knew of that possibility when I, happily, accepted the job. Without complaint, I accepted the reality of it when it occurred. I left with a single comment: "I'm going fishing." I would be less than candid, however, if I did not admit that it hurt. But that's the price of football and politics.*

If, as I believe, my career in the National Park Service ended because I cancelled the special use permit at Biscayne National Monument, I have no regrets; I would do it again.

George Washington's admonition remains, in my opinion, the best standard for a career in the public service. He said:

> Do not suffer your good nature, when application is made, to say 'Yes' when you should say 'No.' Remember, it is a public not a private cause that is to be injured or benefitted by your choice.

Not too long after I was fired, President Nixon left public service, also, but under quite different circumstances. Maybe he and his minions never read or, if they did, forgot to heed Washington's advice.

---

*In 1975, more than two years after my departure, the solicitor's office of the Department of the Interior preferred conflict of interest charges against me, which were promptly leaked to the media. Soon thereafter, another story was planted that while serving as director, I had accepted bribes and kickbacks. Yearlong investigations of these spurious allegations by the Federal Bureau of Investigation, the Internal Revenue Service and the Criminal Division of the Department of Justice concluded there were no bribes, no kickbacks and no conflict of interest.

XX

THIS LAND IS YOUR LAND

A myth endures that the park service alone preserves the national parks. That is its aspiration, but not the reality.

If one reads the journals of the citizen conservation organizations, one may conclude that they preserve the parks. That is their objective, but not the reality.

There are even some romanticists who suggest that the park service and the citizen conservation organizations, together, preserve the parks. That, certainly, is their endeavor, but not the reality.

The reality is that the people through their elected representives in the Congress preserve the parks—or destroy them.

The Congress discharges this constitutionally assigned responsibility in two ways: first by legislation. It establishes park policy and delegates implementing authority to the interior secretary (National Park Service); and second through oversight hearings by its appropriate subcommittees and committees, the Congress investigates how well the secretary (the National Park Service) has implemented the mandated policies.

Oversight hearings and investigations, compared with new initiatives in legislation, are unglamorous and difficult but indispensable tasks, if government is to be efficient, responsive and responsible. To assist in this work, the Congress not only has its own extensive staff but access to the enormous resources of the General Accounting Office.

Through this interplay of authority both the executive and legislative branches act as a check on the exercise of each other's constitutional power. And today, they share responsibility for the endangered status of our national parks.

Each year I served as director of the park service, the House Interior and Insular Affairs Committee (with jurisdiction over the National Park Service) held an oversight hearing. It was an occasion for laying out park problems and for committee members to probe park operations and air their constituents' concerns. These hearings were enormously productive and worthwhile. One year, I remember, the committee was so concerned about financing for parks that it directed its chairman, Wayne Aspinall, and its ranking minority member, John Saylor, to communicate that concern to the House Appropriations Subcommittee. They not only wrote to the chairman of the Appropriations Subcommittee but made a joint personal appearance before the subcommittee on behalf of the park service budget. It was unprecedented.

When I inquired recently of a committee staff member whether such oversight hearings still occurred, he replied, "No, not as much. And they are mostly for education and orientation of new committee members."

There are, of course, many reasons why the Congress has sunk to its present low level of public esteem. One reason, I suggest, is because it has failed in its oversight responsibilities, allowing government agencies and their special interest constituent groups to run amok. Obvious examples are the military/industrial axis and the Iran-Contra affair. But those are only the most visible ones.

The primary responsibility for the breakdown in government oversight is in the Congress, but the ultimate fault lies with the taxpaying public and the media. Despite the obscene excesses of political action committees, a single constituent's voice—by visit, by telephone, by letter—can still be heard and even the Supreme Court reads the newspapers. PAC money may buy advertising but, unlike the days of my youth in South Carolina when two dollar bills or a pint of whiskey could buy votes all day, there are not many places now where one can get away with buying a vote.

Make no mistake: citizen involvement and the spotlight of a probing media can bring about significant improvement in government management. It does not take many citizen complaints, exposés and editorials to turn up the heat on the Congress and the administration. This combination can start a tidal wave of corrective action.

In his book, *Playing God in Yellowstone*, Alston Chase documents the fact that the northern Yellowstone elk herd is in trouble. National Park Service people have told me as much, too.

Mr. Chase attributes the Yellowstone elk debacle to the implementation of the Leopold Report of 1963 contending that the Leopold Committee, "inadvertently replaced science with nostalgia, subverting the goal it had set out to support." Moreover, a high-level official of the park service recently has been assigned by the director to assemble a task force to evaluate whether the alleged thesis of the Leopold Report of "let nature take its course" is still relevant. Neither Mr. Chase nor the director comprehends the Leopold Report.

After articulating the goal of park management—"A national park should represent a vignette of primitive America"—the Leopold Committee said:

The first step in park management is historical research, to ascertain as accurately as possible what plants and animals and biotic associations existed originally in each locality.

The second step should be ecologic research on plant-animal relationships leading to formulation of a management hypothesis.

Next should come small scale experimentation to test the hypothesis in practice. Experimental plots can be situated out of sight of roads and visitor centers.

Lastly, application of tested management methods can be undertaken on critical areas.

By this process of study and pretesting, mistakes can be minimized. Likewise, public groups vitally interested in park management can be shown the results of research and testing before general application, thereby eliminating possible misunderstandings and friction.

Does that sound like replacing "science with nostalgia?"
Does that sound like "let nature take its course?"
Elsewhere, in his book Mr. Chase states:

Senate hearings on the park service's elk policies were convened in Casper, Wyoming in March 1967. Sportsmen's groups united in common cause to promote public hunting. The inquiry was led by Gale McGee, Senator from Wyoming. The night before the hearing, McGee and Secretary of the Interior George Hartzog (sic) had dinner together and agreed on the outline of a solution. According to the new plan, McGee told me recently, "The park service would control the elk population by live-trapping only."

This "solution," however, would not work and the park service knew it. The demand for live elk could not keep up with the supply. Yellowstone had already saturated the market.

That is a half-truth. I did agree with Senator McGee to stop the shooting in 1967; I did not agree that the National Park Service would never shoot again. Quite to the contrary, at hearings in Casper and in Washington we carefully laid out the sequence of our wildlife management policy as articulated in Leopold's report:

(a) Natural predation.
(b) Trapping and transplanting.
(c) Shooting by sport hunters of excess animals that migrate outside the parks.
(d) Control by shooting within the parks.

Senator McGee, in reporting to Secretary Udall on that Casper hearing (letter of March 13, 1967), acknowledged that direct reduction remained a viable management option:

> I am confident that, as a result of the Casper hearing, we can control the Northern Yellowstone elk herd in the future without direct reduction. But even if the kill ultimately becomes necessary, the sportsmen's groups in our area will have a more enlightened and rational understanding of what's going on.

The park service was not left between a political rock and a biological hard place in managing the Yellowstone elk.

Secretary Udall's memorandum of July 10, 1964, recognized three types of areas comprising the National Park System: natural areas, historical areas and recreation areas. In 1970 the Congress confirmed these three categories.

Pursuant to Udall's memorandum, the park service developed separate sets of management policies to guide operations for each category: a green book for natural areas, such as Yellowstone; a red book for historical areas, such as Independence; and a blue book for recreation areas, such as lakeshores, seashores, riverways and artificial reservoirs, i.e., Lake Mead, etc. Wildlife management, especially of ungulate (elk, etc.) populations, was dealt with separately for each type of area.

Some among the paid staff of a few of the citizen conservation organizations never liked the three-tiered policy arrangement. And although the Congress confirmed the three classifications in 1970, they continued to carp and complain.

In 1977, the Carter administration arrived in Washington. Some of the classification opponents were employed as political bureaucrats in the Interior Department. At last they had their opportunity. In derogation of logic and legislation, they junked the three separate management policies dealing with the substantive differences in management of recreation areas, historical areas and natural areas.

In lieu of the necessary differentiations in management policies among the different categories, they promulgated one amorphous policy applicable to such disparate areas as the artificial reservoir of Lake Mead and the wilderness of Yellowstone. Suddenly everything had become the same and, thus, nothing was any longer special—not even Yellowstone. Instead of America's great national parks as crown jewels, all areas in the system were now jewels in the crown.

Gone were the Leopold policies. Gone was cooperative research and programming with the states for managing excess ungulates. Gone was the programmatic sequence for control of excess ungulates. All were junked.

As Mr. Chase suggests, we should ask why there is an elk problem in Yellowstone. But we should also ask some other questions: why were the Leopold policies junked? Why were the unique differences in management policies for natural areas (Yellowstone) reduced to the lowest common denominator of artificial reservoirs (Lake Mead)? How can parks cope with wildlife management without cooperative research and coordinated action with surrounding states and federal agencies?

Mr. Chase is hunting the wrong rabbits; they are not in Yellowstone. They were in Washington, and maybe some of them still are.

Many of the national parks are riddled with privately owned lands, most often identified as in-holdings. The continued existence of these properties not only complicates and increases the cost of management, but also threatens the environmental integrity of the parks.

Since President Reagan's refusal to request appropriations from the Land and Water Conservation Fund, there is no official current estimate of the cost of acquiring these in-holdings. Some knowledgeable estimates, however, indicate the cost may exceed two billion dollars. The problem is manageable if the administration and the Congress would use the money accruing to the Land and Water Conservation Fund to get on with the program.

Not to remove this threat to the survival of our national parks borders on recklessness. The money that accrues to the Land and Water Conservation Fund cannot be used for miscellaneous government programs; it is available only for the purposes of federal land acquisition and matching grants to the states for park and recreation lands and facilities. There is plenty of money available in the fund. While the administration and Congress vacillate, the cost of acquiring these privately-owned lands continues to escalate and the integrity of the parks is imperiled.

Park boundaries are the result of political decisions; that is our process in a democracy. When most of those boundaries were set by the Congress they seemed appropriate. But now we know that life communities exist in ecological boundaries, a wholly different concept from that understood when most parks were established.

Years ago, coal miners carried canaries with them into the mines to detect lethal gases. Today, our national parks are our ecological canaries. And many thoughtful people believe that some of our "canaries" are in trouble.

For example, we have known for decades that the natural range of the elk at Yellowstone, outside the park, has been adversely impacted. Now we know the grizzly bear forages far beyond the boundaries of the park and is slaughtered. Timber harvesting, mining, oil, gas and geothermal leasing that encroach on the park's boundaries disrupt the biotic communities within the park. An organization of concerned citizens, the Greater Yellowstone Coalition, has sounded the alarm: Yellowstone—the world's first national park to be preserved by the people—must not become the world's first national park to be destroyed by the people.

The greater Yellowstone ecosystem comprises approximately ten million acres, almost all of which is in public ownership. Within the boundaries of this major, largely undisturbed geyser basin are two national parks (Yellowstone and Grand Teton), six national forests (Bridger, Teton, Custer, Gallatin, Shoshone and Targhee), two national wildlife refuges, an Indian reservation and miscellaneous ownerships by the U. S. Bureau of Land Management, the states of Idaho, Montana and Wyoming and local governments. The largest public ownership is administered by the Forest Service, whose principal mission is consumptive resource utilization: mineral exploitation, timber harvesting, grazing and sports hunting. Therein lies the challenge to the survival of the grizzly bear, designated in 1975 as a threatened species under the Endangered Species Act. Of the roughly 5.7 million acres of grizzly bear-occupied habitat in the greater Yellowstone ecosystem, approximately 43 percent is in the two national parks, and most of the remainder, approximately 56 percent lies in national forests. These serious economic and ecological problems require a new look at the techniques and procedures for land use management.

The federal government lacks zoning authority inherent in the states and local governments. Thus, historically, the park service relied on fee ownership of the land to control its use. If a problem existed, the boundary was moved over to include the problem area and the land acquired. When the Congress began to establish parks in urban and highly developed areas, this simplistic solution no longer worked.

In the legislation establishing Cape Cod National Seashore, Congress pioneered a new approach. The authority of the secretary to acquire land by condemnation (eminent domain proceedings) was suspended so long as the towns or other local governing bodies zoned the land to conform to standards established by the secretary for protection of the integrity of the seashore. For example, if the standards defined single family housing as meeting the level of preservation needed—and the local government zoned the land in accordance with this standard—the secretary could not use his condemnation authority to acquire the property. If, on the other hand, the local government zoned the land for commercial use, the secretary could condemn the land to achieve the preservation objective of the seashore. This approach has worked remarkably well and has minimized land acquisition costs to the federal government. The success is dependent upon the willingness of local government to compatibly zone the land in its jurisdiction.

In many rural areas there are no zoning codes and many local governments are reluctant to promulgate them. This situation was encountered in the Ozark National Scenic Riverways. The government wanted to maintain the pastoral scenes along the rivers so it bought a scenic easement which obligated the owner of the land never to develop the land with buildings, houses, etc., that intruded on the pastoral scene. Under such easements the public did not acquire a right to use the land for access to the rivers or for other purposes. Where public access was needed, an access easement was acquired in addition. If it was farmland or pastureland, the cost of a scenic or access easement, as opposed to buying the fee in the land, was usually *de minimus*.

Easements work well in rural areas. They are not equally useful in rapidly developing areas, however, where the land may have potential for commercial uses far more valuable than the present agricultural use. Since the easements would prohibit development, the cost of an easement, in this instance, would approximate or equal the cost of buying the full title in the land.

The park service first encountered this problem at Piscataway Park (Maryland) in the Washington, D. C. metropolitan area. The Congress authorized first the fee acquisition of the land, and second the lease-back or sell-back of a right to use the land for purposes consistent with the preservation objective of the park. Later, Congress extended this authority to all areas of the National Park System, except national parks.

Many park preservation problems, however, such as the one at Yellowstone, lie outside of the political boundaries of the parks.

Beginning in the 1960s, we tried cooperative regional planning with the forest service to protect the greater Yellowstone area. Our successes were small and temporary, not because of bad faith, but because the resource missions of the forest service and the park service are, for the most part, incompatible and adversarial. Specifically, the mission of the forest service is consumptive resource utilization—incompatible, in most instances, with the park service mission of non-consumptive resource management. Moreover, there was no final authority to adjudicate between the differing management options and missions. If efforts at cooperative regional planning have not worked, what are the alternatives?

Current National Park Service Director William Penn Mott, Jr., has called for buffer zones around the troubled parks. Under this proposal, Congress could define the extent of the buffer one needed to protect the biotic communities of the park. The secretary of the interior would be authorized to determine—through research, planning and public hearings—the level of protection needed within the buffer zone to insure the objectives of park preservation. Within the buffer zone, the secretary could be authorized to utilize the innovative tools already approved by the Congress for protection of park land within the exterior boundaries of parks.

There is another concept of land protection that has been discussed for several decades but never tried for park protection: compensable land use regulations. After research, planning and public hearings, the interior secretary would issue standards in the form of regulations prohibiting uses within a defined zone that are incompatible with the park's preservation/conservation objectives. An owner aggrieved by the regulations would have the right to sue in the local U. S. district court for damages alleged to have been suffered. If damages were proven, the court would enter judgment against the government. And when paid, the payment would operate to transfer a land interest to the government consistent with the regulation—a result similar to an easement.

If the regulations were consistent with present uses of the lands, damages should be *de minimus*, if any. In the case of their imposition on other federal lands, such as those administered by the Bureau of Land Management and the forest service, costs should be nil. This approach would seem to hold great promise for the survival of the grizzly bear, for one example.

Competitiveness among federal agencies for turf is as intense as between businesses for market share. And where large bureaucratic turfs of competing agencies are at issue, such as at Yellowstone, the Congress may not grant unilateral authority to Interior to direct uses on forest service lands controlled by the Agriculture Department.

This is not unlike the issue that the task force on historic preservation faced in trying to draft legislation to protect our cultural heritage from destruction by competing programs of urban renewal, highways, etc. HUD, the Federal Highway Administration, Army Corps of Engineers and others, would not defer to Interior to adjudicate issues impinging on their bureaucratic turf.

Congress solved the problem by approving a two-step process: first it authorized and directed the park service to establish, maintain and publicize a National Register of Historic Places (buildings, districts, etc.). This register reflected the scholarly, professional judgment of what was important in the preservation and presentation of our cultural heritage. Second, it established a Presidential Advisory Council on Historic Preservation composed of citizens appointed by the president and ex officio membership by such involved agencies and organizations as HUD, Transportation, Agriculture, General Services Administration and the National Trust for Historic Preservation.

The council is charged with the responsibility of advising the president and the Congress on the competing, conflicting demands of use and development vis-à-vis preservation of our patrimony. Even though its authority is advisory, in practice its ability to resolve conflict is comparable to mediation and arbitration. The council has its independent staff to perform its work. The whole concept has worked extremely well with a minimum of bureaucratic conflict and cost.

Surely Yellowstone, Yosemite, Grand Canyon and the other crown jewels among our natural parks are as precious and significant to our well-being as are Independence Hall, the White House and other shrines and memorials of our cultural heritage.

To resolve the competing, conflicting uses that threaten the ecological survival of our national parks, we need a congressionally-sanctioned Register of Natural Places and a President's Council on Nature Preservation such as the President's Advisory Council on Historic Preservation.

Many gaps still exist in the National Park System plan published in 1972. In the lower 48 we are unlikely to complete the effort to preserve the most representative examples of the American landscape unless we look at our opportunities from a different perspective.

Major portions of Shenandoah National Park are classified today as wilderness. This land had been cut-over, burned, grazed and hard-scrabble farmed until it was exhausted and its inhabitants destitute in the '30s. Through the vision of the late Senator Harry Flood Byrd, Sr. and the innovative program of farm resettlement of Roosevelt's New Deal, the land was acquired for park purposes. A half century later, Americans can point with pride to their wilderness park. It is our nation's premier example of a magnificent new creation risen from the ashes of neglect and abuse.

In the region east of the Mississippi River, there are tens

—perhaps hundreds—of thousands of desolate acres that once produced a cornucopia of blessings to nourish the American dream. Today, depleted of their bounty of nonrenewable resources they are in many instances a burden to their owners, a blight to the local inhabitants, and often a threat to our nation's health by leaching poisons into our waterways and air. There are no villains here: we all shared in the bounty of their exploitation.

With super-funds and through stringent new laws and regulations we are attempting to force the reclamation of destitute and nonproductive old coal mines, strip mining areas and industrial sites. The financial burden of doing so has bankrupted many companies. It is inevitable that we, the taxpayers, will eventually pay the costs to reclaim these acres. We will pay through direct outlays, tax credits, hidden subsidies and consumer price increases. But for what purpose will we pay? To enrich a new generation of private exploiters or to endow the national patrimony? The horizon of opportunity for new Shenandoahs hangs over these troubled acres. What we need is a new vision of the possibilities.

I suspect some current owners would welcome the opportunity to donate many of these lands; others could be acquired for a pittance. Perhaps they would be different kinds of parks, preserving resident villages as enclaves with the inhabitants employed to restore the land and encouraged to serve a new generation of visitors.

Reserved and land-banked now, these scarred hills, valleys and plateaus could be the local, state and national parks and wilderness of our future generations.

Mr. Chase in his book on Yellowstone has written a scathing indictment of the management and employees of the National Park Service. Among his many charges is that a "fortress mentality" permeates the park service. In his review of the book for the National Park Courier, Professor Richard Bartlett echoes the charge, saying, "And it is there.

As an outside historian I have felt it, and so have many others."

Director William Penn Mott, Jr. wrote his regional directors on June 16, 1987, saying:

> There was an article from the *Philadelphia Inquirer* in the press clips of June 1, 1987, entitled: "Limits Urged on Park Use." The quote in the article was: "Morale is at rock bottom," said one park superintendent who asked not to be identified, "but we'll outlast them." I am very disturbed by this quote and I would like your comments.
>
> 1. I would like your candid and honest assessment. Is the morale of the service at "rock bottom?"
> 2. If a superintendent is unwilling to be identified, he shouldn't be making comments to the press and, in my opinion, is not worthy of being a superintendent of the National Park Service. I would appreciate your so advising your superintendents.
>
> Now I realize this quote could be a plant by the reporter and I sincerely hope that is the case. My assessment of the morale is just the opposite, but you should know better than I. Likewise, I don't believe any superintendent that I have met would hide behind an "anonymous" statement.

As understanding as I am of the director's chagrin with the messenger (the anonymous superintendent), my concern is with the message: the career park service employees are dispirited, lacking in confidence and marking time ("we'll outlast them"). That's low morale and it isn't good. Why should this condition exist in an agency acclaimed worldwide for dedication to the public service by its highly educated, talented and creative people?

To succeed me, Nixon ordered Secretary Morton to appoint as director the president's advance man, Ron Walker. Charismatic, articulate and energetic, Walker was in the vanguard of White House assistants appointed to a number of strategic positions in the bureaus and departments to make the career bureaucrats toe the line, although no one seemed to know where the line was.

Unfamiliar with park operations, Walker's appointment dismayed the career employees, loyal park service alumni and the citizen conservation organizations. He was greeted with hostility by Nathaniel Reed, the assistant secretary for Fish, Wildlife and Parks, the only interior assistant secretary to survive Nixon's first term. Strangely, many of those Nixon people did not like each other.

Ron brought with him from the White House and the Committee for the Reelection of the President (CREEP) a cadre of assistants and secretaries who isolated him from the directorate while concentrating his efforts on park travel, river floating and public relations events. Lacking experienced park service leadership and, importantly, hostile to it, Assistant Secretary Reed became surrogate director. He transferred one of his special assistants to the park service as associate director for legislation. He neither confirmed the established policy/objectives Morton had approved for my management nor, with the secretary's approval, established any new ones to guide Walker's management. Reed arrogated to himself day-to-day operating responsibilities, including budget allocations and personnel appointments. Operations evaluation was relegated to committees appointed by the regional directors on an *ad hoc* basis for each of their respective regions. The director's office was rendered impotent. Like bass at flood stage, the career employees fled for safety in the deep and murky waters of bureaucratic anonymity. Sensing that park management had become a house divided against itself, the regional directors began to isolate their operations from Washington office park service control. This virulent management style was to bear bitter fruit in the Reagan administration.

Soon after Nixon resigned, Secretary Morton suggested that Ron do the same. He resigned in January, 1975.

Morton then appointed Gary Everhardt, a career park service employee, to succeed Walker. An engineer by training, he had served with distinction in progressively responsible staff and management jobs in the parks and regional offices. I appointed him cochairman of the 1972 national park centennial celebration and superintendent of Grand Teton National Park, where he was serving when appointed director. Calm, competent and cautious, Gary's appointment was greeted warmly by the park service employees, alumni and the citizen conservation organizations. He was the personal choice of Reed and Morton. There was every reason to believe that they would allow him to regain the full authority of the director. Such was not to be the case; Reed kept his former special assistant in place as associate director for legislation, and he continued to dabble in day-to-day operational management. Gary's tenure was beset by the mixed budget policy signals of the Ford administration. Ford had significantly reduced park service budgets, yet in the hopes of saving his floundering reelection campaign, he had gone to Yellowstone to propose a whopping new $2.5 billion program for the parks. The Congress and park people were shocked at the hypocrisy.

Soon after the 1976 presidential election, Chris Delaporte, one of Carter's political operatives, visited me at my law office to say that he was to be the new director of the National Park Service. He did not make it; he was appointed director of the Bureau of Outdoor Recreation. I relaxed believing Gary was safe and that with Jimmy Carter, an acknowledged environmentalist, in charge, times would be better. A short while after the Carter administration settled in, I received a call from Tom Kimball, executive vice president of the National Wildlife Federation, seeking my advice on people to be proposed for consideration as director of the park service. Incredulously, I inquired, "Why? What about Everhardt?"

"Well, he is on the list and he will be interviewed for the job, too," Tom replied.

Everhardt was interviewed by the new assistant secretary. It soon became apparent, however, that his tenure was over. Without explanation or so much as a thank you, he was relieved of his duties in May of 1977. After a period of limbo he was reassigned to the field service as superintendent of the Blue Ridge Parkway.

Everhardt was the third director in succession to be fired in less than five years. Never before in its first fifty-five year history had one park service director been fired. You can bet your boots this inexplicable action reenforced the message to the career park people: hunker down!

William J. Whalen succeeded Everhardt as director. Bill had led the staff of the National Capital Region that inaugurated the highly successful urban park program of Summer in the Parks. For his superior performance he won the Fleming Award for young federal employees. I promoted him to deputy superintendent at Yosemite where urban park problems much like those in the nation's capital abounded. He did a remarkably fine job in that difficult assignment. Based on this record of performance, I named him the first superintendent of Golden Gate National Recreation Area, where he was serving when appointed director. His tenure as director was turbulent, short-lived and scarred by controversy—some self-inflicted.

While Delaporte was not appointed director of the park service he did succeed in getting Whalen shot in the foot. Delaporte convinced Secretary Cecil Andrus to transfer to the Bureau of Outdoor Recreation the dynamic and highly visible external programs of the park service in historic preservation and the federal matching funds used to support cultural restoration by state and local governments and the private sector. He renamed his newly expanded agency the Heritage Conservation and Recreation Service.

When it was learned that Whalen had agreed to this monstrous organizational mayhem—some say as a condition of being named director—his credibility was undermined both within the park service and among its unusually loyal and active alumni. His relations with the regional directors rapidly deteriorated. In the meantime, he poisoned his relationship with the park concessioners by a particularly intemperate tirade which, unfortunately for him, was tape-recorded by the concessioners. When the normally even-tempered, imperturbable Congressman Morris Udall, chairman of the House Committee on Interior and Insular Affairs, read the transcript, he was outraged and demanded Whalen's ouster. Confronted with rising dissension within the park service and the escalating controversy with Udall and the concessioners, Secretary Andrus removed Whalen in May of 1980. He returned to the field service as superintendent of Golden Gate.

In an extraordinary effort to calm the troubled waters, Andrus called a meeting of the regional directors to solicit their recommendations for a new director. Unanimously, they recommended one of their own: Russell Dickenson, director of the Pacific Northwest region in Seattle. Andrus promptly complied by appointing Dickenson as the fourth park service director in less than eight years. In the first thirty-five years of park service history there had been only four directors.

James Watt arrived as secretary in January, 1981 and announced to the delight of one and all—in and out of the park service—that he was going to retain Russ as director. Watt inaugurated a five-year, one billion dollar park rehabilitation and improvement program to correct health and safety hazards in the national parks. Hooray! Watt was not the ogre he had been portrayed—at least for the national parks.

Little did we know, however, the price to be paid for these popular decisions. The balance of Watt's agenda was: for the National Park System, no more parks; for land acquisition for parks already established, no more money; for 50-50 matching grants to the states for land acquisition and outdoor recreation facilities, no more money.

The Land and Water Conservation Fund, authorized by Congress for funding at $900 million annually, was to be apportioned to the states as matching grants for park and recreation lands and facilities (60 percent), and to federal land acquisition programs (40 percent). Among the eligible federal agencies (the U.S. Forest Service, the Fish and Wildlife Service, the Bureau of Land Management and the National Park Service), the National Park Service, historically, had received the lion's share of the federal portion—approximately 67 percent. On this basis the park service share of the available funding for the 1982 fiscal year (the first full-year budget for which Watt was responsible), funding could have been as much as $241 million—the administration's budget was for $25 million—or approximately 10 percent of the authorized funding level. Funding proposed for matching grants to the states suffered even more; it was budgeted by the administration at zero although a total of $540 million was available in the fund for this purpose.

These budget decisions effectively scuttled a major part of the workload of the Heritage Conservation and Recreation Service, which administered the fund. Watt abolished the bureau, transferring its responsibilities, money and highly talented personnel to the park service. He also decreed that there would be no reductions in force. No one would be fired: the National Park Service would assimilate all of them. So much for Reagan's budget-cutting and economy in government. One high-level park service official said of Watt's decision, "It seemed as though he was intent on destroying two of the best professional bureaus in the department."

The work of the National Park Service is operating parks. The work of the abolished Heritage Conservation and Recreation Service was managing the Land and Water Conservation Fund and nationwide coordination and planning of outdoor recreation and cultural resources.

The park service needed personnel, but what was needed were rangers, naturalists and historians in the parks. What it received were high-salaried professional planners and administrators assigned to Washington and regional offices. Regional office staffing ballooned: people had to be reassigned since there was no work for them. But where? To the parks, of course, whether they could be used effectively or not.

Parks that needed rangers and naturalists got planners

and administrators; parks that never had assistant superintendents and didn't need one, got one; parks that had one—and that was enough—got another one or two. One distraught superintendent called to tell me of the chaos. He lamented that he needed another assistant superintendent like he needed a carbuncle.

Inter-larding these planners and administrators, inexperienced in park operations into the park organizations, closed off promotions for park rangers, naturalists, and historians; it derailed the established career ladders up the uniformed ranks to superintendent; and, it aborted promising careers for many young park people.

Not content with the speed with which the park service was assimilating the surplus personnel, the assistant secretary's office intervened to mandate appointments, including park superintendents—the lifetime achievement dreamed of and worked for by every ranger recruit.

Watt removed the deputy director of the National Park Service—a career employee—and replaced him with a Reagan loyalist, Mary Lou Grier. She was strong-willed, inexperienced in park operations and possessed little empathy for the career professionals of the park service. All significant correspondence to the assistant secretary or the secretary, including budget and personnel matters, was routed through her. If she didn't approve, she ordered it changed. If she didn't like it at all she deep-sixed it. Many times the senior career staff lamented: "She won't send on my memorandum and Russ won't intervene."

The successor to Bob Herbst (the assistant secretary for Fish, Wildlife and Parks in the Carter administration) was C. Ray Arnett, Reagan's fish and game commissioner when Reagan was governor of California. He was an ardent supporter of the president and of Watt's programs.

Determined, extroverted and politically savvy, he and Dickenson shared neither the same park philosophy nor management style. Caught between the competence of Arnett and the inexperience of Mrs. Grier, Dickenson found shelter in the eye of the storm. As one park service employee said, "We are grateful to him, lest he leave and a worst fate befall us."

The turbulence of Watt's mismanagement spread beyond Washington. In 1983, John Cook, a third generation career park service employee, was summarily demoted from the regional director's position in Alaska to the superintendency of Great Smoky Mountains National Park. Cook had not failed in his assignment. To the contrary, he had done a superior job in organizing and staffing a new region to manage the vast new national parks in Alaska. In faithfully discharging his mandate to protect the parks, he incurred the wrath of some prominent park opponents. The career employees manned the bunkers: fortress mentality was in place.

On November 21, 1984, Secretary William C. Clark (Watt's successor) announced Dickenson's intention to retire in the summer of 1985 after more than forty years of federal service. He left the director's position in March of 1985 to become a field assistant to the secretary at Seattle, Washington. No successor had been named.

Secretary Clark resigned in February, 1985, and was succeeded by Donald Paul Hodel. In the meantime, in January, 1985, Arnett resigned. Hodel chose William Horn (a former deputy to Hodel when Hodel served as Watt's under secretary) to succeed Arnett. The White House did not immediately send his name to the Senate for confirmation. Hodel delayed choosing a park service director.

In this leadership vacuum, the regional directors moved to complete the isolation of their territories from the control and direction of the park service Washington office. There was no longer one park service—there were now ten. Many senior park superintendents assumed autonomy. Meddlesome day-to-day political management grew beyond the Washington office to the regional offices and the parks. Regional directors and park superintendents were now taking orders from political bureaucrats in the office of the assistant secretary for Fish, Wildlife and Parks. Politics had returned to the parks where Mather and Albright had found them when they arrived in 1916.

Hodel and the White House continued to struggle over who should be the park service director. Several candidates were interviewed but none selected. The name of William Penn Mott, Jr. kept surfacing as the White House favorite for the position. But rumor had it that he was not Hodel's choice because of his age. He is one year older than Reagan.

Among park people, Mott is a legend in his own time. He began his career in 1933, as a landscape architect with the park service. After almost a decade he left to enter local park management in Oakland, California, where he pioneered many innovative park programs. His outstanding performance there attracted the attention of Reagan when he became governor. Bill was appointed California State Park director. He excelled in the job. After eight years of distinguished service he left state government to lead a foundation for the support of park and recreation programs in the Oakland/San Francisco Bay area. He had been offered the park service director position by Nixon in 1969. It was easy to understand why he was the White House favorite.

After much backing and filling the impasse was resolved. The secretary announced the appointment of Mott as park service director effective May 19; the White House sent Horn's name to the Senate on June 21. Mott moved aggressively to replace Deputy Director Grier with an innovative, experienced career park service manager, Denis Galvin. Mott brought with him a well thought out twelve-point plan of policy/objectives, which he reported the secretary had approved to guide his management. Quickly, Mott convened a conference of park people and constituent group representatives to evaluate his objectives and develop programs for their implementation. Park service careerists, alumni and environmentalists alike were euphoric.

This auspicious beginning was soon derailed; Horn's special assistants continued their day-to-day meddlesome ways, bypassing the director to countermand professional decisions of National Park Service career personnel. I was astounded on one occasion to learn that a matter which in my day would have been decided by a regional director had been sent to Washington for review and decision—not by the director— but by a special assistant to the assistant secretary. Horn, from time to time, joined the action. A young resource management ranger, based on his research, recommended a modest change in fishing regulations for his park. The superintendent, regional director and director approved. But before special regulations can be effective they must be published in the Federal Register. Only the executive departments can order publication. The special regulations arrived on Horn's desk. The next thing the young ranger knew, Horn was on the telephone summoning him to Washington to discuss the regulations. He arrived with his research, wondering why neither his superintendent, regional director nor the director was present. Horn challenged his work. Courageously, the young man defended his findings. Horn ended the interview and deep-sixed the ranger's recommendations. In a highly public episode, Horn changed Mott's efficiency rating of Regional Director Howard Chapman from excellent to marginal. Only when Chapman threatened to bring suit to have the performance rating reviewed by federal courts did Horn back down. On another occasion, Horn changed Mott's recommendations for bonus awards to his staff. The changes were so drastic as to be repugnant to Mott. To express his outrage, the director refused to attend the awards ceremony, remaining in his office at the opposite end of the hall from Horn's office where the ceremony took place. Park management remained a house divided against itself, pitting political bureaucrats against career bureaucrats.

Mott proposed a modest reorganization of his top staff. Horn made major revisions in it, including the establishment of a new associate director's position to oversee policy, budget and personnel. Horn had a candidate for the position. While the new position would nominally report to the director, for policy matters it would report to the assistant secretary. It was a thinly disguised ploy to take over substantive park management much as Watt had done with Mrs. Grier's appointment as Dickenson's deputy director. Rightly, Mott was furious. He signed a memorandum to the secretary (written at his direction by deputy director Deny Galvin) protesting Horn's action. The secretary agreed with Horn. The debacle was averted when the Senate majority leader, Robert Byrd, who is also chairman of the Interior Department Appropriations Subcommittee, inserted a provision in the pending appropriations bill which would suspend payment of Horn's salary until the atrocity was corrected. Hodel acquiesced, but not before he gave Galvin a letter of censure for opposing the reorganization. Nothing to Mott! As park service ranger P. J. Ryan opined, "Mrs. Hodel's little boy Donald was not behind the door when political savvy was passed out."

Howard Chapman, the longtime director of the western region at San Francisco—the same one that threatened to sue Horn over his efficiency rating—was harassed into retirement. Chapman enjoyed wide respect among his colleagues in the park service, with the public and with the Congress. He was a talented, highly competent career employee who had distinguished himself as a park ranger, superintendent and regional director. His transgressions were his refusal to sign a certificate attesting that the preservation of Yosemite did not require acquisition of any more of the privately-owned lands within the park and his recommendations to ameliorate the intrusive aircraft noise in Grand Canyon National Park.

In the summer of 1986, I was asked by Congressman Mel Price (Illinois) to testify in support of a bill he had introduced to authorize expansion of the Jefferson National Expansion Memorial into East St. Louis. The expansion will have a dramatic impact upon National Park Service management of this unique memorial. The Department of the Interior witness on the legislation was a bright, articulate young assistant to the assistant secretary for Fish, Wildlife and Parks, accompanied by a staff member of the legislative office of the National Park Service. Neither the director, nor his deputy, nor any associate or assistant director was there.

Soon, thereafter, on another visit to the Hill, I encountered representatives of the Department of Agriculture going to a congressional meeting. Representing the Forest Service was its chief, Max Peterson.

Do these two incidents indicate that the forest service is political; and that the park service is nonpolitical? I think not. Rather, they communicate to the Congress and to other observers, such as me, who the Interior and Agriculture Secretaries believe to be in charge of the respective bureaus.

The power of the director, both in Washington and in the parks, rests equally on fact and perception. If the Congress and the park service constituencies do not perceive that the director is both responsible and accountable, he is ineffective. If the park service career bureaucracy does not know that the director is vested with the untrammeled power and authority of his office, again, he is ineffective.

Many people contend that the position of the director is—or should be—nonpolitical. This is ludicrous. It is the command post on the fireline where politics meets parks. From the birth of the park service in 1916 to the present day, the director's job has been political. That is—and must remain—the nature of the job if a president's policies are to be translated into action.

Mather and Albright's living legacy is not the myth that they removed the director's job from politics, but that they took the politics out of the parks and put it into the director's job. The politics stopped there. To acknowledge this legacy is not to say that the director needs to be a partisan of the political party in power, although that may be the case. He or she must, however, possess other attributes: managerial skills, awareness of park values, respect for scientific knowledge, appreciation of professional integrity and a lively understanding of politics—that medium through which the public gets its common business done. I am not among those who say that only a lifelong park service careerist is qualified to be director. Suffice it to say, I would settle any day for another Steve Mather.

We need a new compact among the president, the secretary of the interior and the career bureaucracy of the National Park Service. The director, once again, will be vested with the full authority of his office and be bound to the political accountability any secretary has the right to expect of a principal program manager. That accountability must begin with the secretary understanding and articulating his policy/objectives for the park service and evaluating the director's performance as measured by results obtained in achieving those objectives—not lapdog fealty. Unless such a contract is renewed for the park service, the Congress should establish a fixed tenure for the director just as it did with the director of the Federal Bureau of Investigation when White House and Department of Justice political meddling threatened its professional foundations: a ten-year term, with no reappointment.

Secondly, when the secretary has established the president's legislative program and budget for the park service, the director and his career associates should have the duty and the responsibility of managing and defending those priorities before all, including the Congress. Do not be deceived: those bright people in the Congress read the tea leaves of power as well as those in the executive branch.

Thirdly, we need to put an end to day-to-day meddling by political bureaucrats inexperienced in professional park management. Let's get the politics out of the parks and regional offices and back into the director's job where it belongs.

The late Alfred A. Knopf, the urbane and distinguished publisher, who served as chairman of the Secretary's Advisory Board on National Parks, traveled extensively in the parks and fought many battles to protect their integrity. Writing of an earlier park service, Knopf said:

XX. This Land Is Your Land

It is hard to imagine more dedicated people than those who run the parks. I have never met a single one whom I would not be glad to meet again, and I have invariably regretted the time to say goodbye. The range of their interests, their high intelligence, their devotion, make them a separate and wonderful breed.

Writing of the more recent park service, historian Everhart said:

The old mystique is nearly dormant, and anyone who today asked an employee to go the extra mile without overtime pay "for the good of the service" might well receive a mocking response. The energy and idealism that have characterized the park service for so long have not vanished, but they do seem to be the victims of a slight recession.

There was no more competent, innovative cadre anywhere than the colleagues I was privileged to serve with in the National Park Service. Questing constantly for excellence, they were determined, strong-willed, sometimes opinionated, always loyal and devoted to the idea and the ideal of America's national parks. There was a time not too long ago when, as Knopf said, they were "a separate and wonderful breed." Their devotion to duty—not time clocks—was as matchless as the majesty of the mountains and memorials in their care.

Today, despite the efforts of Director Mott, the park service is assaulted by political meddling and reeling from slashed budgets—a $60 million reduction since 1981. Its employees can neither serve the visitors adequately nor preserve the national parks. Neglected maintenance, endangered wildlife, environmental degradation and rampant greed of commercial exploiters afflict park visitors and impair our national parks. The responses to these deplorable conditions have been slogans, increased park admission and user fees and "poor boxes" to scrounge nickels and dimes from beleaguered families seeking re-creation in their national parks. These gimcrack responses to the crisis in our national parks have

275

placed our crown jewels at risk. Moreover, only about five per cent of the park service managers and employees in the Washington office have ever pulled duty in the national parks: a condition as absurd as operating the navy with a corps that has never sailed a ship.

Saving the national parks is a compact between the past and the present. The obligation of the contract is that these inherited treasures shall be passed on "unimpaired for the enjoyment of future generations." Our generation must not default on its immutable obligation.

INDEX

index

index

index